Lucid
DREAMING

Gateway to the Inner Self

ROBERT WAGGONER

CHARTWELL
BOOKS

CONTENTS

ACKNOWLEDGMENTS

THE PERSON I NEED TO THANK THE MOST IS THE PERSON WHO CHALlenged me the most, Ed Kellogg, Ph.D. More than any other lucid dreamer, Ed pushed me to search deeper, examine lucid awareness more thoughtfully, and question the apparent limits of lucidity. I found his expertise and insight, particularly in the areas of lucid dream healing, mutual lucid dreaming, and lucid dreams of the deceased simply unparalleled. This book, and chapters 13, 16, and 17 specifically, exist, in large measure, because of Ed's generosity of spirit and friendship.

Many others have provided precious support along the way. My thanks to Lucy Gillis, my coeditor in our quarterly labor of love, *The Lucid Dream Exchange*, and a talented lucid dreamer in her own right; Linda Lane Magallón, who ushered me into using lucid dreams experimentally through three years of monthly lucid goals and then introduced me to the International Association for the Study of Dreams, where I have met many wonderful people and extraordinary lucid dreamers, including Keelin, Beverly D'Urso, Ph.D., Clare Johnson, Ph.D., and Fariba Bogzaran, Ph.D. (to name only a few), and heard fascinating lectures by some of the pioneers of lucid dream research—Stephen LaBerge, Ph.D., Jayne Gackenbach, Ph.D., and many others. I am indebted to lucid dreamer Alan Worsley and researcher Dr. Keith Hearne for providing the first scientific proof of lucid dreaming more than thirty years ago.

The altruistic spirit of lucid dreamers who willingly offered their lucid dreams for inclusion in this book touched me deeply. Though some preferred to remain anonymous (and some I have already mentioned), I also wish to thank Jane Ahring, John Galleher, Connie Gavalis, David

L. Kahn, Ian Koslow, Moe Munroe, pasQuale Ourtane, Justin Tombe, Joscelyne Wilmouth, Sylvia Wilson, and Suzanne Wiltink.

The invitations to speak at campuses and venues such as Sonoma State University, Evergreen State College, the Inner Arts Center in Alexandria, Virginia, and Sheila Asato's Monkey Bridge Arts near Minneapolis, Minnesota, helped me articulate my discoveries and meet others who were using lucid dreams as a path to greater creativity, self understanding, and exploration; my thanks to all who made that possible and for their interest and enthusiasm.

To my editor, Sue Ray, humble thanks for her gracious acceptance of my first book and near infinite efforts and patience in preparing it for publication. Heartfelt thanks to my many, many friends who encouraged me this past year and along life's way. Last, I need to thank my wife, Wendy, for her love and faith, as I pursued this waking dream: a guidebook to consciously exploring the dream state, the Self, and the vast unconscious reality of the mind.

PREFACE

FOR MORE THAN THIRTY YEARS, I HAVE PRACTICED LUCID DREAMING, the ability to become consciously aware of dreaming while in the dream state. During this time, I have had approximately 1,000 lucid dreams, most logged away in dozens of dream journals and computer files.

Like many, I initially considered lucid or conscious dreaming as a fascinating playground for the mind. I could fly over treetops, push through walls, make objects appear, even walk on water (dream water, that is)—all while conscious in the dream state. As the years passed, however, certain pivotal lucid dreams opened my mind to the possibility that lucid dreaming offered a gateway to so much more.

In part one of this book, you will read about my journey into lucid dreaming, beginning with simple experiments such as asking a dream figure to explain the dream symbolism or tell me what it represents. The results contain both expected and unexpected elements. While the expected certainly seemed understandable, I found the unexpected responses troubling. If the lucid dream was a product of my mind, then how did a completely unexpected and shocking response arise from within my own mind?

Probing deeper into this mystery, I and others began to lucidly challenge the boundaries of dreaming as we sought out the unexpected, the unknown, the abstract. Increasingly, we let go of manipulating the dream and directing the dream events as we opened up to the unconscious. Surprisingly, something responded. An inner awareness behind the dream provided answers, observations, insight. Carl Jung theorized that an inner "ego" might be discovered within the "psychic system" of the unconscious; I propose that lucid dreaming has the potential to show that his theory contains fact. Like Hilgard's "hidden observer" in deep hypnosis, lucid dreaming also shows an inner observer with whom the lucid dreamer can relate.

In part two, I explore the limits of awareness available to a lucid dreamer. I show examples, both mine and others', of numerous conceptual explorations as well as attempts to procure telepathic and precognitive information while lucid. And, with the help of research from lucid dreamer Ed Kellogg, Ph.D., I delve into the topics of physical healings while lucid, mutual lucid dreams, and interacting with deceased dream figures.

Those who have experienced lucid dreams will find here numerous techniques, tips, and challenges to consider in their own lucid explorations. For those who have never experienced a lucid dream or do not truly understand the experience, I hope to act as a dream anthropologist of sorts—explaining the lucid dream terrain, the local customs, the rituals, and something of the inhabitants, the dream figures, as lucid dreamers consciously interact with them in the psychological space of dreams. In the book's appendixes, I provide advice and guidance for those who wish to become lucid dreamers or improve their lucid dreaming skills.

Lucid dreaming provides us a means to explore, experiment, and question the nature of dreaming and, as some might say, the nature of the subconscious—the largely unknown part of our selves. For this reason alone, psychologists, therapists, consciousness researchers, and dreamers should have an intense interest in the experiences and experiments of lucid dreamers. As I see it, lucid dreaming is a unique psychological tool with which to consciously investigate dreaming and the subconscious.

In many respects, this book responds to those who claim that lucid dreaming simply involves expectation, which automatically creates mental models to be experienced. By lucidly going beyond expectation and the expected, I attempt to show that much more is going on here. Consciously aware in the dream state, we have access to deeper dimensions of information and knowing that can hardly be explained by expectation or mental modeling. This way is not for the faint of heart or those comfortable with unexamined beliefs.

The journey into lucid dreaming truly is a journey within your conscious and unconscious self. Here, not only will you meet your beliefs, your ideas, your thoughts, and expectations—often materialized in the dream space—but also your fears, your hopes, your limitations, and intents. In responding to those challenges, those self expressions, you make your path. I hope this book helps guide you along the way and gives you insight into your self-creations and the larger dream reality. I wish you well on your journey.

Robert Waggoner

PART 1

THE
JOURNEY
INWARD

1

Stepping Through the Gate

Like many children, I had an intense dream life. Dreams were an amazing theater of the mind featuring both glorious adventures and moments of sheer terror. In one dream, a songbird, a meadowlark, I believe, landed on my chest and sang me its simple song, which I immediately understood and woke up singing. In another dream, I found myself on a fifteen-foot Pogo stick bouncing down the deserted streets, almost flying. On occasion I seemed to be an animal—a dog or coyote, for example—trotting along the dark night's sidewalks in a four-legged gait, totally at peace, seeing the neighborhood from a canine's drooping-headed, tongue-wagging perspective.

With dreams like these, I was a child who had to drag himself out of bed.

In those early years, I remember clearly only one spontaneous lucid dream. In it, I was wandering the local library and suddenly saw a dinosaur stomping through the stacks. Somehow it dawned on me: If all dinosaurs are extinct—this must be a dream! Now consciously aware that I was dreaming, I reasoned further: Since this was a dream—I could *wake up!* I reasoned correctly and awoke safe in my bed.

That youthful experience illuminates the essential element of lucid dreaming: the conscious awareness of being in a dream while you're dreaming. In this unique state of awareness, you can consider and carry out deliberate actions such as talking to dream figures, flying in the dream space, walking through the walls of dream buildings, creating any object desired, or making them disappear. More important, an experienced lucid dreamer can conduct experiments in the subconscious or seek information from the apparently conscious unconscious.

But I'm getting ahead of myself . . .

In those preteen days, before I began lucid dreaming regularly, three experiences kept alive my interest in dreaming and the psyche: occasional dreams that seemed to be precognitive, an unexpected "vision experience," and the very real sense of having access to an inner knowing. Like many, I found life's deepest mysteries in the mind.

For me, the occasional precognitive dream often appeared as small events, like dreaming of someone making an odd statement in a dream, only to hear a real person make the same odd statement a few hours later, or to have a voice in the dream announce an observation that later would be proven correct. Once, the voice explained that the dream symbols meant the dream events would take three years to transpire. I kept track of that date and something incredible did indeed happen in the waking world, directly related to the dream from three years earlier.[1]

Precognitive dreams challenged my budding scientific worldview and disrupted my traditional religious and spiritual views. Strange co-incidences, self-fulfilling prophecies, or unknown information? How was one to tell?

One day in my preteen, church-going mind, I had a mini-epiphany. It occurred to me that if God was the same "yesterday, today, and forever," as they said in the Old Testament, then God must exist outside of time, apart from time, in a place where time had no meaning. And, if that were true, then perhaps dreams were the gateway to a place without time, where time existed in one glorious Now. Yet my young science-educated mind balked at this notion. A dreamt event followed by a waking event could be nothing more than sheer coincidence and didn't necessarily entail any foreknowing. Or perhaps it was like a self-fulfilling prophecy, in which I unknowingly helped bring about the event that I dreamt. And even when a dream voice made an observation that later turned out to be true, perhaps my creative unconscious had simply noticed things and, by calculating the likely outcome of those things, made a clever announcement.

As this spiritual questioning was going on, another fascinating incident occurred. One Sunday evening when I was eleven or twelve, I lay on my bed reading a book and stopped for a moment to think. As I absentmindedly looked up at the ceiling, my head suddenly turned north and I began to see a vision of a Native American setting overlaying the physical scene. I struggled to free myself from this unexpected experience while another part of me took in the vision. Finally it stopped.

At that young age, what do you do with something like this? In my case, I went to the library. I flipped through a number of books about the Old Testament containing commentary on visions but found little of value for me there. I also checked out a few books on Native American culture and discovered the vision quest, a traditional practice by which youth gain insight into their lives. Normally a vision quest occurs in a ritual fashion. The young person is obligated to leave the tribe and travel alone for a period of days of fasting, praying, and waiting for the visionary experience. Yet why would something like that happen to me? Only years later did I discover that our family had Native American ancestry.[2]

Somewhere in this time period, I also recognized the presence of an "inner advisor," for lack of a better term. At certain times, when I considered things deeply, an inner knowing appeared in my mind. It was such a natural thing, I assumed everyone experienced this. It was like having the services of a wise old man inside. For example, after a very simple incident that most anyone would ignore, the inner knowing would make an observation about life or suggest the prosaic incident as a living parable. The comments seemed intelligent, even remarkable. I began to sense that all around me life had meaning, if I only cared to look. Since I lived in the middle of Kansas, far from the centers of world power, the pace of life was slower and perhaps simpler, yet below the surface, at another level, I knew we had everything, all the lessons of life.

Like any teenager, I'd pester this inner advisor—What am I? Who am I? To these questions I was given two answers and then never visited the issue again (although the answers rolled around my mind for decades). In one instance, to my "Who am I?" the inner advisor responded, "Everything and nothing." Okay, I thought, any person in a sense has the potential capabilities of all, but in having them also has nothing, for time or the fates will sweep it all away. In those words, too, I sensed a hidden connection between the rich lavishness of Being and the complete freedom of Nothing. But still not entirely content with being a place marker between two extremes, I continued to pester myself and, by extension, the inner advisor with the question of identity until, one day, an answer came that laid all further questions to rest. "You are what you let yourself become," said the inner advisor. That answer satisfied me completely: *The living of life was an allowing of self.*

Altogether, the precognitive dreams, the vision experience, and my search for spiritual meaning kept me probing for satisfying and complete answers. Obviously, my intense inner life, sparked by thought-provoking dreams, created a persistent desire to accept, abandon, or perhaps bridge one of the two worldviews: the scientific and the spiritual. Which is why in 1975, at age sixteen, I picked up one of my oldest brother's books, *Journey to Ixtlan: The Lessons of Don Juan* by Carlos Castaneda, and embarked on my first lesson in lucid dreaming.

As some readers may know, Carlos Castaneda was an anthropology graduate student at UCLA in the 1960s who sought to learn from native shamans about psychotropic plants in the southwestern United States and Mexico. According to his story, he met a Yaqui Indian sorcerer, don Juan, who agreed to teach him about hallucinogenic plants. In the process, don Juan provided Castaneda with a unique view of the world. Even more important, perhaps, don Juan supplied techniques to experience this new worldview.

The philosophy of don Juan might be summed up in these words, spoken to Castaneda: "[Y]our idea of the world . . . is everything; and when that changes, the world itself changes."[3] Don Juan constantly pushed Castaneda to consider new and world-changing ideas and to become more mentally flexible.

Castaneda has recounted in numerous books his decade-long association with don Juan. While many have openly questioned Castaneda's veracity in storytelling,[4] his many books nevertheless contain a number of provocative ideas and, like many young people, I was intrigued. I read *Journey to Ixtlan* and decided to try just one of the ideas, never imagining how transformative an idea could be.

Don Juan suggests to Castaneda a simple technique to "set up *dreaming*" or become conscious in the dream state. "Tonight in your dreams you must look at your hands," don Juan instructs Castaneda. After some discussion about the meaning of dreaming and the choice of hands as an object to dream about, don Juan continues. "You don't have to look at your hands," he says. "Like I've said, pick anything at all. But pick one thing in advance and find it in your dreams. I said your hands because they will always be there."[5]

Don Juan further advised Castaneda that whenever an object or scene that he was looking at began to shift or waver in the dream, he should consciously look back at his hands to stabilize the dream and renew the power of *dreaming*.

Simple enough, I thought. So, before going to sleep each night, I sat cross-legged in bed and began looking at the palms of my hands. Mentally, I quietly told myself, "Tonight, I will see my hands in my dream and realize I'm dreaming." I repeated the suggestion over and over, until I became too tired and decided to go to sleep.

Waking up in the middle of the night, I reviewed my last dream. Had I seen my hands? No. But still hopeful, I fell back asleep remembering my goal. Within a few nights of trying this technique, it happened. I had my first actively sought lucid dream:

> I'm walking in the busy hallways of my high school at the junction of B and C halls. As I prepare to push the door open, my hands spontaneously fly up in front of my face! They literally pop up in front of me! I stare in wonder at them. Suddenly, I consciously realize, "My hands! This is a dream! I'm dreaming this!"
>
> I look around me, amazed that I am *aware* within a dream. All around me is a dream. Incredible! Everything looks so vivid and real.
>
> I walk through the doors a few feet toward the administration building while a great feeling of euphoria and energy wells up inside. As I stop and look at the brick wall, the dream seems a bit wobbly. I lucidly remember don Juan's advice and decide to look back down at my hands to stabilize the dream when something incredible happens. As I look at my hands, I become totally absorbed in them. "I" now see each fingerprint, each line, as a giant flesh-toned canyon that I float within and through. The world has become my palm print, and I'm moving about its vast canyons and gullies and whorls as a floating speck of awareness. I no longer see my hand; I see cream-colored, canyon-like walls of varying undulations surrounding and towering above me, which some part of me knows as my fingerprints or palm prints! As for me, "I" seem to be a dot of aware perception floating through all of this—joyous, aware, and full of awe.
>
> I'm wondering how this could be, when suddenly my vision pops back to normal proportions and I see again that I am standing, hands outstretched, in front of the administration building. Still consciously aware, I think about what to do next. I walk a few feet but feel an incredible urge to fly—I want to fly! I become airborne heading straight up for the intense blue sky. As my feeling of overwhelming joy reaches maximum pitch, the lucid dream ends.

I awake in bed, totally astounded, my heart pounding and head reeling. Never had I felt such intense feelings of elation, energy, and utter freedom. I had done it! I had seen my hands literally fly up to face level in my dreams as if propelled by some magical force and I realized, "This is a dream!" At the age of sixteen, I had become conscious in the dream state. And suddenly, like Dorothy in Oz, I was not in Kansas any more.

Well, actually, I was in Kansas for another year, until I left for college.

THE PARADOX OF THE SENSES

My first lucid dream felt like a monumental achievement. I had actually become aware in a dream. Moreover, in the don Juan tradition, this first lucid dream seemed filled with auspicious symbols—becoming a speck of awareness floating through my palm prints, maintaining the dream, working on awareness outside of the "administration building" (symbol for my own inner authority, perhaps). I was excited.

Still, it seemed so paradoxical—becoming conscious in the unconscious. What a concept! Like some teenage magician of the dreaming realm, I had done what scientists at the time proclaimed could not be done.

Little did I know, during that same time in April of 1975, thousands of miles away at the University of Hull in England, a lucid dreamer named Alan Worsley was making the first-ever scientifically recorded signals from the lucid state to researcher Keith Hearne. By making prearranged eye movements (left to right eight times), Worsley signaled his lucid awareness from the dream state. Pads on his eyes recorded the deliberate eye movements on a polygraph's printout. At that moment, Hearne recalls, "It was like getting signals from another world. Philosophically, scientifically, it was simply mind blowing."[6] Hearne and Worsley were the first to conceive of the idea and demonstrate that deliberate eye movements could signal the conscious awareness of the dreamer from within the dream state.[7]

A few years later, in 1978, Stanford sleep lab researcher Stephen LaBerge, using himself as the lucid dreaming subject, devised a separate, similar experiment of signaling awareness from the dream state through eye movement. Publishing his work in more broadly read scientific journals, LaBerge became strongly identified with this exciting discovery and a leader in its continued research.

Back in Kansas, each night before I went to sleep I would look at my hands and remind myself that I wished to see my hands in my dreams. Of course anyone who tries this will soon discover that staring at your hands for more than ten seconds is quite boring. When you already feel sleepy, it takes real effort to concentrate. Your eyes cross, your hands get fuzzy, your attention wavers, within a minute or two you may even become so bored and tired as to go blank momentarily. After a few minutes, I would give up and prepare for sleep. At the time, I chastised myself for my lack of concentration and wavering focus, but later I came to feel that these natural responses were actually the best approach, since the waking ego seemed too tired to care about the game my conscious mind wanted to play. In fact, don Juan suggested that the waking ego often felt threatened by the more profound nature of our inner realm. Perhaps a sleepy ego would be less likely to interfere.

My next few lucid dreams were lessons in exquisite brevity. I would be in a dream, see my hands in the course of the dream (e.g., as I opened a door with my hand or as if by some inner prompting my hands would suddenly appear directly in front of me) and immediately realize I was in a dream. I'd experience a rush of exhilaration, joy, and energy. As I took in the dream surroundings, my feelings of joy rose to such levels that the lucid dream would begin to feel unstable and then come to an end. I would awaken, full of joy but mystified by the sudden collapse of the lucid dream.

This brought me to one of my first lessons of lucid dreaming:

To maintain the lucid dream state, you must modulate your emotions.

Too much emotional energy causes the lucid dream to collapse. Years later, I learned that virtually all lucid dreamers realize this same lesson and as a result learn to temper their emotions.

After reading don Juan's exhortation to Castaneda that he should try to stabilize the dream environment and, bit by bit, make it as sharply focused as the waking environment, this became my new goal. Don Juan advised that the dreamer should concentrate on only three or four objects in the dream, saying, "When they begin to change shape you must move your sight away from them and pick something else, and then look at your hands again. It takes a long time to perfect this technique."[8]

In the next dream, I was walking at night and suddenly saw my hands appear directly in front of me. I immediately realized I was dreaming. Lucid, I took a few steps and noticed the colors were extremely vibrant; everything seemed so "real." I felt euphoric and knew that the dream would end unless I could regulate my feelings, so I looked back at my hands to stabilize the dream and decrease my emotional upsurge.

After a few moments, I looked around at the grassy knoll on which I was standing. I seemed to be inside a fenced enclosure that included a building, similar to a military or secured installation. I took a few steps and looked at my hands again to stabilize the dream. There were some small evergreens ten feet away, obviously recently planted. I knelt and touched the grass. It felt soft and grass-like. I marveled at how lifelike and realistic everything looked and how I could think about what I was seeing and choose what to do next. I touched myself and, *Wow*, even I felt real! But I knew my awareness existed within a dream and I was touching a representation of my physical body, which only *felt* like a real body.

Trying to make sense of what I was seeing, I had the intuitive feeling that the building housed computers and was somewhere in the southwestern United States. But where? As I took a few steps toward the building to look for a name, the imagery started to become unfocused. I looked back at my hands but it was too late—the lucid dream collapsed and I awoke.

It began to sink in that knowing it was a dream did not make it seem unreal. The grass felt like real grass. My skin felt like real skin. If I truly focused on something, like the ground, I could actually see the individual blades of grass and grains of sand. When awake, we consider seeing and touching as largely physical activities, but in lucid dreaming, I began to see that seeing and touching were also mental activities and equally real-seeming when consciously aware in the dream state. Which brought me to my next lesson:

> *Our senses provide little distinction between physical reality and the real-seeming illusion of the lucid dream. Only the mind distinguishes between the two realities.*

In later lucid dreams, I tried the other senses—taste, smell, and hearing—and discovered that they, too, seemed real experiences, or at least largely real. Even self-induced pain—pinching myself in the lucid state, for example—actually hurt. But if I pinched myself while telling myself it would not hurt, it didn't hurt. Here I uncovered an odd aspect of the lucid dream realm: My experience would normally follow what I lucidly expected to feel.

Fellow lucid dreamers I've met over the years seem to agree with me that the senses proclaimed each experience as real as waking experience. Yet, experienced lucid dreamers note that if they predetermine or expect *what* to feel or *how* to feel, they can alter the sensory experience in line with their expectations. In other words, "As you believe, so shall it be" is a powerful truth when lucid.

In the lucid dream state, the senses show themselves as the confirmers of expectation—not infallible guides to sensory response—and experience is largely infused with mental expectation about the experience. Just as in studies on hypnosis and pain reduction, the senses somehow bend to the intent of hypnotic suggestion. In both lucid dreaming and hypnosis, the senses don't appear as biological absolutes but more as the servants of the mind.

By age eighteen, I had visited a hypnotist to learn about self-hypnosis. I understood the basic concept that suggestions made to us while intensely focused in a mild trance state influenced the subconscious and affected our perceived experience. Now I could see that being consciously aware in the subconscious (i.e., lucid dreaming) possessed similarities to deeper self-hypnosis.

Our suggestions in a state of hypnosis or self-hypnosis act on the senses. For example, we can make a posthypnotic suggestion that certain foods will taste opposite to their normal taste and experience the suggested taste upon waking. Or we can suggest that we will feel minimal pain during, say, a tooth extraction, and then experience remarkably little pain. Similarly, when lucid in a dream, the senses naturally follow expectation (expectation being a type of natural mental suggestion). In fact, one of the advantages to lucid dreaming involves seeing the immediate results of your suggestion or expectation. If I lucidly dream of a fire, for example, and expect to feel no heat upon walking in it, I'll feel no heat. If I change my expectation to feel the fire's heat, my new expectation will be realized, and I'll feel definite heat.

My lucid dreaming experiences made me wonder how extensively the mind influences perception and sensation while waking. Conscious in the dream state, the influence seems pervasive. During waking, I simply assumed I experienced things "as they actually exist." Yet I knew from my exposure to hypnosis that waking sensory experience could actually be considerably modified.

All dreamers can see how unreliable the senses behave in telling us the difference between waking and dreaming. In almost every dream, the senses don't inform us of the difference between waking and dreaming; rather, they seem to confirm that whatever reality seems to be happening is indeed happening. Dreaming seems real, our senses tell us. Waking seems real, our senses tell us. To sense the reality of our situation requires a new perspective. The lesson:

Only by increasing our conscious awareness in the dream state can we ever realize the nature of the reality we experience.

So, the senses pose a problem. They tell us we exist, but they don't indicate the state of our existence: Are we awake, dreaming, or lucid dreaming? Since the senses don't remind us we're lucid and in a dream, holding onto conscious awareness in the dream state requires considerable training in greater mindfulness.

For example, in many of my early lucid dreams, my hands would appear and I'd realize I was dreaming. Then as I lucidly interacted with the dream, some interesting dream figure would become so compelling and real-seeming that my attention to "the dream as dream" decreased significantly. I'd begin to forget that this was "all a dream." Just as in waking, your conscious attention can begin to drift when lucid dreaming. After a few unfocused moments, you're swept into the dreaming, following its movements, suddenly unaware and no longer lucid. Not only did I need to be consciously aware of being in a dream, I needed to be consciously aware of being aware!

Once again, a new lesson emerged:

Lucid dreamers must learn to focus simultaneously on both their conscious awareness and the apparent dreaming activities. Lucid dreamers who become overly focused on the dreaming activities get swept back into non-lucid dreaming. So too, lucid dreamers who become inattentive to the fact of their conscious awareness risk becoming lost to the dreaming. To maintain lucidity, we must develop a proper balance of mindful, aware interacting *to engage the dream consciously.*

In an environment that appears real, our awareness has to adopt a neutral stance: be *in* the environment but not *of* the environment. Engage the dream, but never forget it's a dream. In my experience, keeping your foot on the tightrope of awareness is an ever-present challenge. In about a third of my early lucid dreams, I would become lucid but eventually, through inattention or engrossment, I'd fall off the tightrope. Each time I fell off, though, it acted as another lesson in the importance of maintaining mindful awareness.

The awareness needed for meditation, at least some forms of it, seems analogous to what lucid dreamers seek to develop. Meditators, especially beginners, have to learn a sense of balance when they turn inward; otherwise, they can fall asleep while meditating or become caught up and engaged with entrancing thoughts. Likewise, beginning lucid dreamers often hold focused awareness for only a short period of time. It takes practice and patience and poise to hold awareness consciously while being confronted with new thoughts or images—the products of the mind.

As you log time in the lucid dream realm, you develop poise, confidence, skills, and flexibility. Your awareness begins to relate differently to thoughts and images. You don't get swept into dream or thought events as easily; rather, you pick and choose what to accept with a greater sense of engaged detachment.

At deeper levels of lucid dreaming, you might discover how to remain aware even when the dream visually ends, and then wait for a new dream to form in the mental space around you, as I did, for example, in the following lucid dream (October 2002):

> I seem to be walking through a small town. I enter a simple restaurant and walk through it into a mechanic's garage. I see a door and decide to slip through it, even though it seems to have a string attached to an alarm. As I get out into the street, I look around and realize, "This is a dream."
>
> Lucidly aware now, I start flying up the street, looking at the people sitting in candle-lit cafes and walking down the street. The detail is incredibly vivid. I sing a funny rhyming song as I look at things. I keep flying farther and end up outside of town with a strong inclination to fly to the right. But then in a moment of conscious choice, I exercise my right to change the direction of the dream and decide, no, I'm going into the darkness, and I turn left.
>
> As I move forward in the darkness, the visual imagery disappears. For a very long while, I feel that I'm moving without any visual imagery—there's only a foggy dark-gray void. I keep moving in this visually empty space and begin to wonder if I am going to wake up. But suddenly a scene appears, bit by bit. First a bush, then a tree, then another tree. Soon the dream fleshes out nicely, and I stand, lucid, on a gently sloped hill, like something you'd see in Britain, with small leafy trees and lots of green grass. I notice that right next to me is a small bush with berries on it. I examine it closely.
>
> Suddenly, I have the awkward realization that my body in bed is having a hard time breathing (even though I continue to see the lucid dream imagery of the green hills). While my conscious awareness is admiring a grassy spot in a lucid dream, I try to feel the breathing

obstruction. With this bifocal awareness, I gently put some mental energy into making my physical head move up and away from the bed sheets or pillow while concentrating on remaining in the lucid dream. This seems to work. But finally, I decide to wake into physical reality and determine what is hampering my breathing.

With experience, you'll realize that sometimes you can be consciously dreaming and also aware of your physical body in bed. To stay in the lucid dream, you have to maintain your primary focus there, but, on occasion, you can check in on the physical body's awareness. In this example, when I woke, the bed sheet really was in my mouth!

As we become more experienced with lucid dreaming, we discover how to maintain awareness even when the dream imagery has all disappeared. In learning how to lucid dream, we learn much more than how to manipulate dream objects and symbols; we learn the importance and proper use of conscious awareness.

2

DOES THE SAILOR CONTROL THE SEA?

BEFORE DREAM RESEARCHERS PROVED LUCID DREAMING AS A DEMON-strable experience and published the results, I spent six years practicing it by myself and often defending the experience of it in conversations with others who routinely told me, "It's impossible to become conscious in the unconscious of sleep." During those years, I was greatly influenced by my father, whose insistence on intellectual integrity helped me accept the validity of my paradoxical experience while also accepting that my interpretation of the experience could be far off the mark. As a result, I continued deeper into lucid dreaming while regarding my interpretation of the experience as a working hypothesis or a "provisional explanation."

In retrospect, this period of my life taught me to view much of science as providing this same kind of "provisional explanation," not the final word. I saw that scientists and the prevailing cultural wisdom can occasionally ignore or explain away what later science or more enlightened times accept. In the case of lucid dreaming, Western science doubted its existence for at least a century, if not longer.

Thankfully, some of my high school friends were open to trying this idea of conscious dreaming and "finding one's hands" in their dreams. It became a challenge of sorts. Within a week or so, one friend reported that while in a dream his hands suddenly appeared in front of his face. As he looked at them, he thought, "Oh, my hands. This is a dream," and decided to wake up.

"Why didn't you do something," I asked him, "like go flying or something?"

"It was just a dream," he said. "It wasn't real. So I woke up."

This cultural bias toward the waking state as "real" and any other state as "unreal"—and therefore unworthy of attention or study—exists as a mental block for many. Yet if we presume that little can be learned from any state other than waking, we largely ignore any state other than waking and thus perpetuate the bias.

"This important phenomenon [lucid dreaming] has been dismissed as a psychic chimera by many authors and derided as a scientific will-of-the-wisp by others," explains J. Allan Hobson, a Harvard sleep and dream researcher. "[The philosopher Thomas Metzinger] knows, as I do, that lucid dreaming is a potentially useful state of consciousness."[1] Lucid dreaming offers insight into the scientific study of consciousness, since neuroscientists could potentially investigate the relation of brain activity to subjective experience while lucidly aware and compare it to waking and dreaming states.

An occasional lucid dreamer himself, Hobson suggests that "an MRI study of lucid and non-lucid dreaming is a highly desirable next step in the scientific study of consciousness. The technical obstacles to the realization of such an experiment are formidable but the main obstacle is political and philosophical." Hobson observes, "Many scientists rule out any study of subjective experience especially one as dubious and evanescent as lucid dreaming."[2]

Overcoming the barriers of science, theory, and culture may be the constant burden of any proven paradoxical experience such as lucid dreaming. Twenty-five years after my first lucid dream, I found myself once again defending lucid dreaming—not so much from scientific researchers who ultimately accepted the official scientific data on the subject, but from concerned psychotherapists and dreamworkers.

At a recent International Association for the Study of Dreams (IASD) conference, psychotherapists began singling me out. It seems another psychologist had mentioned hearing me speak at a conference in Copenhagen during which I wove together lucid dream experiences with comments by Carl Jung and Sigmund Freud to suggest that lucid dreaming may be a means to explore and acquaint ourselves with the larger Self, or collective aspects of the psyche. After hearing my talk, this particular psychologist reconsidered her negative-leaning predisposition to lucid dreaming and realized the potential value in lucid dreaming as a means of psychological exploration and integration.

So now I began to meet the assorted—and yet-to-be convinced—colleagues of this newly swayed psychologist. Most began by telling me that their academic training had taught them to consider dreaming as a message from the deepest part of our selves. To "control the dream," as they assured me that lucid dreamers do, would destroy or pollute the pure message from this deep part of our selves. Though they were too polite to voice it, the suggestion hung heavy in the air—only a narcissistic fool would encourage lucid dreaming.

After a few hallway encounters in which I groped for the words to make my point, an analogy came to me that seemed to bring greater awareness into the conversation. My analogy is this:

> No sailor controls the sea. Only a foolish sailor would say such a thing. Similarly, no lucid dreamer controls the dream. Like a sailor on the sea, we lucid dreamers direct our perceptual awareness within the larger state of dreaming.

Oh, the power of an analogy. Suddenly, I saw in the eyes of my querying psychotherapists the realization that my lucid dreaming experiences were simply attempts to understand the depths of dreaming and, by extension, the Self. Suddenly, we were on the same team—dreamers trying to fathom the beauty and magnificence of dreaming. Now, lucid dreaming had potential for increased awareness, instead of narcissistic flight![3] In fact, as I interacted with these Jungian-trained psychotherapists, I remembered a recent lucid dream with definite Jungian overtones (April 2005):

> My wife and I and my brother (who occasionally changes) seem to be stuck in an old post-Depression farm household that is struggling to keep food on the table. The farmwife comes home with three children, and they put some beans and other items on the stove to cook.
>
> After a while, they serve us at the kitchen table, placing a small portion of beans on our plates. But there seems to be a problem of some sort. Standing behind me, I notice a tall slender black woman who seems to be with us. It seems the farmwife doesn't care for her. We wait.
>
> As I sit there, I look at my brother and then at the black woman; it suddenly occurs to me that this is a dream. Aware now, I stand up and want to know what this means. Lucid, I pick up the black woman and place her in front of me, asking, "Who are you? Who are you?" She looks at me and surprises me with her unexpected response. "I am a discarded aspect of your self," she says, and immediately I sense the

truth of her statement and feel the need to reintegrate her into my being. She seems to evaporate into me, as a brief wisp of light energy.

Many Jungians might suggest this lucid dream illustrates integration with a shadow element, represented by the black woman standing behind me. In Jung's theory, shadow elements consist of repressed, ignored, denied, or misunderstood thoughts, feelings, or impulses that continue to reside in the realm of the subconscious. In some instances, the shadow element appears in a "shadow's position" to the dreamer, normally behind the dreamer.

Jung maintained that these shadow elements may adopt the guise of dream figures to interact with the dreamer as they seek integration or acceptance by the conscious self to create a more fully integrated Self. In this example, the apparent reintegration happens almost immediately, when I lucidly question and understand the dream figure's presence in the dream and accept her openly.

Once I became lucidly aware in this dream, I recognized that something needed resolution. (By this time in my lucid dreaming experience I was aware of the importance of approaching the area of sensed emotion or conflict in the dream, instead of ignoring it.) As I instinctively placed the figure of the black woman in front of me, I *consciously* intended to understand her place in the dream and what she represented. In the process, I received both a conscious answer and an infusion of energy into my awareness. Facing her, I felt the dream figure's energy evaporate into me, as a wispy, colored, light vapor washing toward me. The "discarded aspect" had apparently been welcomed home.

As it happened, in the week after this dream I felt new energy regarding a project that I had discarded years ago as unachievable. The project? You're holding it in your hands. It feels odd to say that reintegrating a discarded aspect into yourself brings a certain energy and imaginative spirit, but after this lucid dream I could suddenly feel the new ideas and positive emotions about writing a book. The wall of doubt surrounding my old goal had suddenly crumbled. Yet to begin work on this project, I had to make other changes that I saw symbolically illustrated and exaggerated in this dream. I had to overcome the culturally ingrained, deep belief about "working to keep food on the table," an issue seemingly represented by this obviously struggling, post-Depression farm family.

At the time of the dream, to concentrate on a book seemed incompatible with a full-time job. Yet, in the year following the dream, the desire grew. I overcame my inner concern about finances, reduced my traditional job responsibilities, and began to focus on this book.

So, no. No sailor controls the sea. Only a foolish sailor would say such a thing. Similarly, no lucid dreamer controls the dream. But like a sailor on the sea moving toward an island or point on the sea's horizon, we lucid dreamers direct the focus of our intent within dreaming to seen and unseen points. In so doing, we come to know the limited realm of our awareness compared to the magnificent depth and creativity of what I refer to as "the dreaming." As a portion of our conscious awareness rides upon the surface realm of the subconscious, we sense the support and the magnificent majesty of the unconscious below.

THE LIMITATIONS OF AN ANALOGY

Sadly, the power of the sailor and the sea analogy goes only so far. Additional concerns about lucid dreaming arose from various viewpoints. While many people understand that the conscious directing of one's focus while in the lucid dream state does not equate to "control" of the dream, they still feel reticent about the idea of lucid dreaming. Underneath it all, three issues begin to surface: 1) a fear of the subconscious and its processes, 2) concern for the dream as sacred message, and 3) using lucidity to escape and to avoid personal growth.

So, let's tackle these three ideas—or as I would call them, misconceptions—about lucid dreaming.

Fear of the Subconscious

In investigating fear of the subconscious, I came to understand that some people, including highly trained psychologists, have what amounts to a basic fear of the subconscious. They simply do not believe that the waking self should interact with unconscious or subconscious elements. The psychiatrist R. D. Laing commented that society has a "psychophobia, a fear of the deeper contents of our own minds."[4] Often, behind this fear of lucid dreaming, lies a hidden concern about "messing up subconscious processes." Which subconscious processes? Well, no one can ever say exactly because we don't understand the subconscious fully enough, leaving me to suggest that, perhaps, with lucid dreaming, we finally have a tool with which to explore it.

A healthy respect for what we call the unconscious or subconscious has considerable value. However, a fear of what essentially constitutes a portion of our being does not seem healthy or respectful; rather, it seems needlessly divisive and limiting. To counter our intense cultural conditioning, we must possess a sense of curious engagement to venture into the unconscious. Even though it's a part of us, it exists as terra incognita or, perhaps more appropriately, psyche incognita—we simply have drawn a sketchy map of the psyche and marked a large segment in frightful red letters, "Mind Unknown." We will never develop a truer conceptualization of the subconscious and unconscious if we only dance around it or consider it from the safe distance of the waking world. Why not let go of fear and interact with the dream (or realm of the subconscious) consciously?

Lucid dreamers have little support from a culture whose psychological theories and cultural views often suggest that the subconscious contains the repository of dark thoughts, repressed feelings, buried anxieties, and ancient antisocial instincts. They often must deal with just these beliefs as they approach lucid dreaming. As a result, they invariably experience unusual things as they attempt to "affirm" their place in the unconscious. As we will see, some lucid dreamers deal with their own doubts and fears (made manifest) as well as the interesting, surprising, and sometimes disturbing phenomena encountered in lucid dreaming. To be in the psychological space of the unconscious requires considerable affirmation of self in spite of numerous cultural conflicts.

Dream as Sacred Message

The viewpoint that dreaming exists as a sacred message from inner portions of our being is pervasive. Any attempt to disturb the dream, to involve the (assumed tainted) ego with it, or bring conscious awareness into it should, according to this viewpoint, be deemed fundamentally profane and a violation of the sacred.

I, too, view dreaming as a profound and creative act that is essentially sacred. But does the sacred prefer I always approach it as a dreamer unawares? Does the sacred have no interest in interacting with me as an aware dreamer, an aware being? Or does the sacred prefer less awareness in its dealings? Rather it seems that the sacred would take joy in dealing with greater awareness, greater consciousness. Wouldn't the sacred appreciate the chance to inform, educate, and instruct at a more aware level?

Further, if we look at our dreams as sacred messages, how many of these sacred messages do we truly understand? For many people, remembering one dream a night seems quite an achievement, even as another four to six dreams slip by unremembered. Then, of the dreams recalled, how many can say they truly understand the sacred message in them? Does our interest in calling the dream sacred simply reflect our inability to understand it? By discouraging conscious interaction with the dream, we limit our ability to improve our understanding of it.

In the lucid dream in which I questioned the woman who announced herself as a discarded aspect of myself, would I have understood this dream if I had not been lucidly aware and able to question her? Would I have experienced new insights and new energy because of it? Only by consciously attending to an important element of the dream did I receive this new level of insight and energy.

Using Lucidity to Escape and to Avoid Personal Growth

Finally, some observers raise a concern about dreamers using lucid awareness to escape or avoid a dream's message and, thus, the opportunity for personal growth the dream might otherwise provide. In some cases, this is true, since in a lucid dream we have the ability to choose and some dreamers do, indeed, choose to escape into an adventure. For example, a lucid dreamer may decide to ignore an angry dream figure and fly away instead, thereby avoiding the issue represented by the figure. More experienced lucid dreamers, however, would stop and engage the dream figure to find out more about the situation, as I did in this lucid dream (October 2004):

> I am walking down a street at night in my childhood neighborhood. I look toward some houses on the right. Suddenly, a big black dog comes running toward me; in a funny way, I expect this. The dog appears menacing and dangerous, but somehow this strikes me as very odd, and I even seem to recognize the mean black dog. I think, "This is nothing. This is a dream." I begin to talk to the dog and firmly know there is nothing to fear. Purposefully, I project love onto it by saying compassionate words. Now, another dog appears. It's a dachshund, like we had when I was a child. Lucid, I begin to fly around the two dogs, who now both seem friendly and happy. Then I decide to take the dachshund flying. I swoop down very low and grab it. Feeling it in my hands, I begin to fly higher but wake up.

Lucid dreamers repeatedly find that when they project love, compassion, and care onto unfriendly dream figures, like the menacing black dog here, the love and concern transforms the image or introduces a new, positive dynamic—or in this case, a dachshund! By taking a direct approach in this dream, I was able to transform fear (represented by the black dog) into something benign, even lovable (represented by the dachshund, a fond memory from my childhood), and quite possibly resolved an emotional issue at the subconscious level.

I argue that though lucid dreams may occasionally lead to escaping issues, most lucid dreamers benefit from recalling more dreams than the average dreamer and, potentially, gain more conscious awareness of inner concerns. At any rate, even for experienced lucid dreamers, the number of non-lucid dreams—"untainted" by the dreamer's interaction—far outnumbers lucid dreams. Most lucid dreamers would say that in less than ten percent of their dreams do they become lucid. In my experience, I recall about three dreams per night, or about ninety dreams each month. In an average month, I may have only three lucid dreams. Proportionally, more than ninety-six percent of my remembered dreams occur in the non-lucid form, and four percent or less in the lucid form. While at one time I recorded thirty lucid dreams in a month (in college) at my prime quantitatively, two to five lucid dreams per month seem the norm nowadays.

Like all dreamers, if we purposely ignore a dream message, it likely returns in another dream or some other form. All dreamers come to know that in the final analysis, lucid or not, there is no escape from the Self.

LUCID DREAMERS WHO STILL BELIEVE IN CONTROL

Lucid dreamers, particularly beginners, can occasionally behave like "Conquistadors of Consciousness," as thoughtful lucid dreamer and writer Ryan Hurd put it,[5] and proclaim dominion over a dreaming that they fail to understand or appreciate. I recall reading of a lucid dreamer who flew into a crowded room of dream figures and gleefully announced, "I am your god!" Oh brother, I thought.

Occasionally, lucid dreamers will come up to me after a talk and proclaim, "But I do control the dream! I fly. I make things appear. I tell dream figures to disappear and they do. I really control the lucid dream!"

My response generally goes something like this: "If you control the dream, who made the grass green and the sky blue? Who created the new scene when you came around the corner or flew through a wall into a new room? Did you control all that new scenery and detail into being?" I also point out that if lucid dreamers control the lucid dream, they wouldn't spend so much time trying to learn how to manipulate things. If they control the lucid dream, their lucid dreams wouldn't suddenly collapse and end. Control suggests a fundamental dominance or authority over. By contrast, lucid dreamers show varying degrees of ability to manipulate themselves within the dreaming.

At this point, the lucid dreamer acknowledges that their "control" seems limited to directing their focus. They don't "control" the color of the various items, the new vista when they fly over a hill, the items in the rooms they just entered, or necessarily the length of the lucid dream itself. Rather, they direct their focus within the larger dreaming around them. When unaware of these points, a lucid dreamer stumbles into the philosophical perspective of the lucid solipsist—one who believes that his or her waking self in the dream is the only reality.

Don Juan cautioned Castaneda that the presumption of control could become a major stumbling block along the path. Since the ego finds security in the feeling of control, it habitually occupies those areas deemed under its control. Any journey into one's depth requires the flexibility and courage to accept a more profound reality and move outside of the area of the ego's control.

When lucid dreamers focus upon what they don't control, they then realize all the things happening without their conscious involvement and understand that they direct their focus but do not control the dream. No sailor controls the sea. No lucid dreamer controls the dream. Like sailors on the sea or lucid dreamers in the dream, we can only direct our focus within that environment, which begs the question: If the lucid dreamer does not create the scene or the objects in the room, what or who does? As we progress deeper into lucid dreaming, this question will become even more pressing.

In the meantime, let's accept our ability to direct our focus within the conscious dream and investigate the mysteries of awareness.

3

MOVING IN
MENTAL SPACE

ADVENTUROUS LUCID DREAM EXPLORERS ARE LIKELY TO ENCOUNTER several phenomena along their path. Out-of-body experiences, for example, are quite common. In fact, a survey of lucid dreamers conducted by The Lucidity Institute shows a strong correlation between lucid dreaming and out-of-body experiences (OBEs). In the study, lucid dream experts Lynne Levitan and Stephen LaBerge report that "of the 452 people claiming to have lucid dreams, 39% also reported OBEs . . ."[1]

In fact, many thoughtful, intelligent people have reported having OBEs. Author, professor, and philosopher of consciousness Thomas Metzinger, for example, wrote of experiencing an "out-of-body (OBE) state again" during an afternoon nap.[2] Lecturer and writer Dr. Susan Blackmore, author of *Consciousness*, "had a dramatic out-of-body experience" that led to her deeper investigation into the nature of consciousness.[3] I also recall a prominent sleep and dream researcher speaking at an IASD conference at Tufts University who mentioned an apparent out-of-body type of experience while recovering from an illness.

My own experience with the out-of-body state occurred within six months of my first lucid dreams. As my seventeen-year-old self lay in bed and began to drift off to sleep, I felt an incredible energy and buzzing around me, particularly around my head. I was startled, but not sure whether I should be alarmed. The buzzing vibration sounded like a thousand invisible bees hovering around my head, or an Australian didgeridoo. I felt incredible energy all around me. Remembering don Juan's advice, I told myself not to fear and just go along with it. Don Juan had told Castaneda that fear was the first barrier to overcome, since the ego used fear as a reason not to explore one's totality and, instead, maintain the ego's dominance of the waking self.

During one of these buzzing episodes, I noticed that I seemed suspended in space. I viewed the room from a perspective about five feet above my physical body, which, of course, seemed extremely odd! How was I getting a view like that, when I knew my body lay in bed with eyes closed?

That summer an even stranger incident occurred. I found myself flying around the sycamore trees in the front yard, doing loop de loops, really enjoying myself in the early morning dawn. It felt very real, not dream-like at all. Suddenly, I saw someone coming down the street on a bicycle. I felt the need to hide, so I flew to the roof of our house and hid behind the peak to watch. Moments later, the young person on the bike threw something at our house! I immediately woke up, alarmed at what I had just seen. It was around 6 A.M. and no one else was awake. I put on some shorts and rushed to the front door. I opened the door and, yes, someone had, indeed, thrown something at our house, and right where I expected—the morning newspaper! I was stunned. Could I have actually seen the newspaper boy ride his bike by our house and throw the newspaper? Could I have witnessed that from the roof of our house while my body lay in bed?

Imagination creates beautiful imagery, so I wondered if this was an interesting case of imagining a scene in a very real and vivid dream-like state that just "happened" to contain elements of a normal daily event. Could I, on some deep level, have heard the paper land in the grass on the opposite side of the house and simply concocted a dream about this subauditory event? I know the experience happened—yet how to explain it?

I decided to ask one of my brothers. He listened to my story, then said, matter-of-factly, "You're having out-of-bodies."

"I have them sometimes," he said, "and normally I fly around the neighborhood. I like to fly around these sycamores, too." I asked him how he knew they were out-of-bodies, and he mentioned a book by Robert Monroe, *Journeys Out of the Body*.[4] He even gave me some advice on dealing with the buzzing and how to roll out of my body.[5]

"Out of bodies"—holy smokes! I didn't recall asking for them. Besides, all the buzzing and humming and energy felt weird sometimes. Comparatively, lucid dreams were fun and easy to understand, since my dreaming self played in the playground of my mind (or so I assumed). Even the term *out-of-bodies* bothered me. It implies that the person's awareness has left the body and now explores physical reality sans body. Yet, I definitely had a body image when experiencing this state—it just wasn't a physical one. For this reason, I came to prefer the term "projection of consciousness," as suggested by metaphysical explorer and author Jane Roberts.

As you can see, while the OBE experience itself may be somewhat commonplace, interpreting the experience is a challenge. If one's awareness seems apart from the physical body, then does one experience a physical realm or an imagined realm, possibly a mental model of the physical realm? If it seems an imagined realm, then how do we explain the rare but occasional instances of apparently valid perceptions of the physical realm? And what does this say about the nature of awareness? Does awareness require a physical body, or does awareness reside sometimes within and sometimes without a physical body?

After reading about and talking with other lucid dreamers, I learned that many developed the ability to lucid dream before experiencing spontaneous, and less frequent, OBE-type experiences. One cannot help but wonder if this coincidence of lucid dreaming and projections of consciousness result from an actual connection between the two experiences or if it relates to the person's interest and involvement in working with awareness. In other words, once we begin to lucid dream, do we then notice similar, subtle experiences of awareness?

On a number of occasions, in my college dorm room, I would take an afternoon nap with the intention of having an OBE. In one attempt, I recall looking very closely at a white, textured surface, just a fraction of an inch above my eye level. When I awoke, I realized that my awareness may have been about eight feet above myself, carefully inspecting the ceiling tile! To check it out, I precariously balanced a chair on my bed and stood on it to reach that same ceiling height. Now, if I could just stick the top half of my head into the ceiling, I could get my physical eyes in the same spot. The view seemed so close to what I had seen while apparently OBE. Just maybe, my awareness had actually moved.

For me, the OBE usually occurred in the local environment (that is, in the general area of where I had fallen asleep). Also I noticed that though I might fly around the neighborhood, I unintentionally "changed" things. For example, if I decided to fly through a house, I might find a window to fly through where no window exists in waking reality. Upon waking and recalling the situation, I would note that I had unknowingly made it easier for myself to fly into the house by mentally perceiving a window where none existed. Realizing this, I came to think of local OBEs as a "reality plus one" phenomenon, meaning that OBEs seemed to mimic a waking-reality model quite nicely, yet held "plus one," or added elements, of apparent subconscious desire or intent interwoven into the imagery.

DIFFERENTIATING LUCID DREAMS FROM OBEs

Invariably, discussions with lucid dreamers yield clear differences between OBEs and lucid dreams. As I see it, there are six clear distinctions between the two phenomena.

First, most lucid dreams occur when one's awareness comes to an understanding of the dream state *while dreaming*—one realizes one dreams within the dream. Most OBEs simply begin at the fuzzy juncture between waking and sleep, and then the person begins the OBE experience "aware."

Second, some OBE reports occur when instigated by physical trauma, illness, or medication, unlike most all lucid dream experiences. In his groundbreaking book *Lessons from the Light*, near-death researcher, Kenneth Ring, Ph.D., reports the story of a woman at Seattle's Harborview Hospital who had a severe heart attack and then went out-of-body during cardiac arrest. Upon waking, she told the hospital social worker how she had floated up to the ceiling and watched as the doctors and nurses tried to save her, then had floated outside of the hospital and noticed a tennis shoe on the third-floor ledge of the hospital's north wing. She begged the social worker to see if a tennis shoe really existed on the ledge of the hospital's north wing. To placate her, the social worker investigated the third-floor ledge and was stunned to find a tennis shoe with the same wear marks and specific details the woman described from her OBE journey.[6] Examples like this fuel the debate that some OBE experiences connect to remote perception in the physical world.

Third, out-of-body experiencers often report buzzing, energy, vibrations, and other phenomena preceding their experiences, which lucid dream reports rarely mention. OBErs sometimes mention "shooting out," or "rolling out" of their physical bodies; again, comments normally never mentioned by lucid dreamers about lucid dreams.

Fourth, as Robert Monroe mentioned in comments to the *Lucidity Letter*,[7] the "most common" difference between a lucid dream and an OBE involved the lucid dreamer's ability to "change" the internally generated environment that they experienced; by contrast, those having an OBE do not report consciously changing their environment. Monroe suggests a difference in how the environment is experienced.

Fifth, as lucid dream researcher, Ed Kellogg, Ph.D., has described, the memory of a long OBE experience seems crystal clear and easily recalled in a linear order, while memory of an equally long lucid dream seems less detailed and more difficult to recall precisely and in order.[8] Many lucid dreamers, myself included, report this hampered memory with long lucid dreams, though my long OBE experiences seem comparatively clear, memorable, and detailed.

Sixth, OBErs usually report "returning" to their body, sometimes with a noticeable reconnection. Lucid dreamers, by contrast, at the end of the lucid dream report waking up, having a false awakening, or the dream imagery "going gray" (that is, losing normal visuals and seeing a diffused dark state).

In short, those experiencing OBEs normally recognize their state from the start; they often report unique vibratory and energy sensations preceding their experience; they seem to accept and not change their environment; they seem to recall easily the details of their experience; and OBE reports contain more reference to "returning to the body."

Lucid dreamers, by contrast, report that lucid dreams normally occur late at night and within a dream; lucid dreamers note a distinct change in awareness from non-lucid awareness to lucid awareness; they rarely report any unique sounds or sensations preceding their lucid dreams; they frequently change the environment; long lucid dreams seem relatively more difficult to recall in exact detail; and, finally, most lucid dreamers report that they decide to "wake up" or realize the dream has ended.

The difficulty in differentiating between lucid dreams and OBEs occurs when you have experiences like my flying around the trees, apparently seeing the newspaper boy. Was I OBE or lucid? On the one hand, I didn't recall any humming or vibrating, but then again I don't recall leaving my body. I didn't change anything, as lucid dreamers report, nor did I recall realizing, "This is a dream!" The experience occurred late at night, like a lucid dream, but I vividly recall every detail, like an OBE. I acted with a sense of awareness, but not like lucid awareness.

My lucid dream illustrates how easily one can become confused about two distinct types of inner experience. As coeditor of *The Lucid Dream Exchange*, I see this same confusion in a small subset of lucid dream submissions. The person doesn't indicate or recall how they became lucid; however they fly around the mental landscape much like in a lucid dream, yet fail to alter the environment, as lucid dreamers normally do.

Tomato, tomat-obe? Maybe so. But as we investigate the varieties of conscious experience and their possible meanings, we must take care to investigate the phenomena's differences and similarities.[9]

Moving in the Lucid Dream State

For many beginning lucid dreamers, few things are as joyous as flying. The fantastic sense of freedom as you swim, glide, or soar through the dream space brings deep satisfaction. Of course, when it doesn't work, when you're unable to fly or do so only with extreme effort, your frustration can mount rapidly. Thankfully, with experience and a bit of insight, you can become an accomplished flyer.

In fact, sometimes the best flying advice comes from dream figures.[10] I clearly remember one such encounter. He was just a kid, maybe twelve years old, thin, with short brown hair. His red flannel shirt, with sleeves rolled up, was worn threadbare. I had seen him earlier in the dream, and now he reappeared on the muddy road of this Depression-era town. Though he spoke only eight words, this boy gave me great insight into moving in dream space (March 2000):

> At this moment I can see mud glistening wet on the road and something strikes me as odd. Then I notice the view in my rearview mirror isn't at all what I thought it should be, since I had just left my old-fashioned hotel. I realize this is a dream.
>
> From my convertible, I announce to the boy, "You know this is a dream." He looks back at me like he already knows this. I ask him if this is the right way back to the hotel. He then offers me a great lesson in the nature of dream space. "Mister," he says, "here, any way is the right way."

I glimpsed the raw truth of this statement and realized another valuable lesson in lucidity:

Almost all movement and flying in the dream begins, proceeds, and ends in the same way—with the manipulation of the mind. Any way is the right way, because there is basically one way, and that way is through manipulating awareness.

In lucid dream space, you are as close to any place as you expect to be. The apparent fifty-foot flight is only a mental act away. So, too, the long-distance flight to that hill over there—you and the hill are only separated by an act of focus and intent.

In one of my first lucid dreams, I became lucidly aware in my childhood front yard, by our sycamore trees. Gleefully, I decide to fly. I leap a few feet in the air and, hanging there in space, I think, "Now what?" I simply could not conceive of how to fly.

For many beginning lucid dreamers, flying in the perceived space is a primary goal. Getting from point A to point B should be easy—after all, you're dreaming this, right? But while many find it easy, others find movement frustrating. They get stuck. They can fly or move only with extreme effort. Why? Normally it's because they bring the expectation or mindset of physical space into the psychological space of the lucid dream. When they want to move in a lucid dream, they walk, they flap their arms, they swim through the air, using physical-type effort. They grow frustrated, not realizing that their belief and expectation in the need for physical action is causing their experience.

The solution to this dilemma involves another lesson in lucidity:

The dream space largely mirrors your ideas, expectations, and beliefs about it. By changing your expectations and beliefs, you change the dream space. Realizing mental space responds best to mental manipulations, you let go of physical manipulations and use the wings of your mind.

How would you recognize that you are relating in a physical way to the mental space of dreams? You would see it in your behavior and thinking in the lucid state. If you find yourself acting in a physical way, it suggests at some level that you believe or feel the dream space to be like physical reality. If, on the other hand, you feel yourself consciously relating to the space in a nonphysical way (you fly through walls, change the couch into a chair, or fly upside down, for example), it suggests that you believe or understand the space as a mental construct.

In some instances, your beliefs automatically overlay and integrate into the mental environment without your conscious awareness. Consider this example: Why does an apple fall in a lucid dream? Or more to the point, why do many beginners fall in a lucid dream? Let me assure you, it isn't gravity.

Whether an apple, or a dreamer, the sense of falling in a lucid dream must be the result of a type of psychological force within the dreaming. Nearly every experienced lucid dreamer would say the lucid dreamer's belief and expectation in falling creates the experience of falling. Lucid dreamers who don't possess that belief, expectation, or focus of falling don't fall. They may simply hang in space, knowing it as the gravity-free space of lucid dreaming. Or if they do move in a downward motion, it's just that—a directional motion—not falling. With apologies to Newton, the only apple that falls in a lucid dream is the one that believes in falling.

But movement, of course, is not always a black and white affair. You may notice this in some early lucid dreams in which movement toward your goal seems extremely difficult. If you take a moment to review it, the quicksand-like difficulty may reflect your ambivalence or conflict about your intended goal. The uncertainty becomes exteriorized as difficulty in movement. In those cases when you feel clear about your goal and are not conflicted, you normally proceed toward it easily. Since the lucid dream environment largely follows the contours of your mind, your mind appears embedded in the environment, the experience, and the experiencer. The difficulty *only appears to be* out there.

So, each lucid dreamer's emotional situation provides an avenue for insight. Whenever you feel frustrated in a lucid dream, it should be a clue that you are approaching the dream in a physical manner or in conflict with unexamined beliefs. Conversely, an easy and successful lucid dream experience shows the proper use of mental principles and a conflict-free mind.

Consider this lesson in lucidity:

The mind, emotions, and mental action precede the effect.

After waking from your lucid dreams, carefully review the effect of each recognized and unrecognized mental action, thought, emotion, or expectation. You will quickly discover that background beliefs, sudden expectations, and new insights create the field from which most lucid events spring.

CFI: MOVING VIA CONCENTRATED FOCUS WITH INTENT

By far, the simplest method to move could be called "concentrated focus with intent." It's a simple two-part process: 1) As the lucid dreamer, concentrate your focus on the place you want to be; then 2) intend yourself to be at that place, feel it, imagine touching it, engage your mind with it. By concentrating on your goal, you naturally dismiss other concerns and thoughts, sharpening your focus. Intent draws the goal and you together.

This method does not consider how one gets there—do I fly like Superman or do I float on a magic carpet, at what speed or in what form? With this method, the focus becomes concentrated solely on the goal, and the movement happens naturally. The lesson:

Concentrating on the goal as your sole focus, then intending yourself there, moves your awareness effortlessly.

What if the place you want to be is far away? How do you "intend" yourself to that mountaintop? In general terms, you focus exclusively on the mountaintop and place your perception there, by either imagining yourself on the mountaintop or, say, by imagining yourself touching the highest rock; in any case, your focus follows your intent, and you find yourself where you want to be. In the following lucid dream, I use this principle to help a friend learn to fly (August 2002):

> I sense that the setting is just "too dreamy" and become lucidly aware. I tell my friend, "Let's fly! I'll show you how," and I grab her arm and we fly about fifty feet. We do this a few more times, going about fifty feet each time, and with each try she gets better. I finally tell her that to fly easily when lucid, you have to see yourself where you want to be. I point to a car far away and say, "See yourself there and then fly, it's easier." I joke with her and we laugh about it. We fly there easily. We go past a gate and into a beautiful garden—it's like a miniparadise.

In this next lucid dream, I see where I want to be and feel myself drawn toward it (May 2006):

> I seem to be on a neighborhood street on a sunny day. Snow covers the ground. I notice one place where water drains down, creating a large hole in the snow, surrounded by fluffy, unreal-looking snow. Suddenly this seems too dream-like and I say, "This is a dream!"

I take off and fly upward. Gaining altitude easily, I see a school building about a half mile away, across a large field. I put my arms out, à la Superman, and tell myself to concentrate on one corner of the building and draw it to me. As I concentrate, I accelerate toward the building effortlessly and arrive there in seconds.

By switching to the method of concentrated focus with intent, you leave behind the days of slow, effortful movement. Just concentrate on the exact spot you wish to be, intend yourself there, and you will feel the graceful flight of intent pull you to your destination.

Soaring through space can feel incredibly joyous and exciting, which is why it remains one of lucid dreamers' favorite activities. However, I once met a dream figure who had an entirely different perspective on Superman flying (August 2002):

I have become lucid and done a number of things. I meet a guy who looks like Robin Williams and tell him I want to know all there is about flying in dreams. He says dryly, "Not that Superman kind of flying stuff."

"Yes," I reply.

He shakes his head and explains, "You've got to understand that there are many different kinds of flying." He pauses. "There's jungamon, hugamon, and tagamon flying, and there's . . ." He continues with four more odd names of flying. He tries to make a point that different types of lucid flying are required for different types of lucid environments. It seems best to use the most appropriate for the environment. Superman flying seems to be a very modest level. He goes on with more information about using thoughts.

Before this dream, I had never considered that the type of flying or movement is related to the environment. It makes sense that certain types of lucid flying would be appropriate in certain lucid dream environments. For example, I still find that I swim through a small room-sized space. It just seems appropriate in that setting. But, in a wide-open space, you'll likely find me flying à la Superman.

PROJECTING YOUR POWER INTO A FLYING OBJECT

In some lucid dreams, rather than flying on our own power, we project power into an object and then use that object to fly. For example, we look for a rocket pack or a magic carpet and then project our belief into its ability to fly. Sometimes we even project power into completely odd things, as in these two short lucid dreams:

> Finding myself lucid in a dream, I grab hold of a blue sandal which I believe can fly—and it does! I hold onto it as it goes zipping around the room. I gleefully hold on, amazed at the speed of the blue sandal.

> * * *

> Standing on a hillside lucidly aware, I decide to touch the wing of an airplane, which begins to levitate, so I use it to take me where I want to go. I hang on and it goes to places that I want to visit. I find this very easy.

While both the sandal and the plane, in some sense, have an association with movement, I still feel surprised by the idea of projecting power into something else in order to fly. Upon waking, I normally remind myself that my belief and expectation alone made the objects fly, even though I projected symbolic power into those items.

And, then, I have to wonder. Why do we sometimes find it easier to project power into an external thing and believe in its ability instead of believing in our own power? Are we predisposed to invest some symbols with power? Or does it follow the outline of our own belief and expectation?

THE POWER OF EMOTION

While flying, many beginning lucid dreamers will realize they're gaining altitude—they see the rooftops or trees below them and can barely believe they're flying!—and suddenly, their focus shifts. They become fearful of the distance to the ground, and they begin to fall. At the moment their focus changed from flying to the distance to the ground, the direction of the lucid dream changed. The lesson:

> *When you focus on your goal, you attract your goal. When you focus on fears, you attract your fears. In a mental space, your focus matters because it naturally draws you to the area of your focus.*

Left alone, your focus naturally follows your beliefs, interests, and emotions. If you focus on fears or have a fearful mindset (e.g., "Oh, I'm getting too high!"), things will go awry. Likewise, if you adopt a limiting belief or expectation (e.g., "I can only go this speed"), the psychological space will adjust to mirror that belief or expectation. Your experience of dream space reflects your focus, which aligns with your beliefs, interests, and emotions.

Lucid dreamers learn that progress involves expanding the mind. By overcoming limiting or negative beliefs and expectations and the subsequent focus on fears or concerns, we open our mind to the possibility of new, broader concepts. When our conceptual mind begins to grow, so do the possibilities of experience. New concepts allow for new creativity.

So, our fears and concerns demonstrate a particularly important lesson in lucid dreams:

Emotions energize the area of focus. If you want to get somewhere in a hurry, just add some emotional energy to it. Emotion shortens the distance between the experience and the experiencer, between the dreamer and the desired.

MOVING INTO APPARENT OUTER SPACE

As you become more accomplished as a lucid dreamer, there may come a time when you wish to travel into apparent outer space, or in the words of *Star Trek*'s Captain Kirk, "to boldly go where no man has gone before."

In this lucid dream experience of apparent outer space, I simply found myself there (March 1997):

There are many people around, like a family dinner or picnic. Somehow I become lucid and find that my flying control is excellent. I effortlessly fly from room to room with grace, precision, and awareness. I play around with moving objects in the rooms. One woman notices me and acts seductively. I choose to ignore her.

I think about what to do and decide to try to fly out into the stars. I begin to fly and keep flying and flying. I'm astounded! I can't believe how far I'm going and everything stays the same. (In previous lucid dreams, when I would fly toward the stars, they would sometimes merge together into various symbols, like interlocking circles, triangles, and so on.)

I continue flying into outer space. I begin to fly past planets. This is incredible! Finally, I decide to stop. I look down about forty degrees and there's a large planet with rings and four moons. I notice that two of the moons seem to have ghostly rings around them while the others don't. The main planet's ring is kind of orangish gold. Two of the moons are to the right, with a third almost halfway behind the planet. The fourth moon is on the left side of the planet.

I marvel at the profound sight of seeing an entire planet hanging in space. It's so incredibly silent and still. I decide to keep going, and do, but don't find anything new, so I turn back with the intent of flying through the outlying rings of the planet. I head toward the rings and, as I do so, I begin to feel energy hitting me as I move through the ring. (Here, I believe I momentarily lose my lucidity or have a total scene shift.) I am back on Earth, still flying. It occurs to me that this has been quite a long lucid dream.

It may require a number of attempts before you make it into outer space. Perhaps on some conceptual level, it poses difficulties in regard to our beliefs. It can be done, however. I still recall the unexpected feeling of energy as I flew through the rings of the planet.

A fellow lucid dreamer once commented that whenever he had lucid dreams of outer space, he couldn't help but wonder if he had really moved deeper and deeper into inner space. The experiences often felt profound and mind expanding, he said, but he wondered if the journey had been symbolic of an inner one. His insight struck me, since I too wondered if these journeys represented a movement of inner depth with the wings of the mind.

Mental space can twist the mind of the lucid dreamer. In one sense, you paradoxically experience the illusion of space and the infinity of space. Your perspective changes as your mind changes, but in that changing, where is space? Does space exist only in the mind? Is space an artifact or epiphenomenon of changing mental perspective? Do you actually venture through space, or would it be more correct to say you venture through ideas, intents, and beliefs exteriorized? Is the movement of consciousness the only movement?

Lucid dreaming offers a new approach to the exploration of awareness and the territory of the mind. Later, we'll travel into implied space and potential space as we explore the far reaches of the lucid mind.

4

BEYOND FREUD'S
PLEASURE PRINCIPLE

"COULD FREUD BE RIGHT?!" I WONDERED, INCREDULOUS, AS MY COL-
lege professor explained the id and the libido. It was 1980, and I was a
psychology major listening to a lecture on Freud's pleasure principle.
As the professor spoke about the id, ego, superego, and libido, I began
to see distinct correlations between these ideas and my first five years
of lucid dreaming.

The professor outlined Freud's theory that the id, or the vast,
instinctual, unconscious system within one's psyche, is the primary
subjective reality of each of us. Through the id, said Freud, flows the
primary source of life-giving psychic energy, or the libido. Because the
id is not governed by reason, culture, or morality, it has one principle
consideration: to satisfy its instinctual needs in accordance with the
pleasure principle of avoiding pain and finding pleasure.

Freud maintained that one way the id released its energy and found
satisfying expression was through the production of dream symbols.
In our dreams, said Freud, the id forms impulsive, magical, selfish,
pain-avoiding, pleasure-loving mental images, which satisfy its need
to gratify its instinctual urges. According to Freud, dreams essentially
represent wish fulfillments. In dreaming, we learn a bit about the ob-
scure nature of the id.

Sitting in class, I wondered if, while lucid, I had interacted with
the id or experienced the libido. I began to make a checklist of my first
five years of lucid dreaming:

When lucid dreaming, did I seek pleasure? Yes!
When lucid dreaming, did I avoid pain? Right!
When lucid dreaming, did I act impulsively? Check!
When lucid dreaming, did I act selfishly? Often.
When lucid dreaming, did I act magically? Yep.
When lucid dreaming, could I feel libido energy? I believe so!

In that moment, Freud illuminated for me two fascinating aspects of lucid dreaming: libido energy and encounters with instinctual urges. On many occasions after becoming lucid, I, and other lucid dreamers, feel an extraordinary energy welling up inside. Suddenly, from nowhere, we experience a vibrant sense of power mixed with pleasure and a feeling of confident mastery, all coupled with the joy of realization. This momentary ecstasy courses through our whole being like an injection of life-giving energy.

It makes you wonder. When lucid, is *that sensation* a conscious experience of libido in its broader sense (i.e., life energy)? Or does it represent something else?

Since Freud associated one aspect of the libido with sexual urges, I had to admit to myself that many of these collegiate lucid dreams involved having sex. In some cases, it simply felt like sex was in the air of the dream, that it wafted in the dream breeze and I caught its scent. Imagine being aware in the dream state and feeling an instinct hanging in the air about five feet to your left. If you accept the instinct, its energy engages you. If you focus on something else instead, it recedes from your awareness.

At other times, I found that lucid dream sex was simply a conscious decision. If I noticed an attractive dream figure and focused on it in the aware state of dreaming, I could internally observe a decision being made. The decision didn't seem instinctual; rather, it followed a deliberate conscious choosing.

Yet Freud's suggestion that the id followed the pleasure principle, with its instinctual element, resonated mightily with my early lucid dream behavior. Though I had tried various experiments suggested by don Juan, many of my lucid dreams involved pursuing pleasure and avoiding pain. I flew joyfully around the dreamscape, magically created things I wished to experience, and delighted in the freedom of this alternate reality. When bothered by a dream figure or situation, I would either ignore it or use my will to pulverize it. (Only later did it occur to me that I might wish to understand and reconcile with disagreeable dream figures.) In some lucid dreams, I even found elements of the superego and its moralistic viewpoint making an appearance. Once while lucidly and passionately entangled with a lovely dream figure along a sidewalk (yes, normal inhibitions disappear when you realize you dream it), two gentlemen walked by and I heard one casually remark, "I wonder if he thinks that is spiritual?" This superego-type comment caught my attention.

In fact, reviewing my early lucid dreams uncovered a lot of id-like behavior. But did I behave like that because of the intrinsic nature of the id *and* the instinctual unconscious? Did the id call the behavior forth? Or did I behave like that because of me, my personality, my focus, my interests? Did the behavior represent my self at the time, in my own private dream realm?

The answer came to me as I began to review my first few years of lucid dreaming. I realized that I had never engaged in sexual behavior in lucid dreaming until I had experienced sex in waking life. Once I had experienced it at an ego level, I brought it into my lucid dreaming experience. I wondered if perhaps the id or the unconscious system was not so primitive and instinctual after all; perhaps we bring from our waking selves what we then discover there in the subconscious—our own ego impulses and desires. To protect our view of our self, we imagine the impulses and desires arise from the unconscious instead of admitting that they are our ego ideas brought into the unconscious.

As time went on, I came to find the subconscious realm of dreaming actually relatively neutral. When lucid, the subconscious seemed to reflect me and my ego issues much more than normally acknowledged by Freud and Jung. The chaotic, primitive, and instinctual expressions of the id failed to appear; instead, the dream space seemed more home to the expressions of the ego—"I."

For some lucid dreamers, these first years actually pose a possible threat to their future development as lucid dreamers. One can become trapped by the pleasure principle, so to speak. Focused on achieving pleasure and avoiding pain, one simply loses interest in going further. Lucid in the unconscious, the considerable pleasures are as enticing as any waking-world pleasure.

In the epic voyage of the Odyssey, lucid dreamers recognize a cautionary tale. Blown off course for many days, the crew finally lands on the island of the lotus eaters. There, they find water to continue their journey. Ulysses sends three men to find out about the local inhabitants, and they discover that the locals spend most of their time eating a delicious lotus plant. When the crew members eat the lotus, they discover its pleasure-giving powers and become apathetic about continuing the journey homeward. Recognizing the danger to the crew from the powerful lotus, Ulysses forces the three crew members back on board and sets sail, lest others discover the lotus and lose their will to journey onward.

For lucid dreamers, the problem is not pleasure so much as abandoning any other goal as they pursue pleasure. When a lucid dreamer habitually uses lucid dreaming only for pleasure, he or she becomes lost, blown off course. It takes considerable determination to pursue lucid dreaming past this first stage of pleasure seeking and pain avoidance. Often at this stage, the lucid dreamer may begin to imagine that lucid dreams have no meaning other than pleasure.

Such was the case with one of my nieces. We met recently at a local restaurant and, after the usual pleasantries, I asked about her dream life. She told me about various dreams she'd had, and I asked her if she was having any lucid dreams. She told me she'd had ten or fifteen of them. "But they don't mean anything," she said.

I was incredulous. "What do you do in your lucid dreams?" I asked.

She explained that when she becomes aware that she dreams, she changes things in the dream. If she sees a run-down building, she begins to fix it up lucidly until it looks nice and new. Or if she finds herself in a park without trees, she demands that nice trees appear, or sometimes moves ones from the background to the foreground.

I knew my niece had an interest in art, but designing lucid dream environments? Interesting. "So you use lucid dreams to design nicer dream settings?" I asked. She agreed with this characterization.

I suggested that if she wanted to find out whether or not lucid dreams have meaning, the next time she became lucid, she should announce to the dream, "Hey dream, show me something important for me to see!"

"Just look up in the dream, and yell it out," I said. "Watch how the dream responds. *Then* tell me if you still think lucid dreams have no meaning."

Within the month, she experienced a big lucid dream containing lots of meaning for her and others. She titles the lucid dream, simply enough, "Meeting My Great Grandmother":

> I was running from a large male lion, scared out of my mind and screaming. A huge boulder was in the front, so I jumped behind it and hid from the lion. I peeked up, and the lion came full force over the boulder. I stood up, pointed my finger at him and in my deepest

voice said, "Don't you dare!" Then the lion was gone. At that point, I thought, "Wonderful, I am lucid dreaming!"

So I stood on the rock and said, "Okay dream world, I know I am in a dream, so give me something good or maybe show me someone I haven't seen in a long while or something."[1]

Then this opening or door opened up into a long, endless transparent-blue hall. At the far point in the hall, I saw the back of a white-haired head, and so I walked toward it. When I stood in front of her, I realized it was my great grandmother, DeeDee. I can't recall everything that she said, but it went something like this. She said, "You have good timing, Honey! I get out of purgatory tomorrow and am headed somewhere wonderful."

She told me not to worry about her. Then she said that I should not worry so much, and that I have many people who love me. After a while, she said she had to leave, and I asked her if she had a message that I could give to anyone. She said, "Tell Susan that I love her dearly, and I will see her shortly. Tell your mom to try to be happy." Then she said, "In fact, tell your mom to remember the old room in the back part of my home. She'll know what I'm talking about." With that, I kissed her and woke up.

The day following this lucid dream, my niece called, very excited. "Uncle Robert, do you remember how you told me the next time I was lucid dreaming, to just stand up and ask the dream to show me something important?"

"Sure," I said. And she began to tell me the story—even asking me to define *purgatory*, since she felt a bit unclear about what that meant. I smiled at that. After she finished with the lucid dream, she wondered out loud, "But what do I do now? Does this mean anything?"

I thought about the most constructive response. "Well," I said, "it may mean something, and it may mean nothing. I don't know." I paused for a moment to let that sink in. "The only way you'll ever know is if you do what the dream figure of your great grandmother suggested."

My niece struggled a bit with this idea and then asked me to explain what I meant.

"The dream figure of your great grandmother—now, I am not saying it was really her, it may be just a symbol—but the dream figure of your great grandmother asked you to give two messages. So you do it."

She asked me how. I explained that it was easy. "You pick up the phone and call your mom. Somewhere in the conversation you tell her you had a strange dream about your great grandmother. Then, just like in the dream, you tell your mom that great grandmother wanted you to remind her of the old room in the back part of great grandmother's home. That's all you say."

For myself, personally, whenever I have dream information like this, I realize it may be purely symbolic and relate only to me. It may have nothing to do with anyone else. In that case, it may be improper or feel inappropriate to even bring it up. But if the feeling in the dream seems largely positive or upbeat, and the information comes from an intent requested in a lucid dream, my inclination is to investigate further. If I decide to tell the person about it, I always mention that this involved a dream and may be completely symbolic. In other words, I "own" the dream.

An hour later, the phone rang. It was my niece. "Uncle Robert," she said excitedly, "you won't believe what just happened." She went on to tell me that she did, indeed, call her mother and that she eventually got round to the dream. "I told her most of the dream, and then I told her what great grandmother said—to remember the old room in the back part of her house. You won't believe what happened next."

She was killing me with suspense.

"Well, she started to cry. She said that the happiest moments of her childhood occurred in that room, because great grandmother kept all these drawers full of old costumes and jewelry there. And whenever she came over with her cousins, they could all dress up and play make-believe. She said that great grandmother let them do whatever they wanted. There were no rules there." My niece stopped for a moment. "I guess those really were the happiest times in her life. I barely knew my great grandmother; I was, like, eight years old when she passed away in the nursing home. I never visited her house."

We talked some more and, as our conversations came to a close, I asked my niece one final question, "So do you still think lucid dreams have no meaning?" She laughed.

This early stage of using lucid dreams for play and pleasure seems only natural. When playing, we learn to enjoy the dream environment and discover things about it. We experience how to manipulate ourselves and dream objects while learning to maintain conscious focus. We develop spatial and movement skills while doing a lot of playful self-education. Eventually, when you realize the fantastic potential of lucid dreaming as a means to explore the unconscious, discover unknown but verifiable information, and interact with one's inner awareness, you notice that the playground of lucid dreams connects to a school of higher education. There you can begin a new stage of learning and experimentation in the lucid dream state as you begin to wonder how deep the unconscious goes.

THE EXPECTATION EFFECT

Beginning in 1981, the first articles about lucid dreaming and the scientific research of Dr. Stephen LaBerge began to appear in popular magazines such as *Psychology Today*. I felt relieved to see that lucid dreaming had finally been scientifically proven and was inspired to do my own experiments with the unconscious. Until this point, most of my experimentation involved trying to manipulate myself in the dream, to fly more easily or make things appear or disappear. Now, however, I began to imagine probing the lucid dream to see how it would respond. Without realizing it, I was entering a new stage of discovery.

One day, I became intrigued with the idea of discovering the meaning of a dream symbol while lucid. Could a lucid dreamer somehow determine the nature of a dream symbol while in the dream? I found this quite an exciting prospect and waited for my next lucid dream (May 1982):

> Dreamt that I was in Minneapolis on a sunny, early spring day. A foot of snow lay on the ground. I am standing at the bottom steps of a porch, while on the porch are four other people. Covering the porch steps are hundreds of amber and emerald gems and crystals.
>
> This seems too odd, which triggers the realization that I'm dreaming. Now lucid, instead of flying around, et cetera, I look up and see my friend Andrea at the end of the porch steps. I recall my interest in dream symbols and excitedly think, "This is my chance." So I bend down and pick up a large amber-colored gem, which I hold between my thumb and forefinger. I look at Andrea and call out to her. "Andrea! What does this represent?" She looks at the gem and then at me and quietly but firmly states, "Hope and consciousness." Excited by my success, I decide to wake up and write this down.

I hadn't known what to expect, but the dream image of my friend responding to my question with a plausible answer seemed incredible. As I considered her response—that the gem represented "hope and consciousness"—I was pleased. For centuries, society had used diamonds and other stones in wedding rings to represent the hope for a bright and durable marriage and used gems in crowns to represent the brilliance and light of royal consciousness.

Perhaps my years of wondering about the meaning of dream symbols was over. Perhaps, lucidly aware, I could gain information about all the symbols in the dream. Yet, my miniature experiment created a host of new questions. At some unconscious level, did I fabricate the answer and subconsciously project it into the comment by my friend? Did the dream figure of my friend simply tell me what on some deeper level I expected to hear?

By this time in my lucid dreaming, expectation seemed a primary force in the dream realm. "To expect was to create" is what I experienced in lucid dreams. This basic rule of lucid dreaming has become known as the expectation effect. In the lucid dream state, I found that, in general, expectations of succeeding led to success, while expectations of failing led to failure. If I expected to fly with ease, I flew easily. If, for some reason, I expected trouble flying, I had trouble flying. If I expected to be approached by dream figures, they approached me. Expectation largely ruled the dream realm.

But this didn't exactly explain my friend's response of "hope and consciousness." Did it simply come from a deeper level of my expectation? Or was it unexpected? How could one tell?

In an odd way, the expectation effect sounded a lot like Freud's idea of wish fulfillment. Freud felt that all dreams are wish fulfillments as the id produces dream symbols to satisfy its need for gratification. But in calling it a wish, Freud sided too heavily on the positive side of expectation, for in my lucid dreams, I realized that expecting unfortunate things led to their creation, too. In a sense, the expectation effect acted as a broader term that encompassed all types of fulfillments—positive, negative, and neutral.

Freud also suggested that for the dreamer's conscious wish to be energized and experienced, it had to succeed in touching something similar in the dreamer's unconscious or "in awakening an unconscious wish with the same tenor."[2] But since lucid dreamers routinely have most every wish or expectation granted, the unconscious seemed to grant *all* expectations. For lucid dreamers, the expectation effect displaced Freud's similar-but-not-the-same theory of wish fulfillment.

So, expectation seemed paramount. But there still seemed to be more to lucid dreaming. Here again, I had to wonder, was my friend's response of "hope and consciousness" an expectation? Or something else?

That same month, I had another lucid dream that resulted in a curious and less than expected outcome (May 1982):

> I become lucidly aware outside, near a white clad office building. Feeling energetic, I glance around and notice an attractive young woman, dressed in a modern style, standing next to a light post.
>
> I go up to her and she looks at me. I say enthusiastically, "I'm dreaming this. I'm dreaming this." She just looks at me, clearly unimpressed. I ask her who she is, but she seems disinterested by my question. In my mind, I assume she can't answer. She starts to walk away.
>
> But then something troubles me. Why did she not behave responsively, as I had expected? I begin thinking out loud about her unresponsive behavior, asking things like, "Is this your dream or is it my dream? Are you dreaming me or what?"

Upon waking, I realized that dream figures didn't always behave as I expected. While some complied with everything that I wished, others looked at me with indifference or even borderline contempt.

I also began to see how expectations even come embedded in our language. In the above dream, I announce, "I'm dreaming this," which presumes that I create, direct, act, and cast the dream because, after all, our language states, "I dream it." But when the woman walks away, I realize that I'm not directing her. So, if not I, then whom? Who directs the actions of dream figures?

Years later, I read about a lucid dreamer who met a much more troubling and unexpected dream figure:

> I cannot remember what induced me to do so, but I told Sandra that she was a character in my dream. This is a very unusual thing for me to do—my dream characters usually think this is rude.
>
> She replied that I'm a character in *her* dream.
>
> To prove her wrong, I did various things such as fly around the room and change our environment.
>
> Sandra did similar tricks. Neither of us could influence the other.
>
> After a bit of this, I was very confused and Sandra commented that she, too, was confused.[3]

When dream figures attempt to prove to you that *you* exist in their dream, you realize how unexpected lucid dreaming can be!

So, while the expectation effect explained many events in lucid dreams, it did not explain them all. Expectation seemed more of a guideline for the dream, not a "law." Lucid dreaming still had many more mysteries to reveal.

Intention and the
Magic of Lucid Dreaming

By continuing to practice lucid dreaming, I developed my skills in maintaining the length and coherence of the dream state. Unlike my early lucid dreams that lasted only a minute or two, I was now experiencing lucid dreams of considerable length and complexity, such that it was hard to recall all the details of the lucid dream. I felt prepared to try more lucid dream experiments.

Knowing that expectation and focus mattered, I began to work with using intent when conscious in dreaming. As don Juan mentioned, intent seemed one of the primary creative tools for lucid dreamers. Through the power of intent, a lucid dreamer could relate to the dreaming in a new, mysteriously magical way. Using intent, you could verbally or mentally suggest an action or object to occur and, somehow, it did. How? Well, like this (March 1983):

> I am in school with friends and acquaintances. I head off to my school room and open the door. In opening the door, I realize that I no longer attend college. "This is a lucid dream," I happily say to myself.
>
> Lucidly aware and feeling energized, I look around the classroom of young people and desks, wondering what to do in this setting. An idea comes to me. Since I don't see enough desirable women in the class, I intend to change that! I shout out to the class, "I want to see more attractive women in here when I open this door again!" I step outside the room and shut the door behind me.
>
> In the hallway, I wonder, "How long do I have to wait out here for more women to appear? Five seconds? A minute?" I feel like a kid on Christmas morning, not sure what to anticipate but hoping for the best. I wait a few seconds longer in the hallway and decide, "That's enough time."
>
> I open the door into the schoolroom and find a U-shaped line of perhaps fifteen attractive young women, completely naked. Amazing! It worked! I walk along and briefly touch each one, awestruck by the ability to create all of this.

Now, although some readers may raise their eyebrows at the content of my "intent" here (please recall that at the time of the dream, I am in my early twenties), one sees the creative power of intent in the lucid dream or subconscious platform. I intended in the dreaming that I wished to experience a specific event in the progression of the dream. And it happened, perhaps even *beyond* my expectations.

Some might be alarmed by this, saying, "Wait one moment! You said that lucid dreamers don't control the dream; rather, lucid dreamers direct their focus within the dreaming! What do you call this?" But look at that lucid dream again. Did I make the women stand in a U-shaped line? Did I determine the number? Did I determine their placement or attitude or height or color or any of that? No. I merely suggested to the dream my general intent. When I opened the door, while not totally surprised, I saw that my directed focus had somehow intended this into being. But my intent did not *create* the particulars; it merely *suggested* a rough outline.

All of which again brings up the interesting question of who is doing the creating while my young lucid dreaming self is standing in the hallway scratching his head and waiting.

To explain the incredible creativity of dreams, some have imagined that dreaming has a *bricoleur*, or tinker behind the scenes, who cobbles together the next portion of the dream out of bits of memory traces and *objet trouves* (found objects) in the mind. With lightning speed and stunning alacrity, the *bricoleur* creates new objects and figures, perfectly detailed and individually unique for examination by the dreamer.

In this lucid dream, did a *bricoleur* or dream-maker determine the scene I was to experience after opening the door? Did the *bricoleur* listen for my intent and quickly throw together an assortment of dream figures with various hair styles, features, and heights? Or did the *bricoleur* extract from the storehouse of my mind some visual imagery and in a few seconds concoct a perfectly acceptable, sensible scene?

The magic of intent seems to be just that—the ability to summon an inner responsiveness, instinctively attuned to you, with creative talents far beyond supercomputing calculations, whose goal seems the appropriate execution of your vocalized desire. In some respects, intent flies far beyond the expectation effect to some deep, rich, formatively creative force to surprise lucid dreamers with an experience previously unknown and basically unknowable. The manifestations of intent arose from something deeper than my waking self's doing.

So while the results of my intent were stunning, they were also mystifying. When I willed something to occur in the lucid dream, I felt a direct connection of willing it. So too, when I expected something in the lucid dream, I saw my expectation take shape. But intent? Intent consisted of throwing a suggestion into an invisible box and having a response suddenly materialize. Intent was the magic of lucid dreams. But who was the magician?

Ten years later when Castaneda's *The Art of Dreaming* was published, don Juan would seek to explain intent, saying, "To intend is to wish without wishing, to do without doing." Pressed by Castaneda for a more detailed technique, don Juan continues, saying that "there is no technique for intending. One intends through usage."[4]

For me, however, doing implies a *do*-er. Creating implies a *create*-er. Behind the curtain of intent, something listened.

I was on a collision course with the doer of dreams, the great Intender.

5

INDEPENDENT AGENTS
AND THE VOICE OF
THE UNCONSCIOUS

AROUND THE TIME THAT I WAS CONTEMPLATING AND EXPERIMENTING
with the issues of the expectation effect and intent, I came across a
magazine clipping about others who wished to experiment informally
in lucid dreams. Linda Lane Magallón, coordinator for The Lucidity
Project, sought experienced lucid dreamers to perform self-directed
experiments. Each month, she would mail out a lucid dreaming goal,
derived from ideas found in The "Unknown" Reality by Jane Roberts
and other sources. The lucid dreamers would then try to become lucid,
recall the goal, and somehow accomplish it. [1]

For someone like me, living in the Midwest and somewhat isolated
from fellow lucid dreamers, it was encouraging to meet others with
similar interests and begin to explore, as a group, lucid dreaming's
potential. I was involved in the project for three years, and it taught me
much about using lucid dreams as an experimental platform. Simply
having a structure developed my skills and brought a sense of purpose
and discipline.

One of the things I quickly realized was that not every month's
goal appealed to me. When I didn't relate to or believe in the goal, I
simply wouldn't recall the goal in a lucid dream. I found that goals
first had to pass through my conscious belief barrier to have a chance
of being acted upon.

One goal that did interest me was "Find Out What the Characters in
Your Dream Represent." Having already asked dream figures to explain

dream *symbols*, I looked forward to having a dream figure explain *itself*. So, while traveling on business near Chicago, I suggested before sleep to become lucid and discover what a dream character represented. That night I had a lucid dream (March 1985):

> Going into an office building, I put my hand out to open the door and think, "My hands! I'm dreaming!" I open the door, wondering, "Now what am I supposed to do?" Then I remembered the goal for the month—that I was to find out what the people in my dream represent.
>
> I walk down the hallway feeling energetic because I have recalled my lucid dream task. I turn to the right through a door and step into a typical office setting. Four people/dream figures are there: a fashionably dressed young woman to my right, a receptionist behind a counter, an older gentleman in a three-piece suit, and another woman looking at a magazine.
>
> I deliberated for a moment and although a part of me wanted to talk to the fashionably dressed woman, I decided to talk to the gentleman on my left. He was looking at a picture on the wall when I approached him and asked, "What do you represent?"
>
> He turned toward me and the oddest thing happened. A voice boomed out of the space above him with this reply, "The acquired characteristics!"
>
> I considered the statement, but couldn't make sense of it. So I asked, "The acquired characteristics of what?"
>
> The voice seemed to hesitate for a moment before it boomed out again, from the space above the man, "The acquired characteristics of the happy giver!" I repeated that to myself and realized I had accomplished my goal. I wondered if I should stay in the dream or come out. Looking at this older man—of medium height, a little overweight, kind of balding with an avuncular, happy, serene face—I worried that I'd forget it if I didn't come out, so I told myself to wake up. I had that funny experience of being in the dream and feeling myself in the bed at the same time—it seemed to last a few seconds.

In all of my past lucid dreams, dream figures spoke (or not) when I addressed them. Now, the *space above* the dream figure blurted out a response—this certainly qualified as unexpected. I had to question the voice ("The acquired characteristics of what?"), to which it provided a complete answer ("The acquired characteristics of the happy giver.").

"Happy giver, happy giver . . ." I played with the response in my mind. Then it hit me. The day before the dream, I had stopped and talked with the head of a local charity. She really surprised me by having such a negative view of the donors to her cause, telling me that they only gave to get their name in the annual report. She was such an *unhappy receiver* that I muttered to myself "The Lord loves a happy giver" as I walked away from her. Now, in this dream, I had met this bit of day residue—the happy giver.

Driving around Chicago that day, I kept returning to the booming voice. Why didn't the dream figure respond? Why did a voice boom out from above? I had neither intended nor expected *that*. The unexpected had recurred, this time in spades.

Because this experience clashed with my assumptions about lucid dreaming, an odd wondering began to form in my mind. If the lucid dream just reflected what I expected to experience, then how could anything unexpected occur? Did the presence of the unexpected mean that lucid dreams derive from outside my waking self's thoughts, memories, and mind? And if so, where did the unexpected come from? And why the booming voice from above?

I had to ponder, was I now consciously experiencing more than my conscious self? Where did these other aspects of awareness come from, since they did not seem to originate from my waking self?

Decades later, I discovered that Jung had considered a very similar point, maintaining that one finds much more in dreams than reflections of the conscious mind and conscious memories. In dreaming, one touches the unconscious, something that extends beyond the waking self. As Jung observed, "Looked at in this way, the unconscious appears as a field of experience of unlimited extent. If it were merely reactive to the conscious mind, we might aptly call it a psychic mirror world. In that case, the real source of all contents and activities would lie in the conscious mind, and there would be absolutely nothing in the unconscious except the distorted reflections of conscious contents. . . . The empirical facts give the lie to this."[2]

At this point, my lucid dream experiences were bringing me to this same realization—the unconscious does not merely reflect a "psychic mirror world" of the conscious mind. Whenever I experienced the unexpected while lucid dreaming, I experienced something beyond the mirror, beyond the conscious mind. The information was not from my waking self; rather, it came from the unconscious, "a field of experience of unlimited extent."

Jung continued, "Because the unconscious is not just a reactive mirror reflection, but an independent, productive activity, its realm of experience is a self-contained world, having its own reality, of which we can only say that it affects us as we affect it—precisely what we say about our experience of the outer world."[3]

Suddenly, I could see that when lucid dreamers ask the dream a question or ask the dream to do something (e.g., "I want to see more attractive women in here when I open this door again!"), the unconscious independently listens and responds. Aware in a lucid dream, one has access to this inner reality of the unconscious and its creativity. But because we lucid dreamers tend to focus simply on our own actions and manipulations in the dream state, and because we assume we create the dream, we never bother to ask the dream itself. To get beyond ourselves, we have to stop focusing on our doings and manipulations and allow the unconscious an opportunity to respond.

Now, within just a few lucid dreaming experiments, I could see a dramatic conclusion developing: *The unconscious was not chaotic, primitive, and archaic. The unconscious appeared to be both conscious and alive.*

KNOCKING ON THE DOOR OF THE UNCONSCIOUS

In the months that followed, I began to have more varied and interesting lucid dreams. Dreaming seemed to open up in step with my curiosity and conjectures; inner connections were taking place at deeper levels. In one of the next lucid dreams, I found myself traveling through space. Whether it was inner or outer space, I wasn't sure (May 1985):

> I'm with some friends in the darkness of space. We seem to be on a platform, but it's nowhere—it's not connected to anything—we're surrounded by space. I think I become lucid at this point and decide to go flying. What an unbelievable trip! I'm flying through space, but suddenly I realize that I'm flying through time as well. At this moment, I know that space equals time and somehow this space puckers; as I move through it, it's thicker in spots than others.
>
> Suddenly a couple holding bright purple-red glowing strings flies past me. I take a string and use it to help me move. Ahead, I see a stunning collection of glowing strands of lights—gold, red, unimaginably vivid colors unlike anything I've ever seen in waking reality. It's beyond neon, even laser light. The strands reach out into the darkness, brilliantly alive.

In lucid dreams like these, you feel that you have gone beyond the conscious waking mind's conception of the world. You know things without knowing how you know. You see things that seem impossible to articulate because they are outside any physical reference point. The inner world, so easy to ignore, now appears more brilliantly incredible and mysterious than ever before.

Yet, I remained troubled. Having more fantastic and awesome lucid dreams only made my curiosity more acute. *What was behind the lucid dreaming?* At each stage of my experience, something *more* appeared in lucid dreaming. The unconscious kept growing in complexity.

Meanwhile, the Lucidity Project's next goal involved the idea of expanding "space" in a lucid dream—a curious idea. As I saw it, the lucid dreamer acted within a mental space. But what were the characteristics of this mental space? Did dream space have limits? What makes space appear in a dream?

Intrigued, I became lucid in a dream:

> I begin to explore a long hallway where some women are working on something they call "the mold of man." Somehow it comes to me that grouping of certain sensory impressions creates "the mold of man." Around on the floor, I see four or five molds of body parts—legs, arms, and part of a torso.
>
> Recalling that my goal this month is to "expand space," I feel a jolt of joyous energy rise up. It occurs to me that by expanding space, the lucid dreamer is engaging the unconscious to create! I begin to run down the hallway, and as I do so, I open all the doors I can find! Peering inside, I know I am expanding the space of the dream!
>
> Opening each door, my quick observing causes something to appear, though I don't know what. Opening the first door, a living-room setting appears. Opening the next, I see an empty office. Opening each door, I basically force the expansion of the space of the dream. But who fills the space with its contents? Do I, or my friend, the conscious unconscious and its now overworked *bricoleur*?
>
> Finally, I run out of the building and into a plaza. Aha, another space! Then I recall Stephen LaBerge's technique of spinning [in which the lucid dreamer spins and expects to see a new dreamscape; often this is done if one senses the dream is preparing to collapse]. I think, "Yes, another way to expand space!" and begin to spin and spin.

I woke feeling gleeful. I began to understand that my conscious focus, or my "observer effect," creates the need for apparent space to come into being. Then that focus somehow prompts the unconscious processes to contribute by filling in the space. If I intended something specific to be in that space, it normally would appear there;

otherwise, the unconscious cobbled together something acceptable or believable.

In the "nowhere" of lucid dreaming space, all was potential, it seemed. Consciously focusing activates the potential of that space and begins the creation process of giving form to the formless. In that brief moment, the dance of unconscious and conscious creation begins. When conscious focus ends, the space collapses back, I presume, into its original form, pure potential.

INDEPENDENT AGENTS

Jung said that people respond in one of two ways when placed in an encounter with the unconscious. One group becomes deflated, realizing the immensity of the psyche's depth and power when compared to their own small ego. The other group becomes inflated, figuring that the psyche's depth and power give strength and energy to their ego desires.

During this period of my lucid dreaming life, I fit into the second camp—those whose ego becomes inflated by the encounter with the unconscious. But things were about to change, as seen in this lucid dream:

> Becoming lucidly aware, I feel that wonderful upsurge of energy and vitality. I immediately take off flying and have a sense that I am over Detroit, or someplace with a similar street layout. Below me, I see a crowd of dream figures and fly toward them to investigate.
>
> Feeling that I have excellent flying control, and not having any experiments in mind, I concoct a game. Each time I fly over the crowd, I decide to knock off one of the men's hats. I swoop down, concentrate, and *poof*, I knock the first one off. Flying back, I descend, select a target, and *poof*, there goes the second one.
>
> Coming back around, I concentrate on a hat in the middle of the crowd, descend, and just as I prepare to hit the hat, a hand reaches up from the crowd and stops me in mid-flight!
>
> Struggling, I can feel the tight grip around my forearm. Shaking free takes a moment, but I succeed in flying away. I continue my lucid adventure.

In the morning, I couldn't get over the experience of having a dream figure stop me in mid-flight. Without any presuggestion on my part, a dream figure acted contrary to my goals. Absolutely unexpected! Until this point, I held the implicit assumption that all dream figures existed as reflections of me and thus were my subjects. True, I had noticed some wouldn't respond to my questions, but by and large, the dream figures were my playthings. This was the first time a dream figure stopped me from acting.

I could feel my ego deflating. Did a dream figure actually rise up independently with purpose and volition to stop me? Or did my unconscious *bricoleur* observe the scene and decide to teach me a lesson? Perhaps there was a third possibility, that something in me acted in opposition to myself, like an alter ego? But how can we explain that if lucid dreams exist by virtue of the expectation effect?

The expectation effect functioned best when used to manipulate objects, settings, or my actions in the lucid dream. When it came to dream figures, however, the expectation effect showed mixed results. Sometimes dream figures did exactly what I expected, while other times, they acted unexpectedly. In fact, dream figures often acted as if they were semiconsciously aware and pursuing their own purposes.

Reading other lucid dreamers' reports, I discovered that their dream figures also showed many unexpected tendencies. Occasionally, dream figures acted in ways as if to prove their independence from the lucid dreamer, as in this case reported by lucid dreamer Connie Gavalis:

> Lucid, I turned to a dull blonde, short, plain, thin, middle-aged woman dressed in a white print outfit. Her hair is stringy, slightly curly and down to her shoulders. I say, "You are not real." She says, "Yes, I am."
>
> I say, "You are in my dream; therefore you are not real!" She says, "Yes, I am."
>
> I say, "This is my dream—notice that I'm flying."
>
> Then I'm flying and the woman is holding me on her lap while we both fly. I think, "This is great fun!" [4]

And as in this case reported by my *Lucid Dream Exchange* coeditor, Lucy Gillis:[5]

> I turn to the girls and say triumphantly, "This is a dream!" Patty is exasperated and says, "You mean to tell me we're all dreaming." I say, "No, I am. You are characters created by my mind." Then I see a bright white light in a narrow horizontal band with black edges flash in my eyes and on my hands. I get kind of surprised.
>
> Patty gets angry and interlaces her fingers with mine. I see more flashes rip through the "fabric" of the dream world and hear a crackle and hiss-like static. The fabric of that reality looks like bad reception in a TV. Patty bends my fingers back. I don't pay attention to her.

Instead, I wonder how my fingers can hurt when I am aware that I'm dreaming.

Examples like these suggest that when conscious in the dream state, dream figures could now be engaged in long-overdue conversations. Instead of tacitly assuming the nature of dream figures and projecting our naive presumptions upon them, lucid dreamers could listen to the dream figures' analyses of the situation. The only problem—dream figures often see themselves so differently than we expect!

The word *conversation* has roots in old Latin with two meanings: 1) "to associate with" and 2) "to turn around." This second meaning, "to turn around," bears special significance as some dream figures literally debate their sense of autonomy with doubtful lucid dreamers. These dream figures exhibit a desire "to turn" us to adopting a new perspective. In some conversations, they turn us away from cultural beliefs and blanket assumptions and ask us to give them status as valid beings with some abilities, aware in the dream space. They converse us toward recognizing them, appreciating them, and ultimately understanding them. Notice, though, that when we refuse to accept their pronouncement and assert our superiority by flying and manipulating the dream space, they do something very rational; they claim their equivalent status by replicating our behavior. Sometimes, they do another very human thing: they get frustrated and show it. I recall reading where a lucid dreamer became upset at the dream figure's repeated claim of awareness and made a final cutting remark; with that, the dream figure sat down on the curb and cried.

Though they may represent a minority, a certain set of dream figures once again show us that the expectation effect only goes so far. By acting unexpectedly, they do much to express their own validity, semi-autonomy, and viewpoint. Consider this lucid dreamer's surprise when her expectation is unmet:

> I was lucid and saw this man, I asked for his name and he replied, "Otto." As planned, I asked, "Can you warn me the next time I'm dreaming?" He immediately replied, "No!" I was really surprised and asked him, "Why not?" Then Otto said, "Because this is real . . ."[6]

Taught to believe and expect that the entire dream exists as our imagined projection, that we dream it into being, many lucid dreamers naturally resist any notion of not completely creating and controlling the dream. Yet, these conversations suggest a new level of inherent complexity in dreaming. With experience, lucid dreamers come to realize that the dream space contains various types of dream figures, behaving with varying degrees of awareness (which I discuss at length in chapter 11).

German psychotherapist and lucid dreamer Paul Tholey intensively investigated the behavior of dream figures and came to feel that some possessed a type of awareness. In general, he based this on three observations: 1) in some lucid dreams, the dream figure's awareness preceded the lucid dreamer's awareness, 2) in at least one lucid dream, a dream figure supplied unknown but later verified information to the dreamer, and 3) the dream figure sometimes developed reasoned and creative responses to various dream tasks such as creating poetry or multiplying numbers.

Tholey states:

> In addition to the lucidity of the dream-ego, the "lucidity" of the other dream characters also plays an important role in their communication. In order to avoid misunderstanding, we can never empirically prove whether or not other dream characters are lucid, only that they speak and behave as if they were. Elsewhere I have argued that many dream figures seem to perform with a "consciousness" of what they are doing (Tholey, 1985; 1989a). Some of our unpublished work on the lucidity of other dream figures (in the sense just described) includes examples which seem to indicate that the dream-ego becomes lucid first. This is followed by the other dream figures attaining lucidity. On the other hand, we have many examples of reverse order. We can illustrate this by means of an example in which another dream character not only becomes lucid before the dream-ego, he also possesses a higher degree of lucidity than the dream-ego [lucid dreamer] later achieves.[7]

In Tholey's 1987 book, *Schöpferisch Träumen,* he recalls a dream figure who became upset with the lucid dreamer's attempt to determine the dream figure's level of consciousness. Tholey writes, "If one asks dream figures themselves if they have a consciousness, it can be that they react annoyed. A [lucid] dreamer got this answer: 'That *I* have a consciousness, I know. But if *you* have a consciousness, I doubt, because you ask such a silly question!'"[8]

As the lucid dream examples in this chapter illustrate, the occasional lucidly aware dream figure plays havoc with our assumptions, since it appears to operate from its own internal purposefulness and directed activity. Whereas many dream figures appear to have very little aware functioning capacity, some appear to possess the ability to reason, remember, comprehend, and perform purposeful actions.

Humbled, perhaps even chastened by the independent agent who stopped me from flying and knocking off hats, I began to see the complexity of dream figures. In fact, I noticed how language perpetuates our simplistic view of them by calling them "dream characters," a term that denotes something fictitious, unreal, and imaginary, like a character in a child's play or cartoon. By calling them dream characters, we prejudge them and dispose ourselves to relate to them as fictions.

Having a dream figure grab me in mid-flight made them more than fictions, more than characters. By acting independently, they suggested a type of awareness, a type of conscious energy. Dream figures, I would find out, were so much more complex than the science of dreaming presumes.

WHAT DOES THE UNCONSCIOUS KNOW?

Encountering independent agents and unexpected events in lucid dreaming can be very troubling. Although at first you might be tempted to rationalize away the events as anomalies or a malfunctioning expectation effect, your viewpoint has been shaken. Lucid dreaming brings you into deeper contact with both the immensity and beauty of your unconscious. With that comes a dawning sense of awe and respect.

Around this time, I read of another experienced lucid dreamer, Scott Sparrow, author of *Lucid Dreaming: Dawning of the Clear Light*, who mentioned his own encounter with seemingly independent dream figures:

> In my own life, I found that at the height of my lucid dreaming, I ran into a brick wall of sorts. Lucid dreaming had become evidence of my evolution, a merit badge of sorts. Of course, I thought I was handling it okay; but I had no idea what I was repressing. Who does? Well, all kinds of very angry people began showing up in my dreams, and turning rather demonic to boot. A black panther walked in the front door and would not go away no matter how much I told him he was only a dream.[9]

For some lucid dreamers, these independent agents may represent personal fears or repressed, shadow elements seeking expression in the dream. In these cases, one wonders whether the dream figures possess actual independent agency or represent personal fears, denied impulses, personal aggression, et cetera, which the lucid dreamer has ignored and now faces in an emotionally charged interaction. Could their seeming independence be only a reflection of their "counter" tendencies to the lucid dreamer's activity? Could a lucid dreamer acknowledge a shadow element and seek reconciliation?

Over the years, there have been numerous anecdotal reports of nightmares being resolved when the dreamer became lucidly aware and asked the nightmarish figure, "What do you represent?" or "What do you want?" So with the proper presence of mind, lucid dreamers potentially can engage the frightful dream figure to discover its meaning in the dream. However, if we expect the dream state to contain repressed material, it may create a situation in which we do meet frightful reflections. Do we meet our expectations personified or something actually inherent in the dream state?

Within the year, the unconscious shocked me again, this time by suggesting, in a lucid dream, a future event, something beyond my conscious knowing. Jung held that the unconscious could "anticipate" events, and much of what we call precognition is simply that, a forward-looking conjecture. Since Jung felt the psyche held the vantage point of both conscious and unconscious knowledge, this allowed it to project a possible course for events that appeared precognitive.

As the following lucid dream unfolded, the future-oriented knowledge appeared to come with the show (April 1986):

> I see something odd, become lucid, and decide to go find my friend Bill (who lives 2,000 miles away). I move through a deep darkness then finally emerge into a nighttime view of his city. It's beautiful! The hills and the city buildings at night seem perfectly reproduced, as I look down from far above.
>
> Suddenly I descend into a restaurant. Bill and his wife are there, seated at a heavy, dark wood table. I sit down and tell them, "This is a dream—we're dreaming!"
>
> I notice his wife has a set of necklaces in front of her. Each strand has a different color. She begins very deliberately to place a necklace over her head, and suddenly I *know* each necklace represents one year of their marriage. With the seventh necklace, she stops. Without any word spoken, I have the distinct impression that their marriage will last seven years.

I wake, wondering if this lucidly sensed intuition could be valid. I didn't think the symbolism into being; I simply knew each necklace was a year in their marriage, but there were only seven necklaces.

Their marriage? It lasts seven years, then dissolves.

FALSE AWAKENINGS TRULY HAPPEN

Though the implications of the occasional independent agent and forward-looking lucid dream both troubled and intrigued me, something relatively simple shook me much more deeply. Lucid dreamers call it the "false awakening."[10]

Many lucid dreamers have had the interesting experience of seeming to wake from a lucid dream, only later to realize that they are not in waking reality but in a new dream scene. Sometimes, these false awakenings are quite convincing. For example, your lucid dream ends, you wake and reach for your dream journal to jot down your lucid dream, only to notice the lucid dream is already written there. Then you think, "How did it get written down already?" At that moment, it hits you—you're still dreaming!

For some people, the false dream setting can seem quite convincing. You may get out of bed, head to the bathroom, and then notice the pink tile. "Wait a second, when did we get the pink tile?" you muse for a moment. In a flash it dawns on you that you are still dreaming.

Sometimes, you wake from the lucid dream but into a new dream scene, like driving down the highway or having breakfast or being at school. You might even begin to look around for something to write your lucid dream on. Eventually you realize, "This is a dream!" Usually, the realization of a false awakening causes you to awaken into physical reality. Usually, but not always.

Once while I was giving a talk on lucid dreams, a young man raised his hand to comment that he had three false awakenings in a row. He was in a lucid dream, felt it falling apart, then woke in bed. Wait a second, he thinks, this isn't my bed! *Bam*, he wakes again, back in his bed. Rolling over, he notices the roman shades. Wait a second, he thinks, we don't have roman shades! *Bam*, he wakes again, a little shaken from two false awakenings. He gets up to go take a shower and then notices the bookcase in the hallway. Wait a second, he thinks for the third time, we don't have a bookcase! *Bam*. Now he wakes . . . in physical reality.

I could tell the young man was quite shaken. And I sympathized with him, because it happened to me. Seven false awakenings in a row. On a beautiful summer morning I had an enjoyable lucid dream and woke from it, only to notice a different nightstand. Oh! A false awakening. But that was just number one. The first two didn't bother me, but then came three and four! Each time, I expected to find my real room, my real bed, but I kept finding very similar realities, close models of my bedroom. Then five, then six! Six false awakenings! My god, what was happening? Where was my world? It felt as if I was bursting through layers of probable worlds as the layers kept giving way! At that final, apparent awakening, my mind swirled in a whirl-pool of memories, perceptions, realizations, and ephemera, grasping for an *actual actuality*! Finally, I slipped out of bed, steadied myself, and touched the light-blue plaster wall, hoping for nothing more than precious stability.

After seven, I told myself that whatever reality I might encounter in the hallway, I would accept—that's how shaken I was—any reality was fine, as long as it *stayed put*. As I've said before, venturing into lucid dreaming takes a certain amount of fearlessness. Encountering the lucid dream reality in all of its complexity and creative splendor can seem almost overwhelming at times.

Maybe that's what happened to me. Maybe like some inner Icarus of the dream world, I had ventured too close to the enormity of the unconscious, only to realize my humanness and fall back. Or maybe my waking ego preferred to be seen as the one in control and felt uncomfortable with the mind-blowing creativity of the unconscious. Whatever the case, something happened, something changed, and I needed a break from lucid dreaming.

Of course, all those unanswered questions about lucid dreaming, the unconscious, and the nature of dream reality stayed alive in my mind and refused to go away. Dreaming had developed aspects of another reality with all the profound complexity and wonder that entailed.

At this stage, I knew that something was "behind" the dream, even when lucid. There was simply more than the waking self conscious in the dream state. The *bricoleur*, the conscious unconscious, the creative system—something—hid behind the creations, yet could be seen in the creativity.

I knew, too, that I directed my focus within the lucid dream. I did not "control" the lucid dream, nor did I control the unconscious and its expressions. I could direct myself and, through "intent," direct the unconscious to some degree.

Finally, I knew that dream figures were much more complex than people realized. Some appeared to possess a type of awareness, a type of conscious volition. Perhaps they were sub-personalities, conscious fragments, or archetypal energies, but their independent agency increased my uncertainty about the dream realm.

So, I stepped back from lucid dreaming to give myself time to reflect. To let the experiences mature in the quiet places of my mind. To prepare for the next, deeper phase of lucid dreaming, when I began to probe the depths of unconscious knowledge and the dream reality.

6

FEELING-TONES AND
REVIEW COMMITTEES

FOR THE NEXT TWO YEARS, I SET ASIDE MY DREAM JOURNAL AND NO longer sought to become lucidly aware. Instead, I thought about what I had experienced and tried to make sense of it. On those occasions when I did, spontaneously, become lucid, I didn't investigate the nature of the unconscious; I simply played around in the dream space. I still needed to process what had happened.

Bit by bit, lucid dreaming was reconfiguring my core assumptions about the nature of dreaming and, in turn, the nature of reality and the ego self. I began to grasp something hard to accept, hard to admit. Like Copernicus, who realized that the Earth was not the center of the universe, I now suspected that the waking ego self was not the center of one's self or even the center of conscious awareness. The waking ego self, it seemed to me, was part of a much larger interrelationship of conscious awareness. Though my waking life revolved around my ego, emotions, and personal concerns, in lucid dreaming, I discovered a much larger sphere of influence—the so-called unconscious that actually seemed very conscious, very responsive, and very much alive.

Consciously aware in the dream state, I saw that I could maintain the illusion of being the center by focusing on manipulating the dream, achieving my personal goals, and refusing to look beyond. But when I opened up and allowed myself to let go, to engage something beyond myself and focus there, what appeared was the larger and more complex, creative, wise, knowledgeable, and encompassing Self.

Now, with what Jung would call my newly deflated ego, I reentered the investigation of lucid dreaming with a more somber view. Something was going on here, and I was determined to find out. On some levels, I felt like my waking ego self unknowingly performed a bit part in a divine comedy, and my only hope lay in lucidly sneaking off the stage and asking the hidden director to explain the mysterious plot, the rationale, the raison d'etre.

It began to seem preposterous that the waking self created the unconscious. How could something as narrowly focused as the waking self create something so unfathomable and profoundly aware? Also preposterous was the notion that the so-called unconscious existed as the repository of all the unsavory and repressed impulses from childhood, primitive instincts, and desires. That was not what I was experiencing as I was lucidly aware and probing the conscious unconscious, nor were my other experienced lucid dreaming friends. Sure, I experienced sexual desire and aggression occasionally in the lucid state, but it appeared to come from my waking self's desire brought into dreaming by me, not something foisted upon me by a primitive unconscious.

If the unconscious naturally contained and was the source of primitive, sexual, aggressive impulses, then every lucid dream would be a fight or conflict with these forces; every lucid dream would demonstrate the battle of the unconscious and its instincts against the waking self and its concerns. This was not the case. On those occasions in which something instinctual arose, the lucid dreamer could focus on it or not; those so-called primitive instincts did not have any power to overwhelm the lucid dreamer. The unconscious seemed a relatively neutral party. If there was a battle, it was one that the waking self had with the alternating desires and self-conflicting purposes of the waking self.

As I considered Freud and Jung, I felt increasingly at odds with their depiction of the unconscious. Though Jung would comment upon the deep creativity, numinous quality, and energetic splendor of the unconscious, he still focused on its dark side and ability to overtake humankind with dark, seething, unleashed forces of repressed emotions. Yet after hundreds of lucid dreams, I felt the vast majority involved joy, wonder, and learning. Only on rare occasions did I feel disturbed or shocked, and rarer still were the lucid dreams in which I felt threatened because, normally, I saw the threatening figure as a personification of my fears, which needed compassion and understanding.

There seemed only one way to get to the bottom of this. Lucid, I set out to probe the responsively aware, conscious unconscious and see how it responds. How much does the unconscious know? Does it have a purpose? Only by engaging the unconscious could I set aside the apparently prejudicial views that culture and theory had placed over it and come to a true meeting with the larger aspect of Self.

Undoubtedly, the primary way for my ego self to interact more deeply with the unconscious involved letting go of directing the lucid dream and inviting the unconscious awareness to lead. Only by letting go of my intent, my direction, my manipulation of the lucid dream could I engage this other awareness behind the dream. Already, I had seen that something existed there. Yet for whatever reason, the something behind the dream seemed largely an observer until that moment when I let go of the dream; then, it would take the lucid dream in new and unexpected ways.

In many of these lucid dreams, I simply asked the lucid dream to show me something and, suddenly, I would be whooshing through the night sky or some foggy darkness and then drop into a scene. In this type of lucid dream, I "surrendered" to the dream or the awareness behind the dream. Yet, surrendering to this unseen awareness did not resolve a deeper issue: Did the unseen awareness provide knowledge and information or just random creativity? I needed to do more than simply surrender to the awareness; I needed to challenge it and seek out the limits of its knowledge.

Around this time, I became curious about a specific concept, put forth in the books by Jane Roberts,[1] called "feeling-tone." As described in Roberts' book, *The Nature of Personal Reality*, feeling-tones "pervade your being."

> They are the form your spirit takes when combined with flesh. From them, from their core, your flesh arises. Everything that you experience has consciousness, and each consciousness is endowed with its own feeling-tone. . . . The feeling-tone then is the motion and fiber—the timber—the portion of your energy devoted to your physical experience. . . . It is the essence of yourself. . . . It is the feeling of yourself, inexhaustible.[2]

Curious about whether this was an actual tone or just a deep feeling, I decided that in my next lucid dream I would ask the dream about it. I knew some type of awareness was behind the lucid dream, and it was responsive, but did it possess conceptual knowledge? Did it understand an idea at a deeper level than my waking self? If I personally didn't get it, would this other awareness in the dream be able to respond and teach me?

So I set out to experiment, hoping the conscious unconscious could explain to me the actual nature of the feeling-tone concept. Turns out, I got much more than I bargained for (February 1993):

I'm standing outside in what looks like my childhood neighborhood. I'm walking with one of my brothers. It's a nice, sunny day.

Suddenly I notice brightly colored fish, about six of them, swimming through the air, about six feet off the ground! At first I conclude, "They can breathe and live in our environment just like we do in theirs." Then I see even more fish swimming by in the air and the incongruity strikes me. I realize, "I'm dreaming! This is a lucid dream!"

I decide not to run off or go flying, but wonder, "Well, what should I do?" I think about trying to find God, but realize that I have tried that before with limited success. (Normally, I begin flying higher and become too emotional and the lucid dream collapses.)

Then I remember: I want to hear my feeling-tone.

I consider how to do this and, on impulse, just look up in the mottled sky and yell out to the dreaming, "Hey! I want to hear my feeling-tone!"

Suddenly, a tiny black dot appears in the sky directly above me. From it comes a barely perceptible humming. At first, it's quite slow and quiet, but it seems to have a familiar sound to it, like a high pitched, vibrating *Aaaahhhh*. Then the dot begins growing in the space above me. As it grows, the humming sound volume keeps sounding—louder and louder. *AAAAAHHHHH!!!*

I can barely believe what I'm seeing and feeling. Simultaneous with the expanding volume, a distinct conical shape begins forming and growing outward from the initial dot and it's headed toward me! The humming sound continues increasing, vibrating the space around me with enormous intensity, and as it does, the conical shape comes closer and closer.

Now the humming *AAAHHH* sound feels like an immense vibrating energy and the sound increases to fantastic proportions. The cone grows larger and will soon be surrounding me on all sides. My whole being is reverberating with this energetic, vibrant humming sound as the cone encloses me! I appear to collapse to a dot of awareness.

At this point, "me," "Robert," simply disappears. From a different vantage point, an awareness watches the scene of the vibrating cone—the feeling-tone, the sound of that person's being. Oddly, a Robert-me doesn't really exist in any normal sense any longer, there is only the vibrating sound of my feeling-tone. Yet strangely, an awareness views the scene of the vibrating cone.

As this continues, something inside that awareness eventually decides that it needs to recapitulate that feeling-tone back into physical form—before "Robert" essentially forgets to exist and loses himself in the sound, the feeling-tone. There's a bit of a struggle here (like a magician pulling a person out of his hat!) as the awareness struggles to recall and recapitulate the memory/form/idea of Robert. The awareness seems to shuffle through various memory/form/ideas until coming upon the one connected to this vibrating feeling-tone.

At once, I, Robert, again perceive, sitting in a lotus position outside in my front yard. I pick up a deck of cards and try to shuffle them, but all of the cards fly out of my hands in an impressive display. Suddenly I recall the feeling-tone sound again, and the tone begins humming, *Aaaaahhhh*. I look down at my thumb and index finger, drawn together like in a yoga mudra, and I can feel the extraordinary energy vibrating through my whole body. I'm transfixed by the sound and notice that my thumb and index finger are starting to glow with a golden light from within.

Simply asking the dream to experience a concept brought forth this immense flood of knowledge from the depths of the listening unconscious. Now I knew beyond doubt—the unconscious is conscious, responsive, and alive. To experience it only requires turning toward it when lucid.

At the time, I had no idea what I was asking for! Requesting to hear one's feeling-tone or vibrational essence sounds rather esoteric, but to experience the concept was, quite simply, utterly profound and beyond belief. I *became* my feeling-tone. I did not intellectually engage the concept, or question it, I *was* the concept.

Most curious was that final moment when the cone of vibrating sound energy set to engulf me completely. At that instant, a sudden transposition of awareness occurred, and the vantage point became this other awareness. As this other awareness watched the vibrating cone of feeling-tone, it then finally tried to recall the memory of Robert, which begs the question, did some small bit of my awareness take refuge in a larger awareness?

Dreaming has the capacity to break through normal boundaries of experience. When waking, experience comes through our senses for the most part, and we "entertain" thoughts and ideas. In dreaming, however, experience has greater direct access to feeling, knowing, comprehending. When lucid, we can see the greater capacity of experiencing available to the dreamer.

Years after this experience, on a business trip to Columbus, Ohio, I had a free hour and stopped at a book store. I stumbled across a book on mantras and yantras. As I began to read the book, I realized that my experience of finding my feeling-tone appeared consistent with some ancient ideas on mantras and the creation of all physical form through sound. Also, the black dot I noticed above me seemed to be analogous to the "bindu," a Sanskrit term meaning "dot" or "point," from which it is believed the creative sound emerges to make the manifest realm of the world. Some religions teach that all manifest matter on another level is simply vibrating sound energy. After my experience, I wondered if this ancient knowledge didn't have a basis in fact.

Had I lucidly reached the level of something like the collective unconscious? Had my lucid request to the conscious unconscious been answered through an inner body of knowledge? How deep could one go when consciously aware in the dream state?

VISITED BY REVIEW COMMITTEES

I continued going deeper, spending more time focusing on the awareness behind the dream, asking the dream to do things, show things, explain things. Some of my lucid dreams involved seeking verifiable information about future events (as I will discuss in chapter 15). Lucid dreaming began to appear as one pathway to the fantastic depth and mysteries of the unconscious. My old curiosity was back and, with it, the energy to pursue a probing of the conscious unconscious.

Around this time, Carlos Castaneda's *The Art of Dreaming* was published. Reading it, I realized that I had lucid encounters similar to those he writes about *before* he wrote about them. One example is the "dreaming emissary," which, don Juan tells Castaneda, is an "energy that purports to aid dreamers by telling them things. The problem with the dreaming emissary is that it can tell only what . . . [dreamers] already know or should know, were they worth their salt." He goes on to explain that the dreaming emissary is "[a]n impersonal force that we turn into a very personal one because it has a voice . . . [you] simply hear it as a man's or a woman's voice. And the voice can tell them about the state of things, which most of the time they take as sacred advice."[3]

Don Juan mentions that most lucid dreamers only hear the authoritative voice of the dreaming emissary speak from within the dreaming. On rare occasions, however, a lucid dreamer might create an illusory dream figure form as the source of the voice.

I began to wonder about my lucid dream (in chapter 5) of asking the gentleman in the office, "What do you represent?" and hearing a voice boom out, "The acquired characteristics!" Was that the voice of the dreaming emissary?

Castaneda complains to don Juan that the voice seemed to know more than he himself did. Don Juan replies, "The emissary didn't tell you anything new. Its statements were correct, but it only seemed to be revealing things to you." When Castaneda insists that he could not know, don Juan concludes, "You know now infinitely more about the mystery of the universe than what you rationally suspect. But that's our human malady, to know more about the mystery of the universe than we suspect."[4]

Because of some earlier lucid dreams, and regular dreams, in which a voice provided me accurate information, I considered this portion of Castandeda's book potentially valid. However, other parts of the book troubled me. For example, Castaneda lucidly encounters knowledge-able dream figures that he calls "inorganic beings." Don Juan warns Castaneda, "There is something the emissary hasn't dared to tell you so far: that the inorganic beings are after our awareness or the awareness of any being that falls into their nets. They'll give us knowledge, but they'll extract a payment: our total being."[5] Although four paragraphs later, don Juan backtracks and states that "inorganic beings can't force anyone to stay with them," still, he warned, a person might find their realm so alluring as to volunteer to stay. This caught my eye. I hadn't been fearful of dream figures before, but now I truly wondered if I had cause for concern. Nevertheless, I continued on and tried one of the book's techniques, which sent me on an interesting adventure that included my first lucid dreaming "review" (October 1993):

> I become lucid and find myself flying around my bed. I casually notice the bodies under the covers, but have a curious disinterest in them. The room looks exactly like it does in waking life. I remember Castaneda's commenting about "when a dreamer learns to wake up in another dream,"[6] so I align myself with my sleeping body (about four feet above it), close my eyes and say, "I want to waken in the next dreaming world." I wonder if there truly could be various levels or realms of dreaming.
>
> Suddenly I feel energized and fly straight up out of the house. The night sky is brilliant with ten thousand stars. I move effortlessly through the night as I fly onward. Eventually, I descend and find myself in an arid region. I notice what looks like some kind of fruit tree and touch its waxy leaves. A cat walks by.

Lucid and energetic, I think how great life is and I marvel at the stars above. I recall that others have flown to the stars and decide, "That's what I'll do." As I fly upward, in a standing position, the stars glow bright and brilliant. Suddenly, the stars do something fantastic—they begin to rush together into patterns and symbols, forming interlocking circles, then pyramidal shapes and something like the Star of David. Other interlocking geometric figures begin to form, all composed of golden stars. They stand still for a moment, then they fly away! This keeps happening—more groups join, make a symbol, then fly away, until finally, almost all the stars are gone.

I begin to have a feeling that the stars and planets exist as symbols of something else. They are more than dust and brilliant burning globes; they have an inner symbolic meaning at another level beyond our normal awareness.

I descend back to the ground, only to find an attractive woman waiting for me. She comes up to me and insists that I follow. Curious about such a talkative dream figure, I follow her, and she leads me to an older, dark-haired woman seated on a chair. This woman begins asking me a series of questions, the gist of which is that she wants to know if I'm worthy of advancing deeper into dreaming—she wants proof that I'm ready! I respond, but wonder why a dream figure would want to question me.

When I awoke from this lucid dream I focused on how profoundly moved I was by the clustering of stars and planets into symbolic groupings in this lucid dream and dismissed the woman's questioning as insignificant. I rationalized to myself that reading Castaneda's book had aroused in me some concern or suspicion about my ability to go deeper into lucid dreaming and that, therefore, the woman and her questioning were simply an expression of my concern.

I continued with lucid dreaming, wondering if I actually was going deeper into myself or deeper into another realm. I seriously questioned the nature of reality and began to read more deeply into Jane Roberts's books. I wondered how one could get beyond the observer effect—the beliefs, the ideas, the concepts—and its influence on perception and see dream and waking "reality" as it truly is. Was there a real reality, or was there only one's specific individual, mentally mediated version? And what about the conscious unconscious? What reality did it call home? Where did it reside?

Exactly one year to the day after my first review, another group appeared who wished to probe me further (October 1994):

I'm walking through a shopping mall and notice some young women. They seem to be dressed up for something. There are some adults, too, but many of the young women have on halter tops that are quite revealing, and that catches my attention. I decide to walk up to one of them, but then it just feels too odd. I realize "this is a dream" and become lucid.

As I walk along considering what to do, three or four people approach and seem intent on talking to me. Lucidly curious, I follow them into a room. It's like a library conference room, with windows. A few more people are there, all middle-aged, quite friendly, and very earnest. They seem to know me and want to interact.

Since I'm lucid, I decide to ask them questions. I ask, "What is my role in life?" And, "What is in my future?" They smile at my questions, and I get an expressed feeling of encouragement as if to say I'm doing fine. Then they begin with their questions for me and seem unusually intent on observing my reactions. They have a long series of questions.

I become amazed at how long this lucid dream is lasting, particularly because it consists of this simple interactive conversation. I keep remarking to myself about this whenever the dream figures talk amongst themselves. Then I hear one of the dream figures conclude that I'm not "as good as Jerdee," but that I'm "conscious" and doing okay or advancing. What did *that* mean? I wondered.

As I listen, I get the feeling that I'm being considered for something or some new advancement. At one point, I realize that I have a bowl of little goldfish crackers in my hand, and that every once in a while I grab and chew some, which makes me wonder if alternating my focus between the conversation and the bowl of crackers is helping to prolong the lucid dream.

Now I definitely wonder whether they are propping up the lucid dream or am I? They set up the conversation, the pace of things, and it seems like it's my duty to maintain conscious awareness and respond to them.

At last, they finish their deliberations. The middle-aged guy to my left, who seems the most friendly, smiles and draws my attention to a book. The volume's cover appears to be white leather. He opens to the contents page and points to a chapter by an "Omar Shemet" or "Omar of Shemet" who has a chapter (number 9?) on the nature of good and evil or decadence and corruption. I wonder why this is being pointed out to me.

After having this lucid dream experience, one or two experienced lucid dreamers mentioned to me their own similar review "meetings," organized by a couple or more dream figures who seem very much aware and curious about the lucid dreamer and, apparently, his or her progress.

I didn't know what to make of being reviewed by consciously aware dream figures. What I did know was that this lucid dream's ending was significant. While I was in the dream, gazing at the chapter title about good and evil, decadence and corruption, I knew this was being pointed out to me for a reason. I had begun to wonder if I was going too far. Lucid dreaming allows anyone to move incredibly deep into the conscious unconscious and even probe the apparent collective unconscious, but in the back of my mind, I wondered if I should be concerned. So, when the man in the committee pointed out that chapter title, he pointed out my unarticulated fear: Would I, at this depth of movement into the conscious unconscious, finally encounter something evil? I had now come face to face with a barrier within myself—an unresolved question that needed to be addressed.

GOOD, EVIL, AND LUCID DREAMING

In the science fiction classic, *Dune*, author Frank Herbert pens a classic line: "Fear is the mind killer." In the realm of lucid dreaming or any investigation of the mind, fear inhibits and restricts. Lucid dreamers who fear can make little progress. Instead, they retreat to "safe," simple lucid dreams, hoping that their fear doesn't find them. Fear becomes one of those self-limiting factors of self-exploration, like narrow beliefs or habitual focus. Fear is, indeed, the mind killer.

I had yet to experience anything remotely evil. Almost all of my encounters with the unconscious were responsive, profound, educational, and helpful. Some, like the feeling-tone experience, may have been a bit overwhelming, but none could be called evil. Still I knew that I needed to resolve the issue for myself personally: Did evil inherently exist? Would I find it lying in the darkest corners of the unconscious? I was simply going too deep into lucid dreaming not to know.

So, I resolved to find out, somehow, in my next conscious adventure, and this is what I discovered:

> I don't recall how I become aware, but I find myself hurtling through the relative darkness of space. At last, I can seek out the answer. I'm determined to go to the ends of the universe to discover whether evil exists. I fly past stars and constellations, deeper into the darkness. I

speed headlong through the cosmos, looking, sensing for something like inherent evil. I continue deeper until, at last, I come to a place where the stars no longer appear. In front of me looms the edge of the universe.

I stop and look intently at the deep darkness. Is there evil in there?

Then, from within, I hear a voice deliver this message: "The light upholds the darkness." And suddenly I know that behind all apparent evil or darkness is light; and that it's light that gives us the sense of darkness.

Then I hear: "Everything is sacred and alive." I intuitively realize that the light is in every living creature as a condition of its existence.

And then I hear something more clarifying: "Even the space between your fingers is sacred and alive." I look at my outstretched hand and see the space between my fingers, that precious emptiness, and know with clarity that I live in a sacred universe, where even the apparent emptiness is aware and alive. With form or without, all is sacred and alive.

My fear vanished.

7

Experiencing the Light of Awareness

THE YEAR 1995 MARKED TWENTY YEARS OF LUCID DREAMING FOR me. Lucid dreaming had enriched my life immeasurably. I had gained insights and experiences that I never could have learned in a classroom and a new, profound appreciation for the realm of dreaming. Moreover, I felt close to this newly expanded *innerness*, since I knew that an observing and responsive, conscious awareness existed there.

My relationship with lucid dreaming had become transformative. Though I could say, like so many others, that "it all happened in my mind," I wanted to capitalize *Mind*, and possibly even *My*. My concept of my own "self" had been altered by these excursions into the conscious unconscious. I now seemed a part of a larger whole, always connected and aware. Not that I personally am divine, but that *everything*, underneath it all, is divine.

As a result, reality began to seem conceptually looser, more ambiguous. We tend to consider dreams as "unreal" and physical life as "real," yet who hasn't woken from a frightening dream with his or her heart pumping wildly? If the dream is unreal, how does an unreal event affect the physical body in such a real, dramatic way? Numerous studies have shown that dreaming engages our cardiovascular and respiratory systems, hormonal production, brain wave activity, and so forth, and that various dream activities often correlate with the corresponding physical system changes. So dreaming is very real in terms of having an impact on our physical body and mental life. It may even account for the frequently cited phenomenon of altering our moods in terms of "waking up on the wrong side of the bed." Similarly, many lucid dreamers report experiencing a "lucid dreaming high" for hours or days after waking from an enjoyable or exhilarating lucid dream.

Dreams are also "real" when they involve mental events that are infused with problem-solving significance. Besides the frequent use of dreams for therapeutic insight, scientists and inventors have pointed to the mental event of the dream as providing creative solutions to real-world problems. One of the most vivid examples of this occurred in 1844. Elias Howe was working on the prototype of a sewing machine but felt perplexed by how the machine should manipulate the needle. He dreamt of being held by savages who threatened to kill him if he didn't finish creating his sewing machine. In the dream, he noticed that the spear tips had an eye-shaped hole and realized that the eye of the sewing machine needle needed to be at the tip for the machine to work.[1] This "real" solution occurred in a dream, and led to the "real"-ization of a world-changing industry.

Even if we don't recall dreams or see any value in them, various neurological viewpoints suggest that any brain or mind event creates a "mass action" that touches the entire brain. Every dream, as a real neurological event, affects the brain and mind in some manner as well as our individual and collective reality.[2]

The deeper we probe the nature of dreaming, the more we realize that referring to dreams as unreal is a false supposition. Moreover, when we consider that in physical life, people report hallucinations, false memories, perceptual errors, and so on, we realize that suggesting that the physical life experience is utterly real is equally unsupportable. Culturally, we have been led to believe an extreme dichotomy.

When we recall that numerous physicists maintain that each so-called real object exists as a conglomeration of energy, of spinning atoms rotating in a field of space, we begin to see that our perceived reality exists as a *version* of reality—one perspective on reality, one sense of reality. In a manner of speaking, our experienced reality is the one largely predicated by our senses. It can hardly be considered the only reality; rather, it is a sensed, mentally mediated reality—in many regards, much like a dream.

When lucidly aware in the dream, a new synthesis appears as the dreamer mixes both reality and illusion. He or she brings the realities of action, meaning, thought, and beauty to the so-called ephemeral, insubstantial illusion of dreams. Suddenly, the boundaries between dreaming reality and waking reality become even more amorphous, as lucid dreaming incorporates aspects of both. The new, synthesized reality begins to call all realities into question and suggest that each is fundamentally a mental construct.

With twenty years of lucid dreaming behind me, I knew that my next step involved becoming lucid about lucid dreaming. I had to "wake up" to lucid dreaming—get beyond this somewhat more aware framework. Realizing that I existed in the illusion of a dream was not enough; I needed to journey beyond all symbol, appearance, and illusion, beyond all self-creation, beyond the lucid dream. I needed to find the source of it all. Only then would I truly know if meaning existed behind appearance.

Around this time of deep questioning and deliberation, something curious began to happen. Occasionally upon waking in the morning, I would try to recall my dreams, but all I could recall was this: blue light. No matter how I pushed my memory to retrieve the dream story, there was none. In fact, there was no action, no objects, no figures, no me, no nothing—just blue light.

One morning I distinctly recall thinking, "Well, what do I put in my dream journal, "blue light"? This really seemed odd. Then, walking down to the breakfast table, my wife asked me, only half jokingly, "Robert, what's happening to you?" I laughed and asked her what she meant. "Last night, I think I woke up and looked at you," she said. "You had this look on your face, I don't know, like pure bliss or ecstasy or something. Are you okay?" I assured her that I was fine, that I was just having interesting dreams and thoughts. I didn't tell her about my deep considerations of reality and the role of the individual in creating the reality experienced or my deep desire to somehow get beyond that.

It occurred to me that the blue light reminded me of something else that was happening to me. For many years, while awake, I would periodically notice a dot of blue light in my perceptual field, normally on the left side. The dot would move around, up and down, so I knew it wasn't a matter of a rod or cone in my eye being damaged. It might hang around for a couple hours a day, and then I wouldn't notice it again for a week or so. Curiously, the dot seemed to appear most often when I was thinking about subjects of interest to me, like the nature of reality, consciousness, or lucid dreaming, for example.

This series of nighttime blue light experiences finally led up to a lucid dream that I jokingly call "The Blue Light Monster" (November 1995):

> I become lucid. The lighting is dim, so I shout out to the dream, "Turn on lights" and things become much brighter. At this point, I notice an area like a white, empty sanctuary. Entering into it, I suddenly see a figure composed of blue light. The figure is about three times larger than I am. At first I'm taken aback, but then I find it comical and begin to laugh—I've encountered a blue light monster! Or, perhaps a blue light god, as it doesn't seem menacing at all, in spite of its height, which seems to me only suggestive of intimidation or power. I have a sense that I need to get beyond it, and so I run to get around it. Just as I pass it, though, a great noise occurs in the lucid dream and I wake up.

I could think of only one association with such an image, and it involved Buddhist paintings, which often include a powerful figure composed of blue in each of the four corners. But why would I dream of that image? I had not studied Buddhism (after having considered all the cultural and translational issues inherent in its study) and therefore lacked any depth of knowledge about it. I did share with it the profound interest in trying to understand the nature of reality and the meaning of life.

As I began to recollect all of my lucid dreaming experiences, a keen sense of certainty formed within me. The reality of lucid dreaming must be just another reality, like waking reality, with its forms and symbols and assumed meanings and preconceptions, but somewhere beyond it there must be an ultimate reality or a base reality from which these realities emerged. There may be an infinity of realities, as don Juan maintained, but behind all of this, something must exist that props it all up.

Something had responded to my intent when I shouted, "Hey, I want to hear my feeling-tone!" But *where* was its reality? *What* was its reality? Beyond lucid dreaming must lie something—some originator, some source reality. To get there, I realized I had to get rid of "me" somehow—my beliefs, my ideas, my concerns, my interests—since these conspired to hook me into the reality that I then experienced. But how does one get beyond one's self? How does one let go of beliefs? Of ideas? Of concerns? Of interests? Until I let go of everything, I would still experience some aspect of self, some symbol, some representation. But how does one exclude one's self? And what would remain? I needed to know. *What was beyond lucid dreaming?*

In answer to my questioning, I experienced something extraordinary. In fact, some experiences simply defy words, and this is one of them. In the first part of this experience, I exist without a sense of self or identity. In the second part, I regain a sense of self. Here's what happened, as best I can explain (December 1995):

As if a floating point of light in an expanse of aware, living light, the self-less awareness exists. Here, all awareness connects. All awareness intersects. All knowledge exists within the brilliant, clear, creamy light of awareness. Awareness is all; one point contains the awareness of all points; nothing exists apart. Pure awareness, knowing, light.

Then, suddenly aware of the black-gray dream space and the lone figure standing there, I try to get my bearings. Recalling the aware light just experienced, I ask the robed figure, "Was that a lucid dream?"

"No," the figure replies. "To enter a lucid dream, go this way." He points to the empty space in front of him.

Knowing intuitively that the entry to regular dreams is to the left, I move right, toward the entry space for lucid dreams. As I cross an invisible boundary, my awareness hurtles through a tunnel of whitish-blue light, along whose surface I see intermittently various raised symbols—ovals, triangles, double triangles, circles. I continue moving until I know intuitively that to enter a lucid dream means going up.

Heading up toward lucid dreams, I feel something I've never before experienced. Around the crown of my head, I feel intense, explosive blasts of energy, localized but moving in a circular pattern. *Bam! Bam! Bam! Bam!* The energy rings in my mind.

Moments later, I know I'm preparing to enter a lucid dream. Until, as if by magic, I emerge through the floor of a dream scene, fully lucid.

I felt completely overwhelmed when I awoke from this experience. What *was* this? I held my head and traced the energy blasts around it. Working my memory backward, I had been in a lucid dream, a tunnel to a lucid dream, then in that gray space (where often only one figure or one or two symbols appear) and talked to the dream figure. But what came before all of that? What was that "aware light"? The dream figure told me that it was not a lucid dream. What was it then?

Within the aware light, there was no idea of self, of me or mine. There were no thoughts, memories, or analysis; no Robert—only a light-filled knowing. Though I had no broader context from which to consider it, it seemed like my awareness had finally arrived at its source: pure awareness, the reality behind the manifest appearances and symbols. The ultimate homecoming. In that aware light, All Is—the essence of everything seemed contained in an ever-present Now. All awareness connected in that pure awareness. In that great nothing, Everything Is.

A few months later, in June 1996, I attended the Association for the Study of Dreams (ASD) conference at the Claremont Resort in Berkeley, California. A session had been set up for experienced lucid dreamers to chat and share ideas. As I sat there with this group of very talented lucid dreamers, Stephen LaBerge asked if anyone had had any "extraordinary" lucid dream experiences.

The group decided to go around the circle and give each person an opportunity to comment. As it came to be my turn, I wondered if I should talk about my experiences of light. I hesitated because, first of all, they didn't seem to be lucid dreams. And, second, there really wasn't anything to talk about—nothing had happened! No action, no acting, only awareness! So, I told the group about my very first lucid dream, twenty-one years earlier, and kept the experiences of light to myself.

It wasn't until two years later, while at a conference in Hawaii, that I started to comprehend the meaning of my experience. At the 1998 ASD conference, on the north shore of Oahu, one of the featured speakers was Tenzin Wangyal Rinpoche, a Buddhist lama from the Bon tradition of Tibet who had just written *The Tibetan Yogas of Dream and Sleep*.

In the late morning sun and a gentle breeze, Tenzin Wangyal stood in his simple attire and discussed the Buddhist Bon tradition's view of dreaming and lucid dreaming, which is based on almost ten thousand years of study. He mentioned his own intense practice of dream yoga as a youth in a monastery, and how he had continued to practice dream yoga as part of his spiritual path.

As he reviewed this rich tradition, he likened the experience of regular dreaming to a blind horse with a lame rider. In this metaphor, the lame rider is one's mind, which sits atop a blind horse, signifying the energy of the dream that dashes about with little control.

By developing greater awareness in the dream state, the rider could overcome his lameness, direct the blind horse, and use conscious dreaming for his spiritual growth. Tenzin Wangyal suggested that the deep practice of lucid dreaming, or yoga of dreams, could assist one in the intermediate bardo state, after physical death. Assuming one had developed sufficient awareness, understanding, and stability of mind through lucid dreaming and dream yoga, one might be able to comprehend the illusory nature of after-death visions and thus avoid another incarnation.

He also noted that with many years of training and experience, the yogas of dream and sleep may "ultimately lead into one another," if the lucid dreaming practice is "fully accomplished," and result in an experience of the "clear light." Unlike a lucid dream, which has a subject and object, in the clear light experience, "the recognition is not of an object by a subject but is the non-dual recognition of pure awareness, the clear light, by awareness itself."[3] He emphasized that in the clear light experience, there is no subject/object duality or sense of self; rather, the ever-present essential, innate awareness appears. Ultimately, the common goal for those who go deeply into either dream yoga or sleep yoga would be to experience the clear light.

Listening, I began to feel that my unusual experiences, after twenty years of lucid dreaming, had a name, a history, and a meaning. I began to believe that my attempt to go beyond lucid dreaming and beyond symbols, objects, and figures may have naturally returned my base awareness to this point of clear light. I found it strange that a Presbyterian lucid dreamer from the Midwest, without expecting or anticipating it, would stumble into such an experience, an apparent glimpse of absolute reality.

THE METZINGER QUESTION

How did the first person to experience the clear light recognize it? How did he or she explain it to himself or herself, since it's an experience of non-dual awareness outside of a subject/object relationship? I wondered, did that first person spend decades trying to comprehend that strange recollection of knowing light? Could he or she deduce an answer?

Many years later, I read *Being No One*, by the German philosopher Thomas Metzinger, and was surprised to find he raised a similar point.[4] He asks, "How can you coherently report about a selfless state of consciousness from your own, autobiographical memory? How could this episode ever constitute an element of your own mental life? Such reports generate a performative self-contradiction . . ."[5]

Though I may be walking on thin ice, and I have no pretensions of being a philosopher or an apologist for Buddhism, I feel my experience may provide an answer or at least a helpful response.

First, to reiterate, I did not expect or anticipate such a state as the clear light. I simply had reached a point at which I deeply felt something must be beyond lucid dreaming. When I lucidly called out a question or intent, something responded. When I lucidly sought unknown and basically unknowable information, a response emerged.

Beyond mediation by symbols, beyond the beliefs, ideas, and expectations of my waking mind, somewhere a base reality must exist that energized or gave rise to appearances, I surmised.

Second, in my report about the self-less experience, one finds that numerous "platforms of experience" appear (e.g., the clear light, the gray state, the lucid dream, and a sense of the entry point to regular dreams). Earlier in the event, I questioned a figure in the dream's gray state who showed me how to enter a lucid dream after informing me that the experience of awareness had not been a lucid dream. So, upon waking, I had some evidence to realize what the clear light experience *was not*. It was not a lucid dream, nor a dream, nor this relatively empty gray state where sometimes lucid dreamers find themselves.

Third, I began to think that perhaps the first person to experience this may possibly have had it explained to them afterward by another awareness. If I had asked a different question to the dream figure in the gray state—"What was that?" for example, instead of "Was that a lucid dream?"—I likely would have received an explanatory response. I wonder if this is how the first person (and others) to experience this came to understand the experience. I have to assume so.

Be that as it may, it still may not satisfy Metzinger's basic question: "How can you coherently report about a selfless state of consciousness from your own, autobiographical memory? How could this episode ever constitute an element of your own mental life?"

So, my fourth point is, I feel the answer may be discovered in my feeling-tone dream (described in chapter 6). In that lucid dream, we see that "awareness" apparently has the mobility to reside outside of the waking self construct. In that dream, I experienced the "waking self as feeling-tone." When the feeling-tone engulfed, expressed, and became my sense of self, awareness stepped aside. Awareness found refuge within a larger awareness, until the feeling-tone ended, whereupon my self and awareness reunited. By this, I propose that awareness can step apart from self, then reunite with self, and that is how you coherently report about a self-less state of consciousness. The self does not experience it; the self's awareness experiences it. Upon the reuniting of self and awareness, the self possesses knowledge of the awareness. This movement suggests that consciousness of self exists as a *quality* arising from awareness, but does not *constitute* awareness.

One afternoon thinking about how to explain this, I intuitively imagined this brief conceptual game:

See yourself in your mind's eye. Now strip away all of your possessions—your house, your car, your bank account, your clothes, your dishes. Strip away the things you own or possess. So now strip away all your emotions, all your feelings, all your likes and dislikes; remove them all. Now strip away all your relationships, past, present, and future; strip them away. Now all of your ideas, your conceptions, your beliefs, let them go; strip them away and cast them off. Now your memories and history must be stripped free, too. Finally, strip away any lingering residue of ideation of self.

As you strip away each layer, something remains—because something preexists your possessions and your emotions; something preexists your relationships and your memories; something preexists your sense of self. When you strip them all away, one final thing remains: Awareness.

You can call it "your" awareness, but it preexists you. The things you attach to awareness—your ideas, beliefs, emotions, memories, all blend together and become the conception of "you" or "yourself." But when you shake them all free, one thing remains: Awareness. The self *has* awareness, but the self is not the Awareness.

Basically, it seems to me that we *clothe* awareness with layers of self conceptions. Then we assume awareness results from or exists by virtue of the clothing of self conceptions! While awareness enlivens the self conceptions, the self conceptions do not create the awareness.

When awareness emerged from the clear light, it could then integrate the experience with or into my waking self and allow the self to claim the experience, though in all actuality, it was my awareness that experienced it, and not my waking self. In large measure, my waking self's involvement consisted of questioning the nature of reality and becoming deeply convinced that some ultimate reality existed behind the manifest realities of waking and dreaming. The experience of pure awareness simply happened. It did not occur as the result of some technique or machination of my waking self.

The experience of light has left me with deep feelings about the interconnectedness of all awareness and what underlies phenomenal reality. Occasionally, it rises to the surface, and I experience in waking reality the sense of interconnectedness. Much of the remainder of this book involves my directly and indirectly suggesting the existence of profound interconnectedness and how lucid dreaming acts as a platform from which one might possibly provide evidence of that interconnectedness.

8

CONNECTING WITH
THE HIDDEN OBSERVER
OF DREAMING

MOST OF US HAVE NO PROBLEM BELIEVING THAT THE DREAM FIGURES we encounter represent aspects of our self, that they may be symbolic representations of our hopes, fears, desires, and other emotions. So, for example, if you dreamt of an angry, black dog and later realized the angry, black dog represented your fear of your boss, you would realize that the image of the angry, black dog was a symbolic construct to express the awareness of this specific fear. If you then came to terms with the fear, you likely would never encounter that dream symbol again. In a sense, the symbolic construct would evaporate once your broader awareness dealt with (or reintegrated) the projected awareness or energy of this specific fear.

So culturally, the traditional self looks at these mental creations in dreams as manifest expressions of psychological energy or awareness. Ingrained in this viewpoint is the assumption that the waking self exists as the "top" or uppermost expression of the psyche. Also ingrained in this viewpoint is the assumption that the waking self is the only reality and that all dream figures are both lesser and illusory.

When we become consciously aware in the dream state, however, this common viewpoint meets severe challenges. As we consciously move deeper into the unconscious, experiences arise to suggest that the "self" exists in much broader terms than the waking ego self alone. In addition to knowledgeable and volitional dream figures (that may represent fragments of conscious awareness or sub-personalities), lucid dreamers appear able to contact something more comprehensive and aware, perhaps what could be called the subliminal self, the inner ego, or the inner Self.

For the first time, the conscious dreaming self can investigate higher up the ladder of consciousness. In doing so, however, the lucid dreamer must do something counterintuitive. He or she must stop focusing on the dream objects and dream figures and direct questions or intentions to a nonapparent awareness behind the dream. As long as the lucid dreamer continues to focus on the dream objects and dream figures (which Western psychology tells us exist as reflections of the self), then the lucid dreamer remains involved with the reflections of the self. To step outside of this self-reflective aspect of lucid dreaming involves an intentional focusing away from the presented dream environment and a redirected focusing toward the presumed awareness behind the dream.

My first clue of this awareness behind the dream occurred years earlier in the "happy giver" lucid dream (as described in chapter 5), when a voice from above boomed out a response. Instead of the dream figure responding, suddenly a nonapparent, mysterious voice responded. This oddity, this slip-up, provided me an initial hint that not everything was on the dream stage; rather, something hid behind the curtain. Attending to the characters in the dream play, I now realized, would never reveal the other awareness offstage.

The problem is, the vast majority of lucid dreamers never consider focusing away from interacting with the dream environment. Why? Well, for reasons I've already touched upon. First, many believe that they completely create and control the lucid dream and therefore presume their action and awareness is the only action and awareness accessible. Second, the waking ego self prefers the sense of primary mastery, manipulation, and control, even when illusory; the waking ego often prefers not to look outside of itself for explanations. Third, to give up control or focus on the unknown can engender fear, and an inflexible waking ego avoids possible fears. Finally, many lucid dreamers become enamored by the pleasure and play of lucid dreaming and fail to experiment or develop their abilities further. In effect, erroneous conceptions, presumed mastery, fear avoidance, and pleasure-seeking act to blind most lucid dreamers to this possibility.

Once the lucid dreamer directs questions or intentions to the awareness behind dreaming, he or she creates an opening from which to engage the subliminal or inner Self. Initially, this may require both a conceptual belief in and an emotional trust of the abstraction behind the dream. The responsive, invisible awareness behind the dream reciprocates in such a profound way as to differentiate itself from dream figures. Its response reveals a creativity, deep knowledge, and mastery that suggest the lucid dreamer has encountered a consciously aware, much larger aspect of Self.

Jung hinted at this distinct possibility when he mused on the characteristics of the unconscious and suggested its creativity and spontaneity pointed to its likely existence as an inner, psychic system. Speculating further, he suggested that if it was a system, then it might possess consciousness: "We have no knowledge of how this unconscious functions, but since it is conjectured to be a psychic system it may possibly have everything that consciousness has, including perception, apperception, memory, imagination, will, affectivity, feeling, reflection, judgment, etc., all in subliminal form."[1]

Jung goes on to suggest the implications of what this might mean:

> If the unconscious can contain everything that is known to be a function of consciousness, then we are faced with the possibility that it too, like consciousness, possesses a subject, a sort of ego . . . [which] brings out the real point of my argument: the fact, namely, that a second psychic system coexisting with consciousness—no matter what qualities we suspect it of possessing—is of absolutely revolutionary significance in that it could radically alter our view of the world.[2]

Lucid dreamers, in their individually unique conscious explorations of the unconscious, often discover (independently of each other) that the responsively aware unconscious has many of these same qualities hypothesized by Jung. Let's consider Jung's list of possible functions that this inner awareness must possess to constitute "a sort of ego."

Perception: In numerous lucid dreams, I and other lucid dreamers ignore the objects and dream figures and simply shout out our requests to the dream, or inner ego.

Now, if no other awareness existed to perceive our requests, we should receive no responses. Or, if our requests were only perceived by a nonstructured or nonsystem chaos (i.e., a primitive archaic realm), we would receive no sensible responses. However, lucid dreamers who shout out their requests to the dream do receive responses. So Jung's first requirement of "perception" is already shown by the responses that result from lucid dreamers' direct requests of the awareness behind the dream.

I want to point out here that I'm referring to asking the *dream* and not a dream figure. Dream figures are not the psychic system, but are, more likely, small elements within it. Similarly, dream figures vary widely in their capacity to respond (as I discuss in chapters 5 and 11).

Apperception: Apperception refers to "the process of understanding by which newly observed qualities of an object are related to past experience."[3] At least one example exists. I submit that my lucid dream in which the dream voice booms out, "The acquired characteristics," and I query, "The acquired characteristics of what?" to which the voice booms out the complete and more comprehensible response, "The acquired characteristics of the happy giver!" hint at this point of Jung's. The inner system or inner ego showed the capacity to re-analyze or reflect upon its earlier response, and it did so upon my query.

Memory: Here, I would have to point to lucid dreams in which the waking intent or curiosity seems preloaded into the pre-lucid portion of the lucid dream. Take, for example, my first lucid dream. My hands suddenly appeared in front of my face, and I realized my prompt. How do we explain this? Did my waking self place my hands directly in front of my face? Or did my subliminal self/inner ego incorporate this waking suggestion and remember to create an extremely rare dream action of hands popping up?

Imagination: This is where the inner Self excels in terms of creativity and imagination, which seems a determining characteristic of any higher system of consciousness. My lucid dream of shouting, "I want to see more women in here when I open the door" definitely qualifies. The responsive agent did an admirable job of creating an attractive and orderly set of young women, creatively arranged and appropriate to my thoughts and beliefs. So too, when I shouted, "I want to hear my feeling-tone!" the experience was light years beyond my expectations and concepts.

If one could suggest an ordering of conscious structures in the psyche, I feel greater and more profound creativity would denote the proper ranking process. As one moves up the ladder of the psyche, one should be able to mark significant gradations in creativity as a key element. As such, the waking ego does not seem the highest-level structure within the lucidly perceived psyche.

Will: Many have "surrendered" their will to the lucid dream or asked the dream, "Show me something important for me to see." In these cases of setting aside the waking self's will, profound lucid dream experiences result, again suggesting the existence of an inner Self's "will" that acts *when allowed to act* by the waking self.

Affectivity and Feeling: In my feeling-tone lucid dream, I experienced an affective response when the presumed inner ego's awareness (in which my awareness sought refuge) had to recall the memories and feelings that constituted "Robert."

Also, that the responses to lucid dreamers' requests seem largely educational and oriented toward assistance suggests an "inner" affectivity or feeling for the waking self.

Reflection and Judgment: My lucid dream's "acquired characteristics" retort is evidence of reflection and judgment. In later chapters, I present many additional lucid dream experiences in which the inner Self responds that the lucid dreaming individual is not adequately prepared for the experience he or she requests or has requested something in error, which cannot be expressed.

My point here is simple. Jung's intimation of "a subject, or sort of ego" within the unconscious appears to be a psychologically and scientifically obtainable goal of lucid dreaming, given an acceptable experimental design. Moreover, experienced lucid dreamers report numerous examples of interactions with the inner ego that can only be characterized as responsive, seemingly intelligent, and educationally oriented (i.e., purposeful). The nature of these preliminary interactions suggests an inner, functioning, perceiving psychic organism or inner Self, accessible in the lucid dream state. Some experienced lucid dreamers already refer to it more poetically, as the Dreamer of the dream, for example.

Already lucid dreamers have independently discovered that the dream state or unconscious seems to function around certain principles (such as the expectation effect, belief, intent, etc.) commonly experienced by lucid dreamers. These commonalities give weight to the idea that a coherent structure exists to the dream state or unconscious. The normal waking-state view of the dream state as "chaotic" has to be reconsidered as consciously aware dreamers begin to interact with that state. Through the aegis of lucid awareness, the dream realm can be observed, explored, and experimented with to determine its operating principles. The fact that its operating principles may be different than physical reality's principles is no reason to ignore or deny its existence or avoid reconsidering its status as a principled environment, a type of reality.

THE INNER SELF IN SPIRITUAL TRADITIONS

Aside from the realm of Western psychology, consideration of an inner ego in lucid dreaming may touch upon spiritual traditions as well. As lucid dreamers provide continuing evidence of an inner awareness, psychologists may be able to draw parallels with the nature of this inner awareness and what various religions have historically called soul or spirit.

Beginning with the ancient Egyptians, most religions have consistently maintained that behind the waking, physical self exists another type of self, a nonphysical, mental, or spiritual self. In lucid dreaming, we may have the capacity to interact with that normally hidden portion of our self and understand it from our waking perspective.

For example, lucid dreaming may allow the waking self to experience what the Hindu called *atman*, or self as soul. As Wendy Doniger O'Flaherty, Professor of the History of Religions at the University of Chicago, explains, Hindu philosophy considered the ego the *ahamkara*. She writes, "*Ahamkara*, literally 'The making of an "I," ' is best translated as egoism; it is a mistaken perception, the source of the whole series of errors that cause us to become embroiled in *samsara* [the world of rebirth, illusion, and worldly involvement]. Once we realize that 'I' does not exist, we are free from the most basic of all illusions. It is the Western assurance that the ego is real that drives us to assume that this is the point from which all other frames radiate outward. . . ." O'Flaherty further explains that Hindu texts suggest something beyond the ego, "The self (*atman*), by contrast, links one not merely to a certain group of other people but to everyone and, further, to the real world (*brahman*) [or the Godhead], which transcends everyone."[4]

In some regards, I feel that a lucid dreamer realizing that he or she continues to exist in a largely ego-reflective illusion even within the lucid dream can use that understanding as the motivating force to discover what persists beyond illusion. By seeking to shake free of the "makings" of the ego, exteriorized as the dream creations of objects, settings, and figures, the lucid dreamer begins to diminish the significance of the illusion of self reflection. By focusing beyond appearances, lucid dreamers increase their likelihood of discovering that which is beyond their ego, presumably their *atman*, or true Self. From there, Hindu literature (if I understand correctly) suggests that a dreamer might continue to an experience of dreamless sleep that provides a glance at the true *brahman*, "the divine mind that does not create."[5]

Through lucid dreaming, we appear to have the capacity to realize our connection with our inner Self as something more than merely theoretical. Lucidly aware, we can finally interact and engage with our larger psyche and experience its reality to some small degree. The elusive psyche may finally be found in the most unlikely of places, the paradoxical nature of lucid dreaming.

A SORT OF INNER EGO: EARLY PSYCHOLOGICAL THEORIES

Jung's suggestion that the inner psychic system's characteristics (e.g., feeling, memory, imagination, and so forth) might exist "all in subliminal form" brings us back to the history of psychology and the idea of more than one conscious awareness in humans.

In his book, *Divided Consciousness: Multiple Controls in Human Thought and Action*, Ernest Hilgard, the late Stanford professor and former president of the American Psychological Association, suggests as much in the book's first sentence: "The unity of consciousness is illusory."[6] Hilgard recounts that in the early years of psychology, many psychologists proposed competing views of consciousness. The German psychologist Max Dessoir, says Hilgard, wrote *Das Doppel-Ich*, or *The Double Ego*, "in which he identified the two streams of mental activity as an 'upper consciousness' and a 'lower consciousness.'"[7] The French psychologist, Pierre Janet, was "the first to introduce the term *subconscious* to refer to a level of cognitive functioning out of awareness that could on occasion become conscious."[8] The American Morton Prince used the term "co-conscious" to denote the idea that "subconscious cerebration is going on concurrently" with one's principal intelligence.[9]

Like many psychologists today, these early theorists point out the complexity of conscious awareness and the likelihood of more than one conscious awareness within the human psyche. However, Hilgard claims that Freud's psychoanalytic theory conflicted with these co-conscious views and "presented an alternative conception of unconscious processes, and substituted repression for dissociation."[10] Essentially, Freud used repression to explain away and negate the need to investigate co-conscious activity. Freud also viewed hypnosis negatively, hypnosis being one way in which subconscious processes could be ascertained to exist concurrently with conscious processes.

With the historic rise of behaviorism, Hilgard observes, the currents of psychological research moved away from consciousness and created a "lack of interest in subconsciousnesses" as well.[11]

Interest in subconscious awareness returned in numerous forms in the 1960s and 1970s as researchers sought to understand the mechanism for multiple personality disorders, popularized in books like *The Three Faces of Eve*. How could psychology explain the appearance of a new ego form or a new conscious awareness? How did it develop? From where did it come? Hilgard notes that Prince's idea of co-consciousness reemerges, since "the concealed (or dissociated) personality is sometimes more normal or mentally healthy than the openly displayed one."[12] This observation of a healthier new ego-aspect refutes the Freudian idea "of a primitive unconscious" ruled by instinctual impulses or repressed emotions, and suggests a natural co-conscious system, as well as an ability to formulate new conscious awareness.[13]

In his research work with deep hypnosis, Hilgard noted a type of co-conscious awareness, which he called the "hidden observer." The hidden observer was first uncovered when a student in a class asked the hypnotist "whether 'some part' of the subject might be aware of what was going on."[14] To their surprise, they discovered a response from an aware information processing part of the self of which the subject had no knowledge. This "other part" or hidden observer could respond to questions, write automatically about its experience, and make requests. Responses from the hidden observer were found to be clear, coherent, business-like, and analytical, according to Hilgard, and not suggestive of any regressive or infantile nature, proposed in psychoanalytic views.

In conversing with the "hidden observer," Hilgard's hypnotic subjects made comments afterwards like these: "The hidden part doesn't deal with pain. It looks at what is, and doesn't judge it. It is not a hypnotized part of the self. It knows all parts." "The hidden observer is watching, mature, logical, has more information." "The hidden observer was an extra, all-knowing part of me. . . . The hidden part knows the hypnotized part, but the hypnotized part does not know the hidden one."[15]

As a researcher, Hilgard realizes that "a reader may think of untapped depths of experience, possibilities of consciousness expansion, unrealized human potential and other rather mystical ideas," which he sought to dissuade as unproven. However, he was quick to point out the "objective, matter of fact, scientific" observations made by the hidden observer were suggestive of some type of inner conscious awareness.[16]

Hilgard's analysis suggested that psychology should refocus on earlier notions of co-conscious awareness, see hypnosis as an experimental procedure to probe this, further investigate attention and its parallel processing, and determine if the "central control mechanism" of awareness has "two aspects"—a monitoring function and an executive or decisive, organizing, and goal-directing function.[17]

Lucid Dreaming and an Inner Observer

The discovery of the "hidden observer" occurred because a student asked if "some part" of the subject might be aware. One can only wonder if the hidden observer exists in all deep hypnotic encounters but remains primarily withdrawn until consciously sought and questioned.

In lucid dreaming, the inner observer appears most likely to be discovered when lucid dreamers turn away from interacting with the dream figures and simply address the dreaming. To some degree, this mirrors the actions of the hypnotist turning away from interacting with the subject to ask if "some part" of the subject might also be aware in that state. Until the focus of the lucid dreamer turns away from the dreaming action, the inner observer or inner Self remains hidden. When the lucid dreamer shifts the focus away from his or her interests and assumed projections and places the focus onto the larger reality of dreaming, the inner observer appears and responds. I have to assume that the inner observer or inner Self exists in all lucid dream encounters but remains hidden until consciously sought.

I want to make clear that the inner observer of lucid dreaming would not normally manifest as a dream figure or an apparent figure or object within the dream. By my experience, the inner observer exists behind the dreaming and can communicate with the lucid dreamer through intelligent and responsive vocalizations, thoughts, information, and the presentation of new dream creations or experiences. Though dream figures may represent the inner observer in part, they do not constitute the larger awareness of the inner observer; just as a leaf, twig, or branch represents apparent aspects of the tree but not a tree's totality.

Questions to the dream's inner observer can be either factual or conceptual, currently known or not yet known, oriented to past or future. Although most questions prompt an immediate response, later we will see examples of some responses that tell the lucid dreamer of the fallacy, inadvisability, or impossibility of the lucid dreamer's request. These thoughtfully explained denied responses indicate the unique and autonomous nature of the inner observer. The lucid dreamer, of course, can counter with an altered request.

Those who feel lucid dreamers only experience what they expect to experience should request something unexpected from the dream. In later chapters, I will discuss how I and other lucid dreamers have pushed dream figures and the inner observer to provide answers to unknowable questions (which thus have no expected answer at the time), listened for the response, and then saw whether it was later verified. The results are surprising and suggest that the unconscious may be more conscious and more broad "minded" than we want to admit.

9

THE FIVE STAGES OF LUCID DREAMING

WHEN I GIVE PRESENTATIONS ON LUCID DREAMING, I NORMALLY BEGIN by asking the audience members to raise their hands if they've had a lucid dream. Around eighty percent of the attendees raise their hands. Then I ask those who've had twenty-five or more lucid dreams to raise their hands. Only about thirty-five percent do so. If I ask those who have had one hundred or more lucid dreams to raise their hands, sometimes I look out and see only one hand in the air. Even among those people very interested in the topic of lucid dreaming—interested enough to go to a lecture or conference on the subject—only a small percentage manages to enter deeply into the actual practice.

This relative lack of experienced lucid dreamers may seem surprising, given that lucid dreaming can be so rewarding. From experience, I know that lucid dreams often result in an immediate sense of joy and well-being that stays with me for hours, sometimes days afterward, leaving me with a type of lucid afterglow. Lucid dreaming can mystify and delight us with incredible sights and experiences that can't be duplicated in the waking world. Ranging from the purely sensual to the intensely spiritual and intellectually profound, lucid dreaming provides fascinating personal experiences. Why, then, do so few progress deeper into the practice?

As I've discussed in previous chapters, lucid dreamers, like travelers on a mythic journey, face many challenges on their path, both external and internal. To begin with, the current culture largely devalues dreams as either meaningless or imbued with personal angst, cloaked in indecipherable symbols. The thinking goes that even if you become aware within the dream state (which society deems basically absurd), what have you accomplished? In the face of cultural beliefs like these, challenging one's self to achieve a dreaming skill can be a lonely affair with little external recognition or support.

In addition, each lucid dreamer will face numerous issues internally as they work on acquiring the necessary skills. Becoming adept at initiating lucid dreams, perfecting lucid dream induction, understanding the mechanics of the lucid dream realm, and persisting in the quest after only intermittent success all can lead many aspiring lucid dreamers to lose interest. Though some may have a natural talent, most find lucid dreaming requires serious effort.

THE FOUR STUMBLING BLOCKS OF LUCID DREAMING

1. A Long Process of Discovery

Like learning a new language or how to play a musical instrument, learning to become a proficient lucid dreamer takes time, practice, and devotion. Becoming consciously aware in the dream state is only the first step. You must then acclimate yourself to maintaining awareness in the dream state as you begin to understand the operational principles of what amounts to a unique alternate reality. Learning how to direct your focus and manipulate your thoughts, modulate emotions, and conduct the most basic experiments can take years.

At a recent IASD[1] conference, I heard a presenter and experienced lucid dreamer say that it took her twenty-five years before she felt like she truly understood lucid dreaming. To some degree, I echo her assessment in my own experience. It is not that lucid dreaming is hard to do; rather, consciously interacting in the dream state begins to reveal the incredible depth and complexity of dreaming and the unconscious. At each stage, the reality of the psyche unveils more profound experiences and insights difficult to articulate.

Present-day lucid dreamers have both an advantage and a disadvantage. On the one hand, lucid dreamers today have the advantage of having other lucid dreamers who can support and encourage them with tips and ideas. On the other hand, the naive acceptance of these tips and ideas often serves to discourage further thought and investigation. The lucid dreamer sees how to achieve a particular goal in lucid dreaming or duplicate another's experience but fails to realize the underlying principles. Inner exploration requires deep understanding, careful analysis, and a probing, curious mind.

2. Temptations, Fears, and Defenses

Consciously aware in the dream state, you can do or experience virtually anything. This is the great blessing and curse of lucid dreaming. A blessing in that it lays open an entry to the reality of the unconscious; a curse in that it then offers so many temptations, distractions, and curiosities to be experienced by the ego self. As I discussed earlier, many lucid dreamers become lost in the psyche's apparent abundance and freedom of experience or get snagged by habitual pleasures, which they return to again and again. In these cases, little progress is made toward greater goals, discoveries, or big-picture realizations.

Because the nature of the unconscious involves a journey deeper into the Self, you invariably encounter more of the totality of yourself, including your fears and concerns. At first in the shallow waters of lucid dreaming, these issues may seem minor, insignificant. But a serious journey requires going into deeper waters, and there you may encounter truly major personal fears and concerns in the guise of menacing dream figures, frightful situations, or seemingly unsolvable puzzles. Occasionally, some lucid dream events may spill out of the dreaming and intrude into waking reality, reminding us of the psyche's broader reach and the curious nature of this realm.

Finally, as you go deeper and feel the immensity of the psyche, you may naturally develop defenses against that immensity. You may ignore clear signals of greater potentials or avoid considering possible experiments because the implications appear too staggering. On some level, your ego self may feel threatened by the awesome depths of the unconscious and what might be discovered there.

3. Assumptions

Possibly the most difficult task of all for lucid dreamers involves the confrontation with our own assumptions. All of us begin with assumptions about dreaming, the nature of the unconscious or the psyche, and reality. These assumptions color our view of ourselves, our experience, and reality. And because assumptions, by nature, are assumed to be true, we rarely examine them and ignore evidence that contradicts them. As a result, along our journey into lucid dreaming, our assumptions often misdirect us. One common assumption, as discussed earlier, is that the dreamer controls the dream. Yet, any thoughtful analysis shows that lucid dreamers direct their focus within the dream but do not control the dream (as the sailor does not control the sea). Those maintaining the assumption of control limit their experience and understanding, unless they're able to see through this assumption and broaden their viewpoint.

Another assumption proclaimed by some lucid dreamers is, "You get what you expect! It's all about expectation!" Again, as already discussed, that assumption works as long as lucid dreamers either ignore the unexpected or fail to set up experiments in which the result must be unexpected. At that point, the assumption begins to falter and you realize that still more is involved.

The assumption, "It's all in your mind," may work for the first part of the journey. Eventually, you will either expand the definition of "your mind" or find yourself unable to explain many experiences adequately. When the conscious mind encounters the unconscious mind, old, limited viewpoints fall by the wayside. Ideally, your conceptual framework adjusts to accept the new encounters and allow for the growth of new ideas.

Deeper into lucid dreaming, we confront situations that conflict with our assumptions, perhaps even our most cherished assumptions. If we let them, our assumptions can blind us to our experience and distort the experience. At this point, our interaction with the reality of the psyche becomes overly interpreted. We can't differentiate the psyche from our own beliefs about it and thus thwart our exploration. We don't see the psyche so much as our beliefs about what "should" be there.

4. Intent and Will

On any journey, lucid or mythic, the individual's intent and will matter. Though we may believe that we journey alone, our intent and will accompany us. Their purity and depth create a path, even when we feel lost or bewildered. On some level, each lucid dreamer's journey follows the dictates of their intent and will.

In that long journey, as the self deals with temptations, fears, and defenses; avoids the dangers of apathy, neglect, and obsession; and persists through provisional assumptions to greater clarity, the self constantly re-creates itself. To a large degree, the lucid dreamer becomes the journey, the realized awareness, the inward probing. By searching for the Self, the waking self becomes more truly its Self.

THE FIVE STAGES OF LUCID DREAMING

I believe the depth of lucid dreaming would be better understood if considered as a progression of developmental stages. The Swiss psychologist Jean Piaget notably developed a model of children's cognitive development stages with approximate time periods and mental functions. Of course, any model of lucid dreaming development has to be much more flexible. Unlike newborn children, lucid dreamers begin at different stages of maturity, knowledge, and awareness. Similarly, lucid dreamers may learn about advanced techniques from others and thereby preempt a natural progression of self learning.

Piaget called children "little philosophers" for their attempts to understand and manipulate within waking reality. Lucid dreamers naturally entertain a second round as little philosophers when they attempt to understand and manipulate consciously within the dream realm. Just like a young child's sincere explanation that the ocean waves create the breeze, beginning lucid dreamers may develop equally interesting philosophies based on limited experience. Over the long run, however, experienced lucid dreamers begin to articulate viewpoints similar to those of other lucid dreamers, regarding expectation, belief, false awakenings, and so on, thereby suggesting the framework of a more coherent philosophy of the dream reality.

Conceivably, a lucid dreamer's development could be divided into five stages characterized by a number of dream behaviors, realizations, goals, processes, and impediments. Like Piaget's stages of cognitive development, the stages become progressively more complex and insightful over time. At the beginning, much like a newborn child, one finds the lucid dreamer focusing on his or her sensory experience, followed by an attempt to develop skills suited to maintaining and manipulating the dream environment. With practice, the lucid dreamer moves into a more skill-acquiring and purposeful period of thought, experiment, and action. This is followed by a new period of greater abstract reasoning and reflection. Finally, the lucid dreamer might consider the totality of his or her experience and posit a realm beyond this system or "beyond the lucid dream."

Stage 1. Personal Play, Pleasure, and Pain Avoidance

At this initial stage, lucid dreamers commonly report marveling at the lucid state, enjoying the sensations of touch and sight, comparing and contrasting the dream with waking reality, and avoiding troubling stimuli. The initial goal revolves around maintaining lucidity by modulating emotions and properly focusing awareness; essentially, the lucid dreamer is learning to remain lucid and understand this realm. Establishing aware focus is the initial principle realized.

Impediments involve a lack of personal control, the appearance of attractions or distractions that preempt lucid awareness, and discomfiture with a mental or nonphysical reality. The lucid dreamer may relate to dream reality in ways appropriate to physical reality such as flying by swimming through the air or flapping arms. At this stage, lucid dreams may be very brief (from seconds to less than three minutes) and involve very limited experimentation.

> **I Dream:** Dreaming reflects only me, my personal realm
> **Behavior:** Play, pleasure, stability, and dealing with attractions and distractions
> **Goal:** Maintaining lucidity
> **Reality Creators:** Focus and emotional control
> **Direction:** If dreaming reflects me, then I must learn to control it
> **Fear Blockage:** Can't control it, unlike physical reality
> **Neutral Stasis:** Lucid dreaming involves fun, pleasure, and pain avoidance

Stage 2. Manipulation, Movement, and Me

Here, the lucid dreamer practices greater movement skills such as flying like Superman but still sometimes reverts to a physical approach (swimming, arm flapping, and so on). The lucid dreamer begins to change dream objects to suit needs or desires and interact with dream figures as mere reflections or playthings. In perfecting the skills to manipulate objects and space, the lucid dreamer learns the basic principles or techniques of expectation and belief to influence the environment.

Impediments involve an inability to manipulate space, dream figures, or objects by improper use of expectation and belief, improper focus, and a resultant concern about one's adequacy. At this stage, the lucid dreamer may experience false awakenings. Most lucid dreams will be brief (from one half to six minutes) and involve a greater sense of experimentation with sensory experience and engaging dream objects such as touching dream figures.

    I Dream: Dreaming reflects me and my control
    Behavior: Manipulation, direction, elongation, and experimentation
    Goal: Manipulating objects and others in the dream space
    Reality Creators: Belief, expectation, and suggestion
    Direction: I can control it if I use more power
    Fear Blockage: Objects and figures difficult to manipulate
    Neutral Stasis: Lucid dreaming involves mental playthings; they are as I expect them to be
    Other Factors: False awakenings occur

Stage 3. Power, Purpose, and Primacy

Now the lucid dreamer may begin to conduct experiments, completely change the dream environment or direction, and show his or her mastery over the dream realm. The initial goal involves the easier manipulation of the objects, figures, and space in the dreaming, often through the use of directed intent and the will. The lucid dreamer continues to treat the dream figures as thought-forms and may ignore evidence of different classes of dream figures as well as unexpected developments.

    Impediments involve inexplicable or unexpected events, the appearance of things beyond control, an inability to conceive of proper experiments to test assumptions, and so on. At this stage, the lucid dreamer may feel very powerful and in control while learning details about the principles of operating in the dreaming realm. However, the appearance of apparent "independent agents" or dream figures acting in purposeful and volitional ways may cause anxiety and concern.

    I Dream: Dreaming reflects me and my power
    Behavior: Creation, destruction, going over, under, and through
    Goal: Complete ability to manipulate objects and others in the dream space
    Reality Creators: Intent and will
    Direction: If my control and power can't do it, there must be more going on
    Fear Blockage: Things do not follow my command; confusion; self as the ultimate limitation
    Neutral Stasis: By will and intent, I can make whatever I want happen

Stage 4. Re-reflection, Reaching Out, and Wonder

Opening up to the responsive element behind the dream provides a new paradox for the lucid dreamer because it suggests the lucid dreamer exists in the dream state with another awareness or larger Awareness. The initial goal involves trying to probe, understand, and respond advantageously to this realization. The lucid dreamer may develop a view that he or she has met the source, the dreamer of the dream, or the aware unconscious. Old assumptions may be discarded.

Impediments emerge as the lucid dreamer deals with this new mystery of another awareness, reconsiders past assumptions, and faces personal and even serious metaphysical concerns. At this much deeper stage, the lucid dreamer may either ignore the apparent, but hidden, awareness or engage it as a means to explore the nature of various realities.

The lucid dreamer also may begin to reflect that the dream realm represents a new type of reality with common principles and structure. Questions may emerge about who or what constructed this new realm, since it seems reflected in other lucid dreamers' experiences but beyond the capacity of the waking self. Some lucid dreamers may be forced to consider what is beyond this realm of lucid dreaming.

> **We Dream:** Dreaming reflects both me and other
> **Behavior:** Surrender, letting go, trust versus fear, the new paradox of awareness
> **Goal:** Trying to understand the complexities of the dream space
> **Reality Creator:** Using the other—the unknown inner awareness
> **Direction:** If more is going on here, then I must be stuck in another system; getting lucid about lucid dreaming
> **Fear Blockage:** Could I lose touch with waking reality? metaphysical concerns
> **Neutral Stasis:** In association with inner awareness, I can explore infinity

Stage 5: Experiencing Awareness

The nature of awareness could be considered a fifth stage, in which the lucid dreamer becomes deeply curious about the foundations of dream and waking reality and going beyond lucid dreaming, beliefs, and expectations. This stage exists outside of the lucid dreamer's control but seems to come as a reflection of the dreamer's intent and curiosity.

At this stage, the lucid dreamer realizes a deep connection with all awareness and a connection to a broader whole. He or she may wake from sleep with a recollection of a self-less experience of awareness characterized by light.

ALL Dream: Beyond me, beyond other; awareness without reflection
Behavior: Awareness
Goal: Understanding what is beyond lucid dreaming
Reality Creators: Deep intent and realizing connection
Direction: Using the analysis of dimensions to move past the representational
Fear Blockage: Loss of connection with representational dimensions
Neutral Stasis: All exist as part of a larger, connected whole

Throughout these five stages, each lucid dreamer progresses as he or she masters the common principles in creating dream reality. First, we come to terms with focus (maintaining balance when lucid) and emotion (not becoming too emotional and losing lucidity). Then, we add belief and expectation as we see that they play an important role in what we experience and what we allow ourselves to experience. Next, we learn to master and use intent and will as we seek to deepen our ability to manipulate the dream realm. And finally, we come to the "other" (or the mysterious inner) when we realize that to go even further, we have to surrender, let go, and seek the presence behind lucid dreaming. Beyond this fourth stage, we reach for something unknown and fundamentally inexplicable.

In the first three stages of lucid dreaming, the common assumption that "I am dreaming this" continues. In stage 4, one realizes that dreaming is definitely a cocreated event, which the lucid dreamer may direct but does not create in total; rather, the conscious unconscious or inner observer participates in the lucid dreamer's reality creation. In stage 5, one basically arrives at an experience of pure awareness as one attempts to go beyond the system of dreaming or lucid dreaming and discover its basis. Because nothing prohibits a lucid dreamer from trying an advanced technique, a beginning lucid dreamer could literally jump to a stage 4 technique and "ask the dream" to show him or her something of importance. Of course, most lucid dreamers will experience the level of their assumptions about lucid dreaming and progress as their conceptions, interests, and technical skills allow.

As you develop as a lucid dreamer, be aware that your regular dreaming and waking life viewpoint may change. You may experience intuitive insights, dream initiations, expressions of newly unblocked energy, and other phenomena that may truly affect your waking self. As your lucid dreaming develops, monitor yourself and progress at an appropriate rate wherein the waking self and inner aspects respectfully cooperate. If at any time you feel unduly concerned by lucid dreaming or disconnected from waking reality, you should set lucid dreaming aside and begin to focus on physical reality. Ground yourself with everyday activities such as taking walks, engaging with friends and family, returning to old hobbies, and reconnecting to the natural world.

MOVING ON

In Part One, I have sought to provide a broad picture of lucid dreaming by explaining some of my experiences and insights along the way. Crucial to my development has been the realization that the lucid dreamer does not control the lucid dream; rather, the lucid dreamer directs his or her focus within the dream. Until I realized this, I assumed that I existed in a "psychic mirror world" that only reflected my waking self.

I have also sought to place expectation as only one portion of lucid dream reality creation, by emphasizing the occurrence of, and seeking of, the unexpected. Through focusing on and courting the unexpected, lucid dreamers engage the greater reality in which they exist and go beyond the mirror world of waking-self reflection—the unexpected hints at the profound depth of the psyche.

When the inner awareness behind the dream began to announce itself, I realized that lucid dreaming involved much more than the waking self alone. As a result, I began to ignore the manifest dream and pose questions and requests to the awareness behind the dream. After deeply considering that something must exist behind the reality of lucid dreaming and waking reality, I sought to go beyond the lucid dream and my self within the lucid dream. At that point, the awareness that enlivens me spontaneously began to have mystifying and self-less experiences of light, a point anticipated by at least one tradition of Buddhist dream practice.

In Part Two, we'll explore how to create dream reality, how to interact conceptually with the lucid dreaming, and how, by seeking out the unexpected, we can begin to learn the true vastness inherent in lucid dreaming and the psyche. We'll also look at a new way to investigate the nature of waking reality, time, space, and the boundaries of identity.

PART 2

EXPLORING THE PSYCHE

10

CREATING THE
DREAM REALITY

AS WE SEEK TO COMPREHEND THE ALTERNATE REALITY OF LUCID dreaming, we may initially feel that we manipulate the dream objects and figures, but ultimately we realize that we actually manipulate our own mind—particularly our beliefs, focus, expectations, intent, and will. By manipulating our mind within the lucid dream, we learn how to create the dream reality that we then experience.

Though many would simply declare the dream an illusion, the dream as illusion still relates to you on an intimate level. Largely, it reflects back your own concerns or wishes filtered through your beliefs, expectations, focus, intent, and will, but in an exteriorized, symbolic fashion. By all appearances, the illusory dream naturally draws events and associations to you that have significance for you. So, as you change, the dreaming changes.

Calling dreams an illusion suggests the ancient Sanscrit term *maya*. However, as psychiatrist and philosopher Gordon Globus points out, maya actually suggests much more.

He writes: "One meaning of *maya* is translated as 'illusion' but it also has its basis in the verbal root *ma*, which means 'to make.' Thus [Wendy Doniger] O'Flaherty calls *maya* 'creative power,' 'artistic creation,' 'the process of creation.' She quotes [Jan] Gonda on *maya* in terms of 'converting an idea into dimensional reality,' which is just what I have called 'formative creativity.'"[1]

As lucid dreamers, we experience this broader meaning of maya directly—the forming and creating of an experienced reality from our feelings, thoughts, and ideas. The Sanskrit expert and scholar Wendy Doniger O'Flaherty points out, "Thus maya first meant making something that was not there before. . . . [M]aya can often best be translated as 'transformation.'"[2] She goes on to suggest, "To say that the universe is an illusion (maya) is not to say that it is unreal; it is to say, instead, that it is not what it seems to be, that it is something constantly being *made*."[3]

The ancient concept of maya, or illusion, alludes to the experiencer of the illusion as formatively assisting in the creation of the illusion. We do not exist in illusion so much as help form illusion. Lucid dreamers come to realize the truth of this as they see their own artistry, their own creative power, their own ideas formed into the dreaming reality that they experience. Like artists projecting their ideas, knowledge, and talent into their paintings, lucid dreamers project portions of themselves creatively into their dreaming. The lucid dreamer embodies and joins forces with the inventive power of maya.

To create the lucid dream most constructively, each lucid dreamer must learn how to apply properly to the dream canvas the colorful materials of their mind. The full "creative power" of the lucid dream creator emerges when he or she masters the principles of reality creating.

In a sense, lucid dreamers accept and even relish their role as illusion makers. Lucidly aware, they learn the process of how they create their own reality, their own maya.

For my part, I have identified six reality-creating principles for lucid dreamers to consider: focus, beliefs, expectations, intent, will, and X, the inner Unknown. Let's begin by examining the nature of focus in lucid dreaming.

BUILDING THE DREAM THROUGH THE CREATIVE POWER OF FOCUS

Focus matters. Imagine yourself becoming lucid in the following dream: Coming out of a park, you see numerous skyscrapers and suddenly realize, "I don't live in New York City. This is a dream!" Looking around, you see fashionably dressed women walking past a pastry shop with incredible desserts in the window. To the left, there's a newsstand with tomorrow's issue of the *Wall Street Journal* next to a man dressed in an orange robe, like a Buddhist priest. To the right, you see a black carriage pulled by beautiful white horses. Lucid, what do you do?

When lucid, you do what you focus upon, according to your state at the time. A hungry lucid dreamer might focus on the pastry shop. A spiritual lucid dreamer might focus on talking to the Buddhist priest. A horse-loving lucid dreamer might focus on the carriage and horses. An experienced lucid dreamer might focus on something not apparent, like flying to the Statue of Liberty, and a more advanced lucid dreamer might ignore the whole scene and focus on an experiment she wished to perform.

When lucid, you can focus on the immediately apparent, the implied, and the potential. In effect, you can focus on the finite or the infinite, the perceived or the unperceived. Focus creates a sense of order out of all these innumerable possibilities. By focusing our attention, we concentrate our mental energy on a limited field of our particular interests and personal priorities.

As the philosopher William James put it, "My experience is what I agree to attend to. Only those items which I notice shape my mind—without selective interest, experience is an utter chaos."[4] So focus performs a selective function by limiting our attention to areas of our own interest and making the experience of any reality practical and personally meaningful.

When consciously aware in the dream state, your focus matters for two fundamental reasons: 1) once lucid, your focus guides your experience, and 2) if you lose focused awareness upon being lucid, then you will shift realities and return to regular dreaming or waking. Focus, therefore, acts as a significant reality-creating principle in your lucid dreaming. By properly using focus, you can radically change your lucid dreaming and create longer, more interesting experiences.

Focus, though, takes time to develop. As you become more adept, you'll find that sharing your early lucid dreams with others feels like showing old photos from grade school—you look at them and think, "Could I really have been that young and naive?" Looking back, it seems embarrassing how short and unimaginative many of my first lucid dreams were. Though I felt excited to be lucid, I didn't understand how to create a stable dreaming reality.

Yet even in their simplicity, every lucid dream demonstrates the reality-creating principles of lucid dreaming. By looking for those principles and learning from them, we begin to realize consciously how to conduct ourselves when lucidly aware. We build a framework of understanding.

While it might be much easier to say, "Do this" or "Don't do that," when lucid dreaming, those directions simply order you around; they don't provide insight. By considering the principles beneath the simple advice, you prepare yourself for a much deeper exploration of lucid dreaming and the unconscious based on something more than simple admonitions or rules. Consider, for example, these lucid dreams from my teenage years:

> Early Lucid Dream #1: At my childhood home, Dad and I and a friend are outside working. We all seem younger than our current ages. Dad gets upset about something and yells, "Hurry up!" This really embarrasses me in front of my friend and I'm just about to react when I realize, "This is all a dream!"
>
> Lucidly aware, I go up to Dad and tell him, "This is all a dream! So it really isn't important what you say, and I'm going to ignore all of your idiotic commands!" Suddenly a policeman appears and takes Dad away.

Notice how I become lucidly aware and totally focus on confronting the dream image of my father. What happens when I say my piece and expend my focus on it? A policeman enters the dream. Did I, the lucid dreamer, consciously call the policeman forth? If not my conscious act, then what explains the policeman's entry into the lucid dream and subsequent action?

> Early Lucid Dream #2: I am walking in an apartment and see my girlfriend lying asleep on the floor near the door to the shower. That strikes me as odd, and I realize I am dreaming. Thinking about what to do, I decide to go and bite her rump, basically to see what this would be like, and if she, as a dream figure, would notice. Grinning I lean over her, and softly bite her rump. Well, this seems fun! So I bite the other side of her rump. It feels so real—just like one would think it should. She continues lying there, asleep. Suddenly, my brother comes to the door and she rises and puts a towel around herself. I feel embarrassed.

In the dream I had decided, while lucid, to conduct an experiment, wondering, "What will this feel like?" and "Will she notice it?" What happens when I conclude my experiment and no longer focus on it? My brother enters the dream, and my girlfriend gets up and puts a towel around herself. Did I, the lucid dreamer, consciously request his intrusion or her reaction? If not, then what explains those actions?

Early Lucid Dream #3: I'm coming up the stairs to a movie theater. I suddenly feel I could move very fast, almost propelled along. I whiz past people. Then right before I come to the door, I realize I'm dreaming and yell, "I can fly!" and I do—zooming around the ceiling of the old fashioned movie auditorium, lucidly aware. I feel great!

Looking down, I announce to the audience, "The world is a belief!" I go on and address the audience, saying that they experience their beliefs and perceptions, and really not a fundamental reality at all. At this point, groups of people start to leave the theater. Suddenly a security guard and a lady manager appear and want to talk with me. I now seem at their level. The manager seems initially mad, but when we are alone, she asks, "How did you do this?" She seemed impressed or surprised in a pleasant way.

This lucid dream came as part of a series of lucid dreams that found me becoming lucidly aware in theaters. Sometimes, I would sit in the audience and realize, "I'm dreaming!" At other times, I became consciously aware onstage. Notice how I lucidly express a fairly interesting idea, but once I finish my important announcement, what happens? The audience begins to get up and leave, followed by the entry of a security guard and manager. Did I, the lucid dreamer, consciously request that?

By looking closely at these lucid dreams, we see how focus relates to creating experienced reality. These simple examples teach the following:

The need to focus, then refocus: In each of the preceding lucid dreams, once I expend my aware focus on the task at hand (reproving my father, experimenting on my girlfriend, making my announcement to the theater audience), my active focus was empty, blank. At that point, new dream figures suddenly enter the lucid dream. Like many beginning lucid dreamers, I failed to refocus on any new objective, which allowed my unconscious to reassert itself and bring new dream figures into my lucid dream.

If an experienced lucid dreamer kept a detailed report, you would read something like this: "Became lucid, decided to do this: did it. Then decided to do this: did it. Then I noticed that and decided to investigate: did so." Experienced lucid dreamers (whether they know it or not) learn to refocus their attention as a means to maintain their creation of the dream reality. Whether through taking action or simply deliberating, experienced lucid dreamers maintain their awareness actively and elongate the lucid dream.

Losing the battle of creating: At that exact moment when the lucid dreamer has expended his focus, something amazing happens: the dream reality continues as the unconscious creative dreaming system returns and introduces new elements, new objects, and new dream figures into the dream, as the policeman in my first example and my brother in the second illustrate. I did not consciously create these dream figures. Their introduction represents the natural, ongoing, creative progression of the dreaming (which comes uninitiated consciously by the lucid dreamer). Once the lucid dreamer's focus diminishes, the apparent creative dreaming system reemerges, causing new dream elements to appear.

At this point, new lucid dreamers often become totally fascinated by the new elements and lose their focused awareness. Within moments, they can become caught up in the swift flow of dreaming and immersed in its offerings. In losing their focus, they lose their creative power over the lucid dream reality and return to regular dream reality.

In effect, an aware lucid dreamer pushes back the ever-present forces of unconscious creation for the right to create his or her conscious creation. As the lucid dreamer's focused awareness emerges, the unconscious creations wane. Conversely, when the lucid dreamer's focused awareness wanes, the unconscious creations reemerge.

So, theoretically, when lucid, we can potentially do anything. As a practical matter, however, lucid dreamers do this:

Beginning lucid dreamers tend to focus on what they find in their dreamscape at the point of becoming lucid. They normally accept the immediate surroundings as their total field of experience.

Intermediate lucid dreamers focus on both the dreamscape and the implied surroundings. They take in the dreamscape but expand the dreamscape as they move or search around the implied area. They may create objects or figures consistent with the dreamscape.

Advanced lucid dreamers often engage the broadest range: the dreamscape, the implied dreamscape, and the potential dreamscape. By the potential dreamscape, they recognize that they can use their focus to attract potentially any dreamscape into their experience, even ones totally disconnected from the current dreamscape.

"Potential" sounds vague in that it suggests the probable, the unmaterialized, the latent. However, the word *potential* comes from the late Latin, *potentia*, meaning "latent power." Latent power exists in lucid dreaming, far beyond what most people can imagine. Even many lucid dreamers find themselves shocked by that latent power once they open up to it. Unfortunately, most lucid dreamers never do open up to it. They either don't progress to the stage at which they can avail themselves of it, or they focus on the immediate or the implied of lucid dreaming and ignore the extraordinary potential.

Of course, don Juan said this much more dramatically. "Dreaming," he told Castaneda, "is the gateway to infinity." However, to venture into infinity requires an ability to focus on a place, a setting, an idea or emotion *that is not evident*. The potential dreamscape awaits those who are ready to birth reality, to create the nonexistent, to call forth the unseen. To focus within the abstract is the gateway to lucid dreaming's true potential.

Understanding the importance of focus as a reality-creating principle can radically transform one's lucid experience from simple pleasure seeking to journeys into unimaginable experience. Focus serves to select our experience from the vastness available to us in the infinity of lucid dreaming. By focusing, we channel our creating powers to produce the dream's likely path.

BELIEFS AND EXPECTATION: WHEN EXPECTATIONS COLLIDE

Consciously aware in dreaming, lucid dreamers see the creative impact of beliefs and expectations in determining the dream experience. The power of expectation is so prevalent, lucid dreamers routinely talk about the expectation effect, meaning the tendency for the lucid dream to follow the mental expectation of the lucid dreamer (which I discussed at length in chapter 4).

The expectation effect carries such import that a lucid dreamer who suddenly changes his or her expectations instantly changes the experience of the dream. When lucid, if you expect to fly through a wall, you normally will fly through the wall. If you suddenly doubt and don't expect to fly through a wall, however, your new expectation will materialize, and you will most likely bounce off the wall.

I recall a lucid dream in which I was flying back through a wall that I had previously flown through. Suddenly, I had just a tinge of doubt about flying through it—just a speck. The result? I became stuck halfway through the wall! Just that little bit of doubt tinged my expectation, and my situation symbolically reflected my mental state. Hanging there in the wall, half in and half out, I realized the absurdity of the situation, and proceeded to "expect" my successful passage through it.

So not only do you get what you expect, you get what you expect *at the moment* you expect it. Changing your mind, even slightly, changes the lucid dream experience to correspond to the minor gradations of your expectation.

When lucid, you realize that the expectation effect (and all reality-creating principles) acts as a self-reflective learning system. If you expect trouble, if you expect punishment, if you expect wrath, the lucid dream responds to your expectation with appropriate images and situations. If you expect love, if you expect joy, if you expect ecstasy, the lucid dream responds in kind. Your experience largely reflects your expectations, which come from your beliefs, thoughts, ideas, and emotions.

You could say expectations come in all shades of intensity, feeling, and depth. Expectations can be both simple and surprisingly complex. You can expect based on seemingly rational conditions; if A, then I expect B, or if A and B, then I expect C, and so on. While expectations appear simple, they emerge from the complexity of our ever changing personal belief system and shifting focus and can mirror that complexity.

Since you can use lucid dreaming to actively go beyond expectation, you ultimately realize that lucid dreaming is not entirely a self-reflective mirror of your waking conscious processes. In going beyond your expectations and allowing the unexpected, you open up to the larger reality and unknown creativity of lucid dreams.

Before Stephen LaBerge had published his book *Lucid Dreaming*,[5] a friend wrote and asked me if I had ever tried spinning in a lucid dream? In the early 1980s, I had never considered it. My friend suggested that I should try it and see what I experienced. At first I thought, "Spinning? Why would anyone want to spin in a lucid dream?" Not wanting to disappoint, though, I reminded myself that the next time I became lucidly aware, I would spin and see what happened. This was the result:

> I become lucid and remember the task. I start spinning myself. A circle of greenish light begins to manifest in the space around me as I spin with eyes open. The environment doesn't change. Then I (or my point of awareness) seem inside a pastel ball of light in which I'm hovering over the floor in a circle around an axis. Unsure about what to expect, I think, "Perhaps, I should look for symbols." Now I see four colored balls of light, vertically arranged in sets of two seeming to spin around their own axes but also around the axis of my aware point. Then four

more balls of light appear. I keep spinning faster. Since this seems so unusual, I decide to wind it down. I wake.

So, was that spinning? Those who have read LaBerge's books realize that he used spinning to create an entirely new dream scene, particularly when he felt that the current lucid dream scene might collapse. At the time of this lucid dream attempt, I did not understand the expected purpose or result of spinning. I spun around to see what would happen and ended up experiencing balls of light—apparently even my awareness seemed inside a ball of light!

Later, when I read LaBerge's book and tried spinning with the accepted expectation to create a new dream scene, I created an entirely new dream scene in my lucid dream, just as expected. Experience largely conforms to expectation.

This line of reasoning leads a person to wonder, do techniques work in lucid dreaming only when the subject knows the expected outcome? What matters more, the technique or the expectation? In the psychologically responsive realm of lucid dreaming, the value of a technique seems equal to its ability to produce an expected result. The true value of techniques may be their usefulness as a focus for expectation or intent, more so than any innate capacity. On some level, my spinning and seeing balls of light made me curious about a "no expectation effect." If we have a technique but no expectation of the outcome, what do we experience then? The underlying reality? The unexpected? An appropriate subjective dream fantasy?

My friend wrote back to explain LaBerge's expected result. Now, however, she proposed another technique to change the dream scene: simply wave your hand while expecting the scene to disappear. She asked me to try it in a lucid dream, which I did (July 1985):

> My friend Paul and I are in a room. I realize this is a dream and remember that I agreed to try the wave technique. I also see a glass vase and almost decide to go smash it to see what would happen but decide not to make a mess. Since the room is kind of murky and not very interesting, I wave my hand to make the scene go away—and it does—but nothing replaces it! Now, all I hear is the sound of Paul's voice in the darkness.

I expected that waving my hand would wipe away the dream imagery and it worked. However, my friend expected something different; she expected a brand new dream scene to emerge after waving away the old. As you can see, I did not expect that or intend that. Once I waved away the dream imagery, I could still hear my friend speaking, but had no visuals other than a deep black field of empty space.

The friend who had suggested the experiment was incredulous that I hadn't understood a new dream image was supposed to emerge after waving away the old. But once again, I experienced what I expected to the degree I expected it. Her initial letter did not make this clear enough for me to include as part of my expectational construct. I experienced my expected mental construct, not hers.

When it comes to expectations, you normally get what you expect, at the moment you expect it, to the degree that you expect it.

THE FIELD OF BELIEFS

Beliefs seem closely tied to expectations in that we expect that which we believe possible. In lucid dreaming (and in waking life, too), beliefs help determine our personal experience, since we focus upon what we believe to be significant and expect only what we believe to be possible. Our conscious and unconscious beliefs help order and structure our unique version of reality.

Jungian theorist Marie Louise von Franz writes:

> As the American psychologist William James once pointed out, the idea of an unconscious could itself be compared to the "field" concept in physics. We might say that, just as in a magnetic field the particles entering into it appear in a certain order, psychological contents also appear in an ordered way within that psychic area, which we call the unconscious. If we call something "rational" or "meaningful" in our conscious mind, and accept it as a satisfactory "explanation" of things, it is probably due to the fact that our conscious explanation is in harmony with some pre-conscious constellation of contents in our unconscious.[6]

To this concluding observation, I would add that our beliefs or belief system may represent much of that "pre-conscious constellation of contents in our unconscious." It seems to me that our conscious and unconscious beliefs create our mental "field," and we accept, reject, and conceive (or allow) each moment's ideas and experiences based on the composition of our individual belief field.

When lucid in a dream, we generally act in accordance with our beliefs. If we believe something is possible, we attempt it; if we don't believe something is possible, we don't attempt it. Our beliefs delineate the boundaries of our experience to a large degree.

Some of our beliefs could be considered our private beliefs, while other beliefs we come to accept from society, our culture, the historic times. We seem to attract to us and hold onto beliefs that agree with those beliefs we already hold. We reject those beliefs with which we disagree and place on hold those that leave us feeling neutral. Considered this way, beliefs hold all manner and intensities of charge—positive, negative, neutral, so to speak—and the beliefs change as we change. Collectively, one might suggest that individual beliefs coalesce into mental constructs, just as electrons form atoms, which combine into molecules, and so on.

In essence, our vibrantly alive beliefs become our psychological homeland, our worldview. Many of us accept our beliefs so completely that they seem self-evident, natural, and utterly true. Our beliefs overlay, and in a sense transform, the reality that we then experience.

As lucid dreamers create the reality of lucid dreaming, they observe how beliefs strongly affect that environment. For example, in college, I read the Russian writer P. D. Ouspensky's assertion that a person could not recall his or her name in the dream state. I wondered about this. During my next lucid dream, I consciously recalled his assertion and lucidly found a pen and paper. "Robert," I wrote easily, and then I began to write, "Watt," hesitated for a moment, thinking, "That's not right," scratched it out, consciously recalled my last name, and quickly jotted "Waggoner."

Stephen LaBerge reports reading Ouspensky's book and notes that lucid dreamers who apparently believed in Ouspensky's assumption failed to announce their name in a lucid dream. He himself, not believing in Ouspensky's suggestion, had no trouble announcing his name.[7]

Undoubtedly, your ideas and beliefs have a major impact on your experiences in the lucid dreaming environment. Though many assert that in lucid dreams you can do whatever you want, as a practical matter, your lucid dream actions will be limited by your beliefs. For example, many lucid dreamers decide that dream figures have nothing to say, or at least nothing intelligent to say. After all, they conclude, "The dream figures are just products of my mind!" To prove that belief, they may point out that in their last twenty lucid dreams, not one intelligent comment was made by a dream figure. But how do they know the lack of response simply reflects their belief and expectation? Similarly, some lucid dreamers announce that the written word always changes in a lucid dream; however, after thirty years of experience, I find the written word to be relatively stable.

When we believe in limitations or difficulties, we help bring them about. So, cultivating an open mind and expansive beliefs about the possibilities in lucid dreams potentially broadens the scope of our experience. To discover the broadest nature of lucid dreaming, we must play with beliefs on numerous levels. Since our beliefs actively affect even the interpretation of our experience, they seem almost inescapable.

I don't so much encourage anyone to adopt what they perceive to be my beliefs as seek their own broader experience in lucid dreams—to consider new concepts, new ideas, and, with integrity, see where they lead in their experience.

INTENT AND WILL: THE GATEWAY TO INFINITY

How do you move beyond expectation? How do you discover that which is outside your experience? How do you engage the unknown? In lucid dreaming, you do this through the use of intent.

Whenever we ask the dream to show us something, we use intent. When we shout, "Hey! I want to hear my feeling-tone!" we express our intent. When we shout, "Hey! I want to see more women in here when I return!" we use intent. The word *intent* comes from the Latin word *intendere*, meaning "to stretch toward." Whenever we ignore the dream figures and ask the dream, our intent stretches toward an awareness behind the dream. We do not command or force or insist. We make a simple request of intent and in that stretching toward, we begin to touch, as don Juan said, the "idea of the abstract, the spirit . . ."[8]

Intent offers the awareness-beyond-the-dream an opportunity to respond. Intent asks that unidentified creative power to show us something of importance—to select from every possible thing, known or unknown, imagined or unimagined, to choose what the lucid dreamer will see at that moment, according to the mysteries of intent and the responder.

And what of the lucid dreamers? In asking the hidden awareness, do they let go of directing their focus within the dream? In that moment of intent, do they announce their openness, their willingness to experience the unknown? Do they allow themselves, at least for a moment, to let go and trust in something beyond the conscious self? In opening to the unknown, do they allow themselves a brief glimpse of that awareness, an expression of their inner Self?

Intent acts as a reality-creating principle, albeit a mysterious one, since we often do not or cannot know the response in advance of its creation. In many respects, intent shows us that reality creation partially occurs "beyond" us, beyond our doing, beyond our waking awareness. It hints at the fact that we cocreate the lucid dreaming reality; we do not create it exclusively. Unlike expectation, belief, or focus, by which we know what we expect to transpire, the use of intent reaches more deeply, eliciting a response beyond our waking knowing.

Will differs from intent. Lucid dreamers often use their will to create deeply desired events in the dream environment. As don Juan said, "Will is something a man uses, for instance, to win a battle which he, by all calculations, should lose . . . Will is a power . . . Will is what can make you succeed when your thoughts tell you that you're defeated. Will is what makes you invulnerable."[9]

In lucid dreaming, inward focus leads you to the will and a powerful means of creating reality. To make the will function requires two things: 1) an inward concentration toward the emotions, and 2) a connection of emotions or emotional energy to a predetermined desire. When that inward wish becomes empowered by emotions, the lucid dreamer experiences a new type of reality creation in the lucid dream. Suddenly, the inner desire literally bursts into the outer experience!

In the mentally responsive space of dreaming, creativity results from a new set of rules. Desire alone is not enough. You have to will that inner desire to the level of emotion. There, your will, combined with emotional energy, explodes in a flash of creation. Through the use of the will, dream reality can be made to bend your way, as I experienced in this lucid dream (June 1984):

> My fiancée, Wendy, and I are, I believe, on a school's stairway. Suddenly my hands are in front of me and I realize I'm dreaming. I look at my hands, then look away, then at my hands, back and forth, trying to stabilize my lucid state. After a while, I turn to her and say, "I'm having a lucid dream. I want to teach you how to have a lucid dream. First look at your hands. Now when they start to get fuzzy, look away at the scenery, and when *that* gets fuzzy, look back at your hands. And keep doing that."
>
> We do this for awhile. Since we stand at the bottom of the stairs, I decide to will myself to the top of the stairs. I concentrate inwardly and suddenly float to the top. I look down at Wendy and tell her to use her will and come up here. She tries and she does it.

At the next landing, I intuitively know that I can't fly to the higher landing. Frustrated for a moment, I determine to use my will to bend and pull the metal banister at the top of the stairs down to me. It curls like a ribbon toward me as I grab hold of it, then it rebounds back in place, taking me with it. After a moment, Wendy does the same. Eventually, we leave the building and go elsewhere. I remain lucid while noticing a number of Chinese men at the new location. We become amorous and the dream ends.[10]

ACTIVELY USING EMOTION AND THE WILL

Interestingly, the will often emerges most easily when the lucid dreamer feels frustrated. At that moment, your frustration automatically moves you closer to emotions. If you can quickly connect that emotional energy toward your goal, you can perform a kind of lucid jujitsu and manifest your desired reality. By consciously directing available emotional energy to a willed outcome, your desires appear in the lucid dream state instantaneously.

Like the invisible air in physical reality, we rarely notice emotional energy in lucid dreams except when we become frustrated and it rises to the surface. Emotional energy seems to compose one of the building blocks of dream reality, ever present but hidden within the structure. The emotional substrate provides, I presume, some of the energy to prop up the dream objects and figures, along with perhaps mental energy.

Recently, I acted on this premise with surprising results. Aware in a lucid dream, I began to collect all of the energy of the dream and reclaim it, calling the energy back to me in sweeping motions. After waking from that lucid dream, I recorded three more lucid dreams that same night.

In those moments when you use the will, it seems almost ontologically creative as it suddenly bursts forth with incredible creative energy. The will wipes away all obstacles. You don't control the will so much as become one with its expression. It acts like the big bang of creation; everything yields to the pure expression of the will in that moment.

A subtle aspect of intent and the will appears after many years of lucid dreaming. The dreaming begins to encourage the lucid dreamer. Events happen, as if purposefully designed to assist the lucid dreamer in becoming more aware. Messages appear, words are spoken, helpful dream figures arrive in the lucid dream, all to encourage and support the lucid dreamer. At those moments, you feel the accumulated years of striving for greater awareness is beginning to be acknowledged. The will of the lucid dreamer touches something—the abstract, the spirit, the inner Self—and that something responds. When that occurs, you realize that your intent and will help create the path that you follow.

Of all reality creators, the will stands closest to emotion. It feeds off emotion's energy to vitalize its mission. The will, when it bursts forth, realigns dream reality, carrying the dreamer's perception with it. That inward drawing of focus acts to compress the desire's expression until a powerful release occurs. In that moment, one experiences the birth of creation.

X, THE INNER UNKNOWN

When you use intent to "ask the dream," most lucid dreamers come into contact with an inner, aware responsiveness, which I consider the inner ego or the inner Self.

When that inner awareness responds, it often creates or introduces an unanticipated new dream environment. For this reason, I consider X—the inner ego, the inner Self, or the inner Unknown—to be a reality-creating principle, which lucid dreamers can work with to alter the lucid dream normally beyond any preconception of the waking self. The existence of this inner Unknown and its reality-creating powers means that lucid dreamers are cocreators of the dream reality. As much as our waking ego would like to take credit for all lucid events, we must accept that the lucid dream reality is frequently a creation of this inner awareness.

Because it goes beyond the waking self's conception, this aware X or inner Self does not seem a "product" or outgrowth of the waking self. Rather, it seems to me the organizing awareness or inner ego within each person's dream space and, likely, mental space. It exists beyond the waking self, so to speak, while understanding, appreciating, and responding to the waking self. By all appearances, it seems greater than the waking self, though primarily functionally engaged in its own dimension of mental space.

In upcoming chapters, a number of lucid dreams will show this inner awareness's responsiveness and apparent independence from the waking self. In some examples, the inner awareness explains why the lucid dreamer's request cannot be expressed or should not be expressed at that time. In those episodes, we again see an element of independent and responsive awareness far beyond the waking self's wish fulfilling expectations. Collectively, these lucid dreams do not show a sub-personality or something lesser than the waking self; rather, these lucid dreams show something greater than the waking self.

As we investigate the reality-creating principles, we discover the initial meaning of maya—how we make, form, and create the illusory realm that we then experience. In regular dreaming, we forget our part in the dream's creation; in lucid dreaming, we begin to see our role in maya. Through manipulation of our belief, expectation, focus, intent, and will, along with X, the lucid dreamer works to create the lucid dream reality, using the underlying energy of emotion and ideation as its raw materials.

In manipulating the mind, the lucid dreamer experiences the Mind.

It seems clear that the reality-creating principles so evident in lucid dreaming have a wider application to the making or maya of the waking world.

11

VARIETIES OF
DREAM FIGURES

As EXPERIENCED LUCID DREAMERS WILL TELL YOU, DREAM FIGURES exist in much greater complexity and variety than most dream theorists imagine. When lucid dreamers consciously engage and converse with dream figures, the dream figures frequently surprise them with their knowledge, observations, and rational comments (as we saw in the examples in chapter 5). As such, lucid dreaming provides for an entirely new perspective on the nature of the dream realm and dream figures.

Some dream figures appear to be simple thought-forms or symbols, representing some idea, expectation, or emotion in the lucid dream; this group has little or nothing to say. Other dream figures, as previously discussed, argue logically and convincingly for their autonomous existence in an environment they perceive as real and resent the lucid dreamer's comments about "creating" them. Still other lucid dream figures go beyond this and actually act in such a way as to be seen as independent agents with an apparent agenda of their own, sometimes in contradiction to that of the lucid dreamer. As we shall see, on rare occasions dream figures will appear and spontaneously announce they are guardians or helpers, there to assist or watch over the lucid dreamer; they sometimes even provide useful advice or suggest ways to manipulate the lucid dream environment.

Dream figures don't appear to possess the same broad abilities of the inner awareness behind the dream; those abilities seem to be specific to the inner awareness alone. Instead, the variety of dream figures manifest as points of increasing complexity and functionality along a broad continuum of awareness, knowledge, and ability to change the dream environment. By contrast, the inner awareness, when consulted by the lucid dreamer, responds with a much deeper sense of awareness, insight, and knowledge plus the ability to create an entirely new dream environment that expresses concepts and abstract ideas in direct response to the lucid dreamer's request, such as in my "Hey, I want to hear my feeling-tone!" experience recounted earlier.

Differentiating between the types of dream figures requires considerable skill, since our apparent physical senses in the lucid dream have little discriminative ability. To get a more accurate reading of the variety of dream figures, lucid dreamers have discovered that they must literally interact with them, through conversations, questions, or suggestions, sometimes literally face to face. In a lucid dream years ago, for example, I found myself having sex with an attractive woman dream figure. While part of me enjoyed the physical thrill and building passion, another part lucidly wondered, "Is she merely a thought-form?" To resolve the question, I raised myself up and authoritatively announced, "All thought-forms must now disappear!" Suddenly, she was gone. As I lay there in the semidarkness, hanging in a missionary position that had seemingly lost its mission, I lucidly wondered how someone apparently so real, so tactile and responsive, could be nothing but a thought-form.

Before I could ponder too long, another woman had taken her place! While not as captivating as the first, she seemed to know the part quite well and we continued the scenario with passionate gusto. Again, I consciously felt her skin, touched her hair, and pressed her lips, yet I had to wonder, "Could she be a thought-form?" With that, I declared again, "All thought-forms must disappear!" And *poof!* She too vanished.

In the semidarkness of the lucid dream, I became alarmed. She had felt real, as real as my body felt in the dream. But she too disappeared. How could one tell then? How could we distinguish between a dream figure as valid as our own self and a thought-form? Or are all dream residents merely thought-forms?

Before I could finish the questioning, a third woman lay underneath me! Not as engaging as the first two and with a bit of an attitude, nevertheless she seemed intent on fulfilling the mission. But as I felt her skin, her bones, her muscles, seeking some imperfection that would clearly indicate her status in the dream state as either equivalent to mine or just a thought-form, I realized my senses had a record of unreliability. Formulating the dreaded question, "All thought-forms must now . . ."—she was gone before I could say "disappear."

I have tried this same announcement—"All thought-forms must now disappear"—in a number of lucid dreams. Occasionally, all the dream figures disappear, but sometimes they don't. I recall once making the announcement to two groups of about four dream figures; one group suddenly disappeared, while the other group looked at me with something close to utter disdain as if to say, "Can't you tell the difference?" and continued with their project.

In many lucid dreams, we find the more common assumption that the dream figures represent elements of the dreamer borne out. By consciously asking, "Who are you?" the lucid dreamer allows the dream figure an opportunity for expression. Consider this lucid dream, in which lucid dreamer Connie Gavalis poses that same question:

> A man appeared. I asked him, "Who are you?" He said, "I am a part of you." He took my hand and led me through grayish darkness. We were in a room like I've never seen previously—kind of old—like outdated—from the past. The corner was decorated with streamers or something. Then, another man walked in. He had a beard and looked like an explorer of old. He stood in the corner where things were hanging. He said, "I'm a part of you that stakes out territory and uncharted areas." I laughed and said, "Oh yes, I do stake out my territory and nobody else better come into it." He said, "That's right, that's you." He said, "We are going to go over all parts of you."
>
> Then I saw other people walking in, all different types of people. I looked around and said, "I wonder where the teacher is?" I meant the teacher in me. Then, I saw a nun dressed in gray come in. They said, "That's the you who is too religious and too good. That's the nun in you." I became annoyed and said, "I'm not a prude. I'm not a goody, goody girl." I couldn't understand why the nun was there.
>
> I got very anxious to know all these things about me. I asked, "Why do I want to know all these things about me?" They said, "Because then, you can be a complete, single entity—a whole person." I was delighted because I wanted to know all about myself—to be real. I wanted to correct what perhaps is wrong in my understanding of myself."[1]

As the lucid dreamer's waking self questions the action, "a part" of her takes her to a place where her "explorer" part announces, "We are going to go over all parts of you." She then sees "all different types of people" and learns that by understanding the various parts of herself, she then "can be a complete entity—a whole person." In many respects, this type of experience suggests Carl Jung's individuation process in which, by knowing and accepting all parts of our self, we become our complete Self.

EDUCATING THE LUCID DREAMER

Curiously, some dream figures have a distinct interest in educating the lucid dreamer. When consciously aware, we notice the purposeful nature of their actions. I encountered one figure at a dream library who seemed intent on showing me something profound (October 1996):

> My wife, Wendy, and I are outside a building in Houston it seems. Standing there, we see the couple from an the earlier dream, which strikes me as odd. I decide to go inside and find the area incredibly well lit and interesting—it's a library. Suddenly I realize, "This is a dream! This is a lucid dream!"
>
> I start running forward, gleeful. I turn back to three or four women sitting near the entrance. They are very serene and welcoming. One is holding a book. We talk briefly and I look directly into her eyes, very close. I notice that the coloration is a gray-blue swirl but doesn't change colors as I continue to stare. I ask the women to come fly with me but they decline.
>
> I turn and go flying down the aisles of books. Suddenly, I take a right and fly up to a young woman sitting alone. She has long brown hair, a very soulful expression, and deep brown eyes. I implore her to come flying with me. She hesitates, but finally agrees.
>
> We hold hands and go flying up and through the ceiling. I think how easy it is to fly with her and begin wondering whose energy and willpower is being used in the flying, mine or hers?
>
> We go through the ceiling into an attic. She stops me and directs my focus to the scene below. Interestingly, we can now see through the building to the basement of the library. Though the basement floor has dusty rubble on half of it, I look closer and notice a fascinating design. I see a large circle outlined, and then, within that circle, a square, touching the circle at four equal points. On that square sits an equilateral triangle (I believe) and standing upright in the middle of that triangle, I can see a softly marked rectangle. The rectangle stops at a point on the triangle where it creates three new smaller triangles: the top point and alternate triangles pointing either way.

I intuitively sense the outline has mathematical meanings that connect the geometric images proportionally. Then, as I look again, it somehow dawns on me that these geometric figures symbolize the ancient knowledge or wisdom that exists as the foundation of human knowledge. That it's half covered in dust and rubble suggests that we exist only half aware of our true selves.

I look at the woman and then realize that she brought me here to show me this. She wanted me to be aware of this.

Years later, I finally realized that I had been shown a yantra symbol in this lucid dream. Similar to the auditory mantra in my earlier feeling-tone lucid dream, a yantra is a geometrical design that some Eastern religions believe contains both profound symbolic meaning and inherent energy. Yantras are often composed of circles, squares, triangles, bindu (center dot or seed symbol) and may have lotuses or mantras in them. By meditating on these visual images, some Eastern religions believe one may spontaneously have intuitive insights into the nature of the phenomenal and spiritual world.

Incredibly, this dream figure made an independent effort to point this yantra out to me, even though I had no conscious awareness of the Eastern tradition of yantras and their meanings. Gazing at it, I intuitively sensed it held meaning. Yet, how do I interpret the dream figure who pointed it out? As an expression of me or my higher awareness? As an independent agent with a desire to educate and instruct?

In the next lucid dream, I wondered how these more aware dream figures viewed the lucid dreamer. I used my time to ask about *their* perception of dream interactions (January 2005):

After noticing an odd airplane, I begin to realize this is a dream, and I pull my awareness fully into the dream. (Sometimes this seems like pulling a full bucket from a deep well—it's almost a physical sensation.)

I decide to ask the dream residents some questions. . . . Incredibly, I have an unusually long lucid dream with lots of discussions with various dream figures. As I go on, I realize that it is hard to remember some of the earlier conversations.

I begin talking to some of the dream residents about my situation in the dream and their situation in the dream. The basic conversation develops that in the dream state I appear to them as a type of awareness, and each of them appears to me as a type of awareness as well. The conversation is about how one needs to show an understanding of and appreciation for the dream figures' own valid awareness. When the lucid dreamer doesn't demonstrate this, the dream figure doesn't care to interact with one so unaware and unknowledgeable. The dream figures suggest they need to be treated thoughtfully in order to respond thoughtfully.

In this brief exchange, you might take away the following: 1) since some dream figures have a type of awareness, you should approach them on this basis, and 2) based on their responsiveness, you can determine what type of further interaction seems warranted.

Marc Ian Barasch, author of the award-winning book *Healing Dreams*, mentions a lucid dreamer who becomes befuddled by the unexpected knowledgeable awareness of seemingly autonomous dream figures:

> I'm in some sort of clinic. I ask the woman behind the counter, "If this is a dream, can I touch you?" She says, "Yes." I reach out and shake her hand. To my amazement, her hand is warm and solid and feels just like the outer world. Then I turn to a nurse walking down the hallway, and she gives a glance to the woman behind the counter, sort of like, "Oh, she figured it out." I get a tremendous feeling that this is their life, walking around in dreams, just like we have jobs out here. The nurse says something like, "Now that you know this is a dream, you know that we have a lot of information on you." [2]

Many lucid dreamers find it shocking to discover that a subset of dream figures seem to possess a type of awareness, knowledge, and action. While you may vaguely suspect that some dream figures have conscious awareness, nothing prepares you for the more convincing encounters.

Recurring dream figures occasionally appear in lucid dreams. In fact, they often prompt the dreamer into conscious awareness. Once, I watched a small group of dream figures enter a restaurant door two or three times before the strangeness of that made me realize, "This is a dream!" Once lucid, they came over to me, and we had a fascinating discussion. In fact, I consciously listened as some of the figures disagreed with the assessment of the other dream figures! On a different occasion, I saw three dream figures walking separately, but all wearing the same outfit. That struck me as so odd I instantly became lucid. And this lucid dream of recurring dream figures happened while I slept outside in the Grand Canyon on a rafting trip (August 2003):

> I'm walking down a hallway and pass a woman and her teenage daughter on my left side. Something seems odd (the woman's eyes, I

believe) and I become lucid as I say, "You are the woman that was in my dream last night!"

She grabs my right hand to focus on the palm print and points at it, saying, "Look!" As I look, I notice various gemstones lying on my hand at certain places. In the very center of the palm is a round yellow sapphire. An emerald-colored stone sits at my thumb's base, and a ruby-colored stone on the opposite side. An inch below the index finger, where the life line and head line begins, there's a diamond.

As I watched, small pieces of the diamond began flaking off and drifting into the skin. I felt an exquisite tingling, almost painful but exhilarating energy as the diamond flakes dissolved. I felt newly energized and woke up.

Besides the interesting symbolism, the fact that the dream figure recurred on successive nights caught my attention. In such cases, it feels that we're being set-up to achieve awareness. Does the dreamer's inner Self set the dreamer up to become lucid or does the dream figure possess the initiative to reappear as a semi-independent awareness within the lucid dreamer's mind?

Though recurring dream figures who prompt lucidity seem fairly rare, the main exception involves seeing deceased relatives, who appear quite regularly for some lucid dreamers. The presence of the deceased often initiates awareness that one must be dreaming. (In chapter 17, we will consider this unique topic at length.)

Besides recurring dream figures, lucid dreamers also occasionally dream of doubles. By that, I mean seeing two dream figures of the same person. In the following example, lucid dreamer Joscelyne Wilmouth describes her lucid dream encounter with an identical Joscelyne dedicated to educating Joscelyne:

> After I became lucid, I was one of a pair of identical twins who never previously knew each other that interacted; my lucid self showed the other how to control her environment. We had a great time with each other, learning and teaching, and now I am excited to see how my nightly dreams turn out from now on. I usually have very vivid, vivid violent dreams. It was great to see that when my lucid dreamer self showed my non-lucid dreamer self how to deal with potentially dangerous situations, how stunned she (the non-lucid dreamer) became and also how excited.[3]

This lucid dream vividly suggests that the conscious waking self can receive instructions in manipulating the dream realm from his or her inner counterpart, symbolically portrayed.

GUIDES AND GUARDIANS

One particular group of lucid dream figures I personally found hard to accept initially is guides and guardians—designations, by the way, the dream figures themselves provided when questioned in the lucid dream. For me, this just sounded too spiritualistic. Invariably, however, experienced lucid dreamers seem to encounter these self-described guides who spontaneously appear as relatively knowledgeable dream figures that offer assistance or support. Here's an example of a self-professed guardian appearing in one of my lucid dreams (June 2003):

> Suddenly it occurs to me that having tea in an English garden is too dreamy and I say, "This is a dream." I begin to fly and ahead I see a totem pole with figures standing on top of each other. I fly to it, then realize that the top figure of a woman in a red silk outfit is actually alive. As she comes to life, we begin to talk.
>
> She states that she is a type of guardian. She says that she watches over us and is there to help us. She has some other comments; she mentions something about the "deadman's day."
>
> She then hands me another totem-like figure—this one of an Asian male priest-like figure with a red silk outfit and boxy red hat with a tassel or feather on the right side. Suddenly he comes to life and becomes life size. We all then talk.

Notice how the dream figure explains her designation and purpose; I did not consciously project upon her or label her a guardian. Notice, too, how the dream figure exists on the top of a totem pole. For many native people, totem poles honored a respected, deceased elder or symbolized an encounter with a supernatural being. In this situation, portions of the totem become alive.

Oddly, the lucid dream's Asian male figure had appeared repeatedly in other interesting dreams. Normally, he would comment on my dream activities from the night before and often gently correct me or praise me for my dream actions. Knowing little about the symbolism of Asian dress, I asked a knowledgeable person about this red outfit and was told that only scholars were allowed to dress like this. For me, that unknown-to-me detail reconfirmed the teaching aspect of this recurring dream figure.

Not all guides or guardians appear in bodily forms. In this wonderful example taken from an interview in *The Lucid Dream Exchange*, lucid dreamer Clare Johnson, Ph.D., reports consciously meeting an awareness that exists as a ball of light:

One night there are drunk students in the corridor outside my room and they wake me up. When I fall asleep again, I go directly into an exceptionally vivid lucid dream. I am standing in my room and everything is totally clear. I announce, "This is as real as reality and I am dreaming." As if in response to a password, a ball of light starts to form across the room by the wardrobe. I watch it swirl and then stabilize. It is beautiful.

The light coming from this ball is orange and yellow, and it has a distinctive female energy. I ask it what it is, and (without words) I am told it will always be there to help me in my dreams. If I need it, I just have to call. It then gives me some sort of power word which I know I'll never forget. Then it disappears. I stare at the place where it was, and experience a rush of joy which propels me up and out of the window. I fly on the cool air and shoot up into the stars. For a long time, I swing across the air currents enjoying the feeling of the wind on my skin and wondering at the startling reality of this dream. Then I wake up, and can't for the life of me remember the power word.[4]

Ultimately, most lucid dreamers come to accept that certain forms of self-designated guide and guardian awareness exist in the lucid dream state. While they might be symbolically clothed in the fashion or taste of the individual dreamer, this set of aware dream figures normally have very similar messages, such as the following:

I watch over you.
I'm there to help you.
I can teach and advise you.
Call on me, if you wish.
I have something for you.

In general, the various messages are attentive, caring, and instructional.[5] Also, the interaction seems initiated by the guide or guardian dream figure. (By contrast, the much more common thought-form dream figure rarely initiates interaction with the lucid dreamer.)

Jung mentions meeting a few specific recurring dream guides or teachers over the course of his life. One such figure, Jung called Philemon. Painting him as an elderly man with wings, wearing a simple robe, Jung wrote, "Philemon and other figures of my fantasies brought home to me the crucial insight that there are things in the psyche which I do not produce, but which produce themselves and have their own life. Philemon represented a force that was not myself. In my fantasies I held conversations with him, and he said things which I had not consciously thought. . . . Psychologically, Philemon represented superior insight."[6]

Jung indicates that some special dream figures exist beyond the production of the waking self. Conscious in the dream state, lucid dreamers have met similarly aware dream figures and made a similar analysis. For any dreamer, such meetings have radical implications about the nature of mind and psyche. In Jung's case, they likely factored into his ideas on archetypes, the collective unconscious, and the nature of dreaming.

THE INEQUALITY OF AWARENESS: YOU AIN'T NOTHING BUT A THOUGHT-FORM

By engaging, conversing with, and challenging lucid dreamers, dream figures argue for a broader appreciation of their existence. In numerous examples, a distinct set of dream figures use the following types of methods to persuade lucid dreamers of their awareness:

1. Employ logic or reason

2. Provide information that is unknown to the lucid dreamer but verifiable

3. Behave in a manner equal to the lucid dreamer's (for example, they fly when we fly to demonstrate a type of equality)

4. Question the lucid dreamer (for example, "What's that book in your hand?")

5. Return again as if to suggest their ongoing existence

6. Initiate action toward the lucid dreamer (for example, actively pointing out to me the yantra symbol at the base of the library in my earlier dream)

Similarly, lucid dreamers consciously engage various, distinct classes of dream figures who possess dramatically different awareness levels and behaviors in the following areas:

1. Conversational ability: to varying degrees, can converse freely, ask questions of the lucid dreamer, respond to questions, initiate conversations

2. Purposeful action: to varying degrees, can act or behave in a purposeful manner (for example, teach the lucid dreamer, direct the focus of the lucid dreamer)

3. Education or knowledge of the dream state: to varying degrees, can reason with the lucid dreamer, provide information

Therefore, lucid dreamers need to take into account behavior, knowledge, purposefulness, and ability to reason when interacting with dream figures. At their simplest, some dream figures exist as thought-forms, which briefly express a symbolic representation of an idea, thought, intent, or emotion. The thought-forms may have very little durability, limited functional capability, and appear only as an expression of a thought, idea, or emotion. These figures may be incapable of replying to questions or may respond with gibberish.

Some dream figures may be considered aspect-forms or symbolic representations of some semipermanent issue for the dreamer. They possess the greater energy of a larger issue and may be able to respond about or initiate action regarding that issue. Since they represent an aspect of the dreamer's psychological reality, they may be able to relate to the dreamer on a limited basis.

Some dream figures may exist as core aspect-forms or symbolic representations of some permanent feature or issue of the dreamer. They may feel at home and alive in the dreaming as fragmentary consciousnesses with responsive purposefulness to our waking and dreaming life. Core aspect-forms may achieve considerable psychological complexity and function as the building blocks for greater ego awareness. I believe they may emerge intermittently into waking reality such as when we "don't seem ourselves" or "act out of character." One or more of these core aspects may develop even further to continue a workable identity in waking reality, particularly when a new ego leader is required, as in multiple personality disorder or dissociative identity disorder.

On very rare occasions, some dream figures may directly represent the inner ego or the inner Self, which may have a deeper understanding or perspective than the waking self about certain issues and try to communicate. These figures may be capable of other means of expression via concepts, emotions, light, and energy.

And finally, though obviously complex, some dream figures may represent something outside our conception of our waking ego self. These dream figures may represent or actually be the mental form of the deceased, other dreamers, aspects of greater consciousness, and so on, or they may be the symbolic representations of that knowledge presented telepathically or in an unknown manner.

In effect, dream figures occur in a wide spectrum of actuality, from ephemeral thought-form to those that have a functional reality similar to the lucid dreamer in that state. In any given dream, you may meet a variety of dream figures with differing actualities—just as you may see a number of different "figures" in my living room, such as a news announcer on the TV, a portrait of a figure on the wall, and me sitting in a chair. In our waking world, we know enough to differentiate the figures based on their vastly different capabilities. In lucid dreaming, however, we're only beginning to learn this lesson. All dream figures are not created equal.

Some may wonder if the lucid dreamer's awareness attracts certain types of dream figures, much like a street lamp at night attracts moths who circle about. Or does the lucid dreamer's awareness reflect itself in the dream figures, making them only seem more aware? One can find many examples in which dream figures appear to be consciously aware *before* the lucid dreamer achieves awareness. Such experiences suggest that the dream figure's awareness is not dependent upon the lucid dreamer's awareness; rather, the dream figure's awareness likely continues functionally separate from the lucid dreamer's.

Lucid dreaming offers the field of psychology insight into the complexity of the Self and the myriad fragments of awareness that appear to compose one's larger consciousness. As the physical body is composed of various organs, muscles, bones, and fluids all working together and supported by complex cellular and chemical interactions, so too may the contents of the mind be composed of a large variety of psychological structures all interacting and supported by the processing of ideas, information, experiences, and emotions, occasionally embodied as dream figures. Behind all of this psychological complexity, from the simplest thought-form to the most aware dream figure, lies the synthesis of that composite: not the waking self, but the more comprehensive inner Self. Conscious in the dream state, we have the means to appreciate the distinct elements and vastness of our larger psyche.

GUIDELINES FOR CONVERSING WITH DREAM FIGURES

To experience the vast nature of dream figures, you must cast off limiting beliefs and expectations and allow for the possibility of a more complex milieu. Once you open yourself to a real, conscious interaction, consider the following guidelines:

1. Don't limit the dream figure by expressing prejudiced assumptions, such as "You're a creation of my mind!" or "Do you know I'm dreaming you?" Most dream figures just stare at you when you say these things. Instead, ask them an open-ended question, like "Who are you?" or "What do you represent?" or "Why are you here?" Then listen for their response.

2. When you have a choice, look for the most appropriate, aware, or intelligent dream figure to talk with. If you see Aunt Nelly but remember that Aunt Nelly was always confused, asking her questions will, most likely, lead to questionable results.

3. Develop your most important question, or series of questions, in the waking state. Sometimes in the excitement of being lucid, you may be unable to think of anything appropriate to ask.

4. Recognize the expectation effect and your influence in the process. If you expect a nonsensical reply, don't be surprised when you get it. If you get something unexpected, don't toss it away and ignore it. Don't be blind to what you don't expect (or want) to see.

5. If confused by the dream figure's response, ask for clarification!

6. See the answer in broad terms. It may come as a feeling, an image, words, a symbol, or all of these at once.

7. Asking general questions ("What is my purpose in life?") may lead to cryptic responses ("To live."). Instead, ask specific questions such as "What does this white horse symbolize?" or a question that has an unknown answer, as in "When the Cubs play next, what will the final score be?" Or, get some advice about how best to manipulate the dream.

8. Come to the conversation with a sense of openness. Come with a desire to learn, not a desire to *tell*. Experience the magic of consciously being aware in dreaming.

12

FISHING FOR INFORMATION

AT A DREAM CONFERENCE A FEW YEARS AGO, A FRIEND COMMENTED that lucid dreaming shared a common feature with the introduction of the microscope. "How so?" I asked, never having imagined such a connection. He explained that although the microscopic world has always existed, few had a means to explore it properly until around 1668, when a Dutch businessman, Antony van Leeuwenhoek, learned to grind glass lenses more accurately. With that, van Leeuwenhoek increased the simple microscope's magnification to more than 200x, which allowed him to observe the microscopic world of protozoa, bacteria, blood cells, nematodes, and so on. Even though van Leeuwenhoek had no university or scientific degree, his curiosity had driven him to perfect the tool that would allow deep investigation into the unknown, yet always present, microscopic world.

Likewise, my friend continued, the dream realm has always existed, but until recently no one had a good tool to explore it deeply. With the scientific acceptance of lucid dreaming, science finally has a tool; lucid dreaming is a kind of psychological microscope to probe inwardly. Finally, the unknown world of dreaming can be explored, tested, and experimented with consciously to determine its true nature. Only lucid dreaming allows for experimenting with the dream *in situ*, in the place it happens as it is happening.

But, my friend cautioned, just as in van Leeuwenhoek's day, many people were shocked to hear of his discoveries and scarcely believed their eyes when they peered into his high-powered microscope. The dogma and belief system of the period held such sway that it took time for van Leeuwenhoek's observations to be broadly accepted.

Like van Leeuwenhoek's high-powered microscope, lucid dreaming opens up a perplexing realm and shows it in a more accurate light. The nature of dream figures, the principles of influencing the dream environment, the various types of dream space, even the end of the dream and the emergence of a new dream can all be explored consciously. Already, lucid dreamers compare their personal notes, and most agree on basic principles and experiences regarding dream objects, settings, and figures. Yet, many lucid dreamers still have not fully accepted the idea of using lucid dreaming to focus on nonapparent but potentially accessible concepts and conceptual information. By looking past appearances and posing questions to the dreaming, something unanticipated and unexpected happens; an inner awareness responds to the question. For millennia, artists, writers, and scientists have proclaimed that many of their most profound ideas and creations came to them suddenly, fully conceived, like a gift from the muse or, perhaps, the unconscious. Have experienced lucid dreamers discovered a means to tap the level of unconscious information from which those concepts emerge?

In the remainder of this chapter (and at various points in other chapters, too), we will be considering numerous instances in which lucid dreamers have shifted from focusing on dream figures, events, and so on, to focusing on "asking the dreaming." And, as with any tool or technique, the usefulness of asking the dream works best when the lucid dreamer follows certain practical guidelines. By taking these guidelines seriously, lucid dreamers can better fulfill their personal goals for acquiring information and accessing the conscious unconscious.

THE IMPORTANCE OF WORDING

The first guideline in "asking the dream" involves the importance of properly wording the request. The words selected convey the intent of the request and strongly affect the forthcoming response, so exact wording is crucial. A fascinating example of this comes from poet and painter Epic Dewfall, who has used lucid dreaming as a means to discover new artwork to create. As he prepares to visit his own "inner art gallery," wording is key to what the dream reveals to him.

"I get ideas for my paintings from lucid dreams," he says. "About once a month when I'm dreaming, I will realize I'm dreaming, and when I do, I then walk around in the dream looking at art on the walls. I usually find many paintings on every wall. By the time one of these lucid dreams ends, I usually have one or two good paintings memorized . . . I've been doing this as a hobby since 1986." When he stops to look at a particularly interesting piece, he says, "I'll wake up after I have been looking at it for about six seconds; I suspect this is because I've stopped moving from painting to painting."[1] As lucid dreamers know, staring at an object for an extended period of time will normally collapse the dream.

Now here's the important lesson: Experience has taught Dewfall to phrase his lucid dream incubation such that he will look "*at* art" and not "*for* art." (*Dream incubation* refers to the practice of intending to dream about a particular topic by concentrating on it before sleep.) When he suggested to become lucid and to look "for art," he found himself doing just that—literally looking for art—trying to find art somewhere in his lucid dream! Thus his whole lucid dream would become a futile search "for art." This misdirected wording taught him to incubate a lucid dream in which he would become aware and look "*at* art." He then found himself lucidly aware in a room with works of art all over the wall. The conscious unconscious responded to the exact wording of the request. By all appearances, the dreaming awareness took into consideration the precise meaning of the preposition, *at* versus *for,* and weighed the intent of the wording in its response.

In addition, when lucid and we "ask the dream," the response arrives in direct relation to the form of our request. If we ask the dream "to see," then a visual display appears. If we ask "to hear," then an auditory event occurs, just as in my "Hey! I want to hear my feeling-tone!" experience.

Again, the wording of the request appears to be crucial in the materialization of the response. A poorly worded request and its fuzzy intent can alter the resulting experience away from the waking goal of the lucid dreamer. As a lucid dream figure once told me as I sought the principles of flying, "In the form is the outcome." Curiously, a major criticism of Hilgard's hidden observer in subsequent experiments concerned the significant response differences by the hidden observer to slightly different wording by the hypnotist. Critics felt this showed the hypnotized person was actually responding to subtle verbal cues (a process called *demand characteristics*) and that no hidden observer existed. The experiences of lucid dreamers show that actually the inner awareness displays a high degree of verbal acuity. A change of word or phrase that seems minor to us is critical to the inner awareness's response.

For example, a lucid dreamer might verbally or mentally announce that now she will project her consciousness "into a bird," and suddenly she views the scene from the bird's vantage point. Contrast this to the lucid dreamer who announces that she will "become" a bird or "totally experience what it feels like to be a bird." This second lucid dreamer may suddenly feel wings, a beak, talons, and a tail and experience "birdness" at a more profound level than the first dreamer. To the dreaming, the intent and wording of the request join together to delineate the response.

The founder of the popular lucid dreaming website LD4all.com, pasQuale Ourtane, recalls her attempts to become various animals. In an interview with *The Lucid Dream Exchange*, she recounts a lucid dream in which she intended to "change into" a bird:

> I tried to change myself into a bird to see what that feels like. Sure enough, I felt my body change, felt I had a tail and a beak. The eyesight also changed, like very wide vision that came together in the middle.
>
> Shortly after that I tried to lay an egg to see what that feels like, it was actually quite pleasurable; [my] realization: of course it is [pleasurable], nature wouldn't make it unpleasurable.[2]

On another occasion, Ourtane attempts to become a specific bird by mentally desiring to "transform into" an owl:

> (Lucid) I'm in a backyard of some sort. I see two beautiful owls flying. I decide I want to try and transform into an owl as well.
>
> I want myself to be an owl; I spread my arms and they become wings. I feel the feathers on my wings and try to be in an owl's body.
>
> I fly on silken wings. So softly through the air with no sound at all. Even though it is dark, I have no problem seeing. I swoosh through the trees in the forest.[3]

"I feel I succeeded (only) in half," Ourtane comments, "because I still felt myself being human as well. But I felt smaller (as an owl) and that experience of flying silently through the air was wonderful. It has made an impact, this dream, because the owls were so beautiful. It was a barn owl. I did some research and it turns out the barn owl flies indeed silently through the night, I never knew that."[4]

As we see in Ourtane's lucid dreams, subtle differences in wording affect the materialization or experience of the intent. The desire to "change into" something resulted in a different level of experience than the desire to "transform into" something. Also, the result is affected by the desired goal; a generic bird implies a different experience than that of a specific bird such as a barn owl.

By becoming more specific about experiencing the concept or object, you can experience it at different levels or in different modes. For example, imagine being lucid and telling the dream, "I want to experience the complete absence of gravity!" Now become more specific and tell the dream, "I want to experience gravity as if I were on the moon!" You can continue with other examples, gravity on Mars, gravity in a black hole, the variations are endless. Concepts have depth of experience, and the conscious unconscious seems to have unfettered access to them.

When a lucid dreamer wishes to experience a concept, he or she has a choice of intent: either to sense the concept or to become the concept. Intending to sense the concept will normally result in the concept appearing in some sensory way, involving sight, sound, touch, taste, or smell. We can then point to it as something apart from us, something we sense. When we intend to become the concept, however, we may literally be swept up into the experience such that it seems to displace the experience of self as the concept expresses its reality.

For many of us, it's relatively easy to deal with a sensed response, something materialized. We can imagine a lucid dreamer ignoring the dream figures and shouting, "I want to see unconditional love!" In response, a profoundly emotional scene may appear for the lucid dreamer to look at visually and absorb. Contrast that to the lucid dreamer who shouts, "I want to become unconditional love!" He or she may then begin to feel intense emotion, bordering on the mystical, and swoon into the depths of unconditional love. Depending upon the concept we seek to become, the intensity of "becoming" may approach the overpowering and all consuming.

Lucid dreamers exploring concepts for the first time, therefore, may wish to ask to sense the experience. Sensing allows us to learn about it, become familiar with it, yet still stand apart from it. Lucid dreamers shouldn't ask to become a concept until they feel ready to let go fully. By becoming a concept, you essentially ask to experience it on all levels, to take it on completely, to live it. While fascinating, the unprepared may find it overwhelming as their normally separate viewpoint takes on the immensity and strangeness of being a concept. Some concepts may be just too difficult to experience. We may have wrapped the concept with so much emotional energy and so many ideas that we barely understand our intent in even relating to the concept. Or the concept may be inherently unfathomable. For example, consider experiencing the concept of God. Beyond any personal religious or spiritual beliefs, the idea of God simply may be too profound or complex for the beginning lucid dreamer to experience fully. Take, for instance, this early lucid dream in which I ask to see God (May 1985):

> I'm riding my bike across the sidewalks on the lawn of my old elementary school. I see another bike rider doing something odd and realize, "This is a dream!" I ride along saying "this is a dream" every few seconds to maintain my focus. Other kids are riding their bikes, too. I start to do figure-eight patterns; a portion of me senses a connection of the figure as an ancient symbol for eternity. I almost run into someone, which causes me to close my eyes for a second (this breaks me out of my lucid apathy). I suddenly decide, "I want to see God," so I call out for God—and I start to fly upward! But the emotional surge is too much. I wake up quite excited, with my ears ringing.

We may do best initially to seek simpler concepts. Instead of asking to see God, we could announce to the dreaming, "I want to feel divine grace!" or "I want to experience inner peace!" The dreaming will likely respond to these requests with a profound experience, far beyond any waking-self imagining, but probably not one as overwhelming as we're likely to experience when asking to see God.

The concepts to be experienced need not be spiritual; we can "ask the dream" for virtually anything. A theoretical physicist might lucidly ask, "Hey, I want to experience being an electron in hydrogen" or a neurochemist might lucidly announce, "Hey, I want to experience how a gene transfers into a Purkinje cell!" The resulting experiential mindtrip might provide the insight of a hundred labor-intensive lab experiments.

In effect, asking the conscious unconscious provides you an inner virtual reality experience that far exceeds any (physical) virtual reality laboratory. Inside the unconscious, we have inner knowledge and comprehension far beyond waking knowledge or computer models. Moreover, we get the experience in the realm of lucid dreaming, where sensory and intuitive awareness seems considerably heightened.

TRUST, ACCEPTANCE, AND LETTING GO

Over the past ten years, as I've gone more deeply into lucid dreams, I often mentally hear words of encouragement and solace, such as "Trust" or "Nothing to fear." Usually, I hear these words when lucidly venturing into totally new and unknown activities. In the following lucid dream, for example, I first experience an unknown force coming into the dream as white light, then watch as an ancient roman-looking helmet begins to split apart vertically as the white light cracks it. At this point, I become lucid in an extremely powerful dream (October 2004):

> Lucidly aware, I begin to sense all of the energy around me and feel the movement of the air and the power behind the dreaming. I begin to say very strongly, "I accept the power," and feel the energetic power of the lucid dream starting to funnel toward me, like a vacuum. Then I spontaneously say, "Nothing to fear," as I recognize that the energy seems powerful, good, and natural.
>
> I then begin to announce these phrases boldly, as the funnel of energy is coming toward me and into my body, "I accept the power!! Nothing to fear!!" I notice that the palms of my hands feel very hot, and I feel that the power is becoming encased in me. It all seems odd but natural, like I have finally opened up to the enormity of lucid dreaming's source.

Other lucid dreamers in this same situation might have been overwhelmed by the extremely intense energies coming at them, but at the time of this dream, I had been considering the idea that dreaming requires energy of some sort and, thus, it may be possible to reclaim the energy when lucid, so I had gone along with the experience to feel what that might entail. As I've said, going deeply into lucid dreaming requires a certain degree of fearlessness and trust. Although these are inner experiences, the sensory experience can test our limits.

Of course, we can always call a halt to things. If the experience in this lucid dream had become too much, I could have announced to the dream, "Stop!" or "Too much," and I would have seen an immediate lessening of energy.

ACCESS DENIED: PLEASE TRY BACK LATER

Not every request presented to the dreaming receives the desired or expected response. In fact, the lucid dreamer may instead receive a lesson in making requests.

Lucid dreamer pasQuale Ourtane recalls discovering an interesting way to explore the dream space. As a reality check, she would often push her finger through a dream mirror to make sure she was dreaming. Then, in one lucid dream, she spontaneously decided to step through a mirror to see what would happen. Incredibly, she found entering the mirror took her to amazing places. Now she jumps into dream mirrors simply to experience the joy of exploring. She feels the mirror can also work when "you see in the mirror, where you desire to be, and then dive into the mirror to end up in that scene you just saw in the mirror."⁵

Recently, a lucid dreamer proposed to Ourtane's LD4all.com website readers a conceptual task to explore time and "to see the beginning and the end of the universe." In her resulting lucid dream, Ourtane used the mirror as a means of dream exploration. Here's what happened when she made this conceptual request to the dream:

> Right in front of me is a huge mirror. I walk towards it and look at myself and pinch my nose, and yes, I can easily breathe [she performed this as a reality check to make sure she was dreaming]. I remember the task and decide to use the mirror for it.
>
> I say to the mirror, "Show me the beginning and the end of the universe." My plan is then to jump though the mirror to be there. I press my head against it to better see inside.
>
> A voice says, "The Universe has no beginning and no end, the Universe is an everlasting cycle."
>
> Well, that was that then. I decide to do some time travel just in case to complete the task. So I jump through the mirror and call out something like "let me travel in time, let me be in the universe." I now whoosh through a space with light dots in it, it goes very fast and feels a bit scary, I realize I have no idea where I want to go (or more accurately, "when"), I know I'm traveling to the past.
>
> At some point I fly over a landscape and see houses disappear while I fly over it, and the landscape change through time. In the back of my mind I think oh, I can go to ancient Egypt or something! But then I have already landed and I know I'm still in Holland. [She then converses with some young people who seem dressed like the 1950s, but can never get them to provide her a year or date.]⁶

In many respects, asking the mirror seems to function as a means to engage the conscious unconscious or inner ego behind the dream. As usual, a response occurs, though sometimes unexpected. In Ourtane's case, the voice disagrees with her original intent and its premise, announcing, "The Universe has no beginning and no end, the Universe is an everlasting cycle." In effect, the dream has denied her request! When she reconsiders her options and announces a different intent, "let me travel in time," the dream responds.

In another case, lucid dream researcher Ed Kellogg flies along and recalls his intent to see a superstring. He announces, "By the power of Alkahest, let a superstring manifest!" Moments later, he receives a response. "I hear a voice," he writes, "that tells me 'it does not seem a good idea to do an experiment of this type, at this time, as you still seem too unfocused and distracted.'" He considers this and then the voice begins again by explaining how to remedy the situation: "To do an experiment of this kind requires careful consideration beforehand as to what to do, and clear mindful intentionality while doing it." At this point, Kellogg reconsiders: "[L]ooking up at the sky, I intend/shout, 'Cancel.' The clouds lighten and begin to disappear. I intend/shout, 'Cancel' again, and the dreamscape returns to normal."[7]

In some instances, nearby dream figures explain to the lucid dreamer the risks or problems associated with the request. In one example, the lucid dreamer persisted with a risky request to the dream and ignored the advice of the concerned dream figures, which resulted in the alarmed dream figures acting in such a way as to make the dream collapse.

Once in a lucid dream, I started to fly and announced my intent to visit a friend. As I began to head in his direction, I noticed a strange black zone that I intuitively knew was impenetrable. As I got closer, the lucid dream unexpectedly collapsed. Talking to my friend the next day on the phone, I mentioned the failed lucid visit. He told me that he had intentionally determined not to be bothered by others in his dreaming that night because he was working on a dream project. He was glad to hear that his intent appeared to counter my intent!

The fact that not every intent or request is granted seems reassuring somehow. That an inner awareness knows or seems to respond in such a way to stop or redirect our intent shows a caring or responsible aspect to the inner observer.

Those situations in which the voice directs the lucid dreamer to reconsider his or her intent suggest an awareness capable of analysis and insight about the lucid dreamer. Again, I find this comforting. In nearly every case, the purpose behind the response seems purely educational, helpful, and intended to assist the lucid dreamer. In general terms, then, we would be wise to heed the advice of this inner awareness in the lucid dream. It appears to have our best interests in mind.

SETTING GOALS:
PREPARING TO ACCESS THE UNCONSCIOUS

Because the wording of your intent has such major implications for the experience, it's a good idea to prepare the exact wording while awake. Write out your request and see if each noun, preposition, and verb reflects your actual intent. As you mentally repeat your phrase, see what imagery it evokes in you. As Ed Kellogg suggested to me, let your intuition tell you whether your intent poses any problems.

Remember that it's best to request to *sense* the experience and not to *become* the experience until you're truly prepared to let go of normal modes of self reference. Gradually acclimate yourself to the depth of the conscious unconscious. Since it apparently exists there behind the lucid dream, it will be available in future conscious explorations. Then, when you become lucid and feel the time and setting are right, ignore the dream figures and objects and simply announce your intent to the dream. Lift up your head and shout it out. Then, stand back and wait to see what happens next.

Actually, sometimes you don't even need to shout. All you really have to do is wonder intensely, like I did in this memorable lucid dream (February 1999):

> In a small Midwestern town in the early evening, I come to an intersection and look around. It just seems too odd, and I suddenly realize, "This is a dream!" I walk up and down the street, laughing at the things I see, their "unreality." I go up and talk to an older woman about being lucid, but she gets upset and doesn't want to hear.
>
> Back out on the street, I wonder what to do. I decide to call for Ed Kellogg and see if he will appear. I look up and down the street to see if he has come. Then I tell myself, "No thought-forms! I want the real Ed." But I have the feeling that Ed isn't available.
>
> I decide that I'd like to make "energy balls" or *chi*. I put my palms about six inches apart and tell myself I'm making chi. I can feel the energy and start to chant "Making Chi To See Ed!" (Earlier that week in a phone call, Ed Kellogg and I reminisced about our mutual lucid dreaming attempts; he suggested that perhaps we needed more chi, hence my odd chant.) I do this for quite a while, then I put my palms outward toward the nearby plants and feel energy moving. I laugh and keep up my chant.
>
> Walking out of town toward some sandy ground, still chanting, I begin to wonder seriously, what is chi?
>
> Now in the far distance, I see two areas of bright, bright lightning-type light that doesn't disappear; in fact, it slowly seems to come my way. It changes a bit as it turns and spins and sparks blue and violet colors. I am amazed and wonder if these spinning funnels of light represent chi. Oh boy, I think, what have I done? I keep up my chant "Making Chi To See Ed." The two spinning funnels of light begin to

move my way, coming closer and closer and growing taller as they do so. The swirling seems more distinct now, and I notice that the twisting funnels are actually composed of plumes of light. Some plumes are colored light blue, some violet, and some white as they all twist together yet remain distinct colors.

The incredible light keeps growing in size and speed until it's more than a hundred feet tall, towering over me. I feel an incredible energy and begin to laugh. The counterclockwise swirling pillars of light seem to have little dot-like shapes on them. I decide to allow myself to merge with one of these pillars of light and start to fly upward, freely—the energy is incredible and loving. I let go and merge with it.

SEEKING CONCEPTS IN A LUCID DREAM

An infinitude of conceptual experiences are possible when consciously aware in the dream state. The following represent just a few of the simple and complex approaches taken to access the wisdom inherent in the conscious unconscious.

Meditating in a Lucid Dream

The following is my one lucid dream experience with meditating (November 2003):

> As I go along, it occurs to me that I have never tried to meditate formally in a lucid dream, and I recall my waking curiosity about this. I stop on a hillside and sit cross legged. I decide to simply quiet my mind. I find this extremely easy in the lucid state—it seems I reach a deep mental emptiness almost instantaneously.
>
> Suddenly in the sky, I notice brilliant streaks of white light all over—almost like intense white shooting stars in the daylight with lingering streaks of brilliant white. This continues, and then my mind restarts. Remembering my goal of meditation, I decide to cut down on external stimuli. I close my eyes. Visually the scene goes gray—but I feel somehow truly expansive now—like I have become "at one" with my self/Self.

Becoming a Color

In an interview for *The Lucid Dream Exchange*, Minnesotan David L. Kahn, author of *A Dream Come True*, relates how a type of foreknowing often precedes the lucid experience:

In a recent lucid dream, I had a very bizarre experience . . . [I was] standing in front of a bathroom mirror when I became lucid. I noticed that the shower curtain was blue, and I also noticed geometric shapes on the shower curtain. I knew that I would be blue when I looked back at the mirror. Indeed my skin was very blue, except for my neck in the area that I recently had surgery. I looked away from the mirror for a few seconds, and when I looked back something very strange happened. I *became* the color blue. It wasn't just my skin color. I was actually the color, as though without me blue would not exist. This is one of my most difficult dreams to express in words, because it is hard to describe what it feels like to be a color.[8]

Solving an Important Problem

In a lucid dream taken from *Exploring the World of Lucid Dreaming* by Stephen LaBerge and Howard Rheingold, we find a computer programmer who keeps good company as he works on practical issues of programming while lucidly aware:

At night I will dream that I am sitting in a parlor (an old-fashioned one that Sherlock Holmes might use). I'm sitting with Einstein, white bushy hair—in the flesh. He and I are good friends. We talk about the program, start to do some flowcharts on a blackboard. Once we think we've come up with a good one, we laugh. Einstein says, "Well, the rest is history." Einstein excuses himself to go to bed. I sit in his recliner and doodle some code in a notepad. Then the code is all done. I look at it and say to myself, "I want to remember this flowchart when I wake up." I concentrate very hard on the blackboard and the notepad. Then I wake up. It is usually around 3:30 A.M. I . . . start writing as fast as I can. I take this to work and usually it is 99 percent accurate.[9]

Going to Infinity and Beyond

As part of an eight-week course on lucid dreaming, Ed Kellogg presented a weekly lucid dreaming challenge to go "to infinity and beyond" while lucid. To interest his students in the topic, Kellogg presented various mathematical, numerological, and esoteric perspectives on infinity. Participant Justin Tombe lucidly recalled the concept while dreaming (April 2004):

[Initially confounded by missing objects] I then realized that I dreamed, exclaiming to my friend, "It's O.K., this is just a dream." I then remembered my dream task and flew up out of the room. I looked back one last time over my shoulder to see a hazy image of my friend standing in the room, looking around in a confused manner.

I turned my attention to the dream task, and repeated "To Infinity and Beyond!" several times, and then became aware that I was now floating in a vast emptiness. I was clearly aware of my (dream) body, but all else was emptiness, void. Sound, light, color, movement were all absent in all directions in what FELT like an infinite distance.

Finding this somewhat disappointing, I decided to try another approach suggested in our group. I traced the mathematical symbol Aleph Null with my hand in the space in front of me, and immediately became aware of a whole new subset of perceptions, existing simultaneous and implicate to the empty void. This new perceptual data was in the form of a churning, turbulent "sea" of geometric wave fronts, emerging from a multiplicity of points, spiraling and unfolding in distinct motions, interpenetrating each other on multiple dimensions, and then falling away, or dispersing into fractal fragments. Each wave seemed to have its own unique geometry, much of it fractal, and rate and manner of unfolding. In addition, the leading edges were composed of bands of color, much like a rainbow, but with astonishing diversity, and they each also resonated a tone or set of tones. Surprisingly, the whole array somehow conveyed a sense of being very subtle, and in some fashion encoded, implicate, or beneath the surface of the vast emptiness. [Justin continues his lucid dreaming by intending to find Ed Kellogg and suddenly finds himself in a cluttered room.][10]

Justin writes in his notes: "Several interesting factors were brought to light after further exploration. Of note, this entire dream sequence happened between 7:00 and 7:08 A.M. (between when my alarm first sounded and the snooze went off). This indicates that my perception of the passing of time was occurring at a different rate in the dream state than as measured by the clock in WPR [waking physical reality]."[11]

Notice how Justin literally announces his intent to the dreaming. He doesn't ask a dream figure or interact with a dream object; he simply makes a request and waits for the response. And what a response! Suddenly surrounded by an infinity of empty space, he traces the sign of Aleph Null, which stands for the countable infinity set of natural numbers (1, 2, 3 . . .); in the tracing movements, he physically expresses a new intention of a specific kind of infinity. Once again, the dreamscape transforms itself with waves of geometric forms, spirals, tones, and colors.

Incredibly, over the course of eight minutes, Justin enters a dream, becomes lucid, and performs numerous tasks in which he manipulates dream space through the simple act of intending. In my experience, lucid dreamers would have much greater success with intentionality in dreaming if they simply directed their intention to the dream, as Justin did. By asking the dream, we show our lucid awareness of something behind the dreaming—and that *something*, in turn, responds.

Experiencing Reality without Preconceptions: the Phenomenological Epoché

Ed Kellogg describes a fascinating experiment in which he sought to experience the lucid dream without preconceptions (along the lines of the phenomenological view[12] proposed by Edmund Husserl). In this endeavor, Kellogg manages to suspend his judgment about the perceived environment and experience it free of assumptions, functioning intentionality, and preconceptions (February 1999):

> Flying along through a bizarre dreamscape. I remember my task to try to focus on what I directly experience, without preconceptions. I perform the phenomenological *epoché* (even saying *epoché*, eh-poe-kay, out loud to help focus my intent) to suspend judgment and become fully lucid, marveling at the strange shapes and geometries.
>
> I fly down a sort of flat smooth valley between massive strange layered structures looming on either side of me, towering twice my flying height, like oddly shaped cliffs. After 10 seconds of this at most, the dreamscape snaps into focus as a gigantic office storage room space, with a smooth flat floor with shelves and racks of supplies to either side of me. In relation to the room, I seem about 6" in height. I now perceive and mentally note racks of paper office supplies, an old safe. I feel I have become more lucid.[13]

Kellogg comments: "However, at this point [seeing it as an office storage room] my Functioning Intentionality has become activated, automatically 'making sense' of the dreamscape. I do not even consider the possibility that I might now incorrectly impose this giant 'office space template' on an unfamiliar environment."[14]

It appears that his attempt to see the lucid dream reality without preconceptions works for a brief time. It may be that, as he supposes, his waking self innately sought to make sense of the weird shapes and geometric experience. As soon as it did so and functionally conceived the environment as an office storage room with the usual items, the reality became as he conceived it to be. Linguistically, the seemingly automatic desire to verbalize the thing or the experience may have also taken part in undoing the direct experience. Normally, lucid dreamers wish to experience the environment but also to create a dream report at the conclusion. In effect, the desire to understand the environment comes as the undoing of the nonconceptual experience of the environment.

Not every request to the conscious unconscious can easily be rendered into experience or words. Frequently, lucid dreamers remark that words fail to encapsulate the incredible nature of the experience they request. Certain concepts, when experienced, fall far outside of simple expression.

DREAM-ART SCIENTISTS

The acquisition of conceptual information through asking the unconscious may have been presaged by Jane Roberts in her 1977 book, *The "Unknown" Reality*. There, she broaches the idea of the "dream-art scientists," that is, consciously aware dreamers who would seek out information in the dream state for use by science.

Already lucid dreamers have repeatedly validated that this theoretical possibility could be a practical actuality. Speaking for the personality essence known as Seth, Roberts states:

> The trouble is that many in the sciences do not comprehend that there is an inner reality. It is not only as valid as the exterior one, but it is the origin for it. It is that world that offers you answers, solutions, and would reveal many of the blueprints that exist behind the world of your experience.
>
> The true art of dreaming is a science long forgotten by your world. Such an art, pursued, trains the mind in a new kind of consciousness—one that is equally at home in either existence, well-grounded and secure in each. Almost anyone can become a satisfied and productive amateur in this art-science; but its true fulfillment takes years of training, a strong sense of purpose, and a dedication—as does any true vocation.
>
> To some extent, a natural talent is a prerequisite for such a true dream-art scientist. A sense of daring, exploration, independence, and spontaneity is required. Such a work is a joy. There are some such people who are quite unrecognized by your societies, because the particular gifts involved are given zero priority. But the talent still exists . . .
>
> A practitioner of this ancient art learns first of all how to become conscious in normal terms, while in the sleep state. . . .

The true scientist understands that he must probe the interior and not the exterior universe; he will comprehend that he cannot isolate himself from a reality of which he is necessarily a part, and that to do so presents at best a distorted picture. In quite true terms, your dreams and the trees outside of your windows have a common denominator: they both spring from the withinness of consciousness.[15]

Lucid dreamers have already discovered that this "inner reality" has the capacity to respond thoughtfully and abundantly to questions posed to it. If scientists were to approach this inner reality proactively, they would discover a new means of accessing available unconscious knowledge and creative ideas.

As we probe inwardly to the conscious unconscious and the various manifestations in dreaming, we begin to discover, like van Leeuwenhoek and his microscopic reality, an inner mental reality that has existed there all along. Through perfecting the tool of lucid dreaming, science has the means to investigate the conscious unconscious and understand the larger nature of the psyche. In doing so, we begin to lay the groundwork for the introduction of the "dream-art scientist."

13

Healing Yourself and Others

DREAM WORKER AND MINISTER JEREMY TAYLOR TELLS THE SURPRIS-
ing story of lucid dreamer "Dan," who dreams that he attends a lively
party at a fashionable penthouse. Suddenly, Dan realizes that he's
actually sleeping at a "cheap rented room in Chicago" and becomes
consciously aware:

> [Lucid now, Dan finds that an attractive woman sits on his lap and]
> asks him if he is having a good time. He laughs and replies that he is
> having a great time, but that he will have to leave soon—his alarm is
> about to go off and wake him up. The woman asks him in surprise
> what he means, and he replies that all this is a dream and none of it
> is real.
>
> "You mean you think I'm not real?" the woman asks in some
> annoyance.
>
> "That's right," he replies.
>
> With this, the woman becomes even more annoyed. "I'll show
> you who's real or not!" she says, and crushes her lit cigarette out on
> the back of the dreamer's right hand. Instantaneously the young man
> awakens in the rented room with a terrible pain in his right hand. He
> turns on a light and sees a round burn the size of a cigarette on the
> back of his right hand.[1]

It's almost unimaginable—a lucid dream incident crossing the
boundary into waking reality. Obviously, such an experience further
extends the preliminary conclusion reached by Stephen LaBerge, after

studying the physical body's response to lucidly dreamt events, that "dream events are closely paralleled by brain events."[2] Various studies show a strong correlation in physiological measures between a waking event and the same event performed in a lucid dream.

This cigarette-burn example is reminiscent of experiments with hypnosis. In hypnotic studies, as I discussed in chapter 1, some subjects have shown the ability to manifest physical changes—burn marks have appeared and disappeared, bleeding has increased or decreased, pain has been experienced vividly and then seemingly turned off—simply through the use of concentrated focus and suggestion. In Dan's case, he may have shown the heightened suggestibility achievable in the lucid state and the dramatic potential to alter the physical self.

Which prompts the question, if the body can be influenced by events in the lucid state, could a consciously aware dreamer heal his or her physical body in a lucid dream? Incredibly, the answer appears to be yes.

Numerous examples exist of attempts at physical healing of self and others while lucidly aware in the dream state. Some lucid dreamers who attempt healing in the lucid state report very limited success or no effect on their symptoms. Other lucid dreamers, however, have reported considerable success at achieving one or more of the following: 1) a reduction in the severity of physical symptoms, 2) a surprisingly rapid healing experience, and 3) on occasion, a disappearance of the health issue altogether. Why do some lucid dreamers succeed, while others don't? My research into instances of successful and unsuccessful lucid dream healings has made clear to me the importance of the reality-creating complex of belief, expectation, focus, intent, and will (as discussed in chapter 10). A constructive use of these elements seems essential in creating a positive outcome.

Another success factor appears to be the healing method itself. Lucid dreamers have approached the task of lucid healing by using a variety of methods, such as the following:

1. Symbolically and literally entering and manipulating the dream body

2. Directing healing intent, which often manifests as an unexpected light

3. Directing affirmations, chants, or sound energy

4. Creating symbolic, healing imagery

5. Seeking information about the cause or meaning of the illness

6. Seeking a dream doctor, medicine, or healing environment

Obviously, techniques varied. Some were direct versus indirect, others literal versus symbolic, while some showed varying degrees of internal and external loci of control. Nonetheless, each lucid dreamer used some form of projective technique to create a healing experience, though some techniques appear to be more effective than others.

INSIDE THE DREAM BODY

It may never occur to many lucid dreamers to manipulate their dream body.[3] Normally, we focus our energies outward to the dream scenes and figures. Other than looking at our hands in lucid dreams (to become lucid or to stabilize the lucid dream) and touching things with our hands in the lucid dream, it seems rare to consider the lucid dream body at all. We normally "assume" the body into being as the presumed locale for visual perception and then forget it as we go about our adventures. When it comes to improving one's physical health, however, some lucid dreamers do focus upon manipulating the dream body, often with impressive results and in dramatically different ways.

Let's look at some examples of healing in the lucid dream state through manipulating the dream body. In the first example, Patricia Garfield, author of *The Healing Power of Dreams* and an experienced lucid dreamer herself, describes the healing experience of another lucid dreamer, Mattie. Mattie's ankle fracture was severe enough to confine her to a wheelchair for months. To assist in the healing process, Mattie decided to use her lucid dreaming ability. Garfield tells the story:

> Whenever she became aware that she was dreaming, Mattie pictured herself "going inside my ankle." There she looked around and saw "all sorts of junk." In these lucid dreams, Mattie busied herself with removing from her injured ankle the debris she found—screwdrivers, bolts and all sorts of tools. When she was awake, she found her condition improving. For the first time since her injury, Mattie was able to walk.[4]

Notice how the lucid dreamer found "all sorts of junk" inside her ankle. So the "going inside my ankle" was represented visually, in a symbolic manner, and the removal of the symbolic "junk" led to rapid improvement in her condition. This lucid dreamer didn't interact with literal imagery of ankle ligaments, muscle, and bone as a surgeon might have seen. Rather, she saw her own unique symbolic expression of her severe ankle fracture as "screwdrivers, bolts and all sorts of tools" to be discarded.

We can only speculate as to whether Mattie's encounter with her ankle existed as an overtly symbolic event because of her belief that the encounter must be symbolically portrayed. As you will see, other lucid dreamers manipulate the lucid dream body not symbolically but directly, as if a representational model of the physical. In the following example, for instance, an experienced lucid dreamer, Keelin, discusses an interesting lucid experience in which she works directly on the dream body:

> Last year, I was having a serious health concern with out-of-control menstrual bleeding . . . the problem recurred and hysterectomy was on the horizon . . . When the final decision was imminent, I had the following dream:
>
> Sitting on the couch in the living room of my home, I'm braiding the left half of my hair, which I suddenly notice is longer and thicker than it is in waking reality. This cues lucidity and I feel the familiar, chilly vibrations that often accompany the onset of dream awareness. I remain calm, thinking I can always spin to prolong the dream state, but I'd rather not risk the possibility of landing in a new scene, and I don't want to become distracted from my pre-intended goal of directing healing energy to my body. I decide that continuing to braid my hair will keep me well enough engaged in the dream, so complete the left side and begin with the right. When I'm almost finished braiding my hair, the dream feels stable enough to get on with my goal.
>
> Touching my face with both hands, I marvel at the realistic sensation, the lack of distortion. Lightly I stroke the tip of my nose where I'd found an area of concern recently (referring to skin cancer), feel it smooth and healthy. This is a spontaneous gesture (not part of my original plan) as is my next action.
>
> Gently I insert my fingers directly into the center of my chest. There is no pain or blood, only the sensation of the pressure of my fingers moving slowly into my body without resistance. I touch my heart while holding in mind thoughts of healing and serenity. After a few moments, I remove my fingers and then insert them into my uterus (the original plan). Again, there is no uncomfortable sensation, no resistance, just an awareness of an extraordinary freedom to perform this feat so easily in a dream. *While placing my fingers and palms against the uterine wall, I hold a thought I've had on several occasions both in and out of dreamland—there is healing in my hands* [emphasis added].

Other than this exact phrase, I have no other word thoughts but, instead, a spreading becalming sense that accompanies my touch. I wake peacefully, in rapt wonder.

Without scientific data, there's no way to prove that this dream had any physical effect; however, the bleeding did stop, and it's not gotten out of hand since then.[5]

Notice how Keelin spontaneously follows her intuitions first, by stroking her nose, touching her heart. Afterward, she continues with her original intention to bring healing to her uterus. She marvels "at the realistic sensation" of touch in the lucid state and actively intends thoughts of "healing and serenity" to her heart and uterus, firmly believing "there is healing in [her] hands."

Like Keelin, many experienced lucid dreamers have learned to follow intuitional impulses as they sense their way through the inner realm of lucid dreaming. Though they may have a general plan or goal, a sense of spontaneous knowing often leads the way and sometimes results in new insights about the situation. Often by letting go of the waking self's approach and allowing the inwardly felt direction, lucid dreamers discover the most constructive path for their intent.

In Keelin's case, while the healing touch occurs on a dream representation of her physical body, it appears here that the brain responded with appropriate adjustments on the actual physical body. Through some mysterious translation, the combination of healing touch and healing intent moves from her symbolic body to her physical body to create a significant physical improvement.

MANIFESTING LIGHT: ENERGY, ELECTRICITY

Lucid derives from the Latin, *lucere* meaning "to shine." For many lucid dreamers seeking to project healing energy for the first time, it comes as quite a shock to find themselves, without any conscious intent, projecting light from their hands. Even more shocking, perhaps, comes the realization that other lucid dreamers with similar goals have also spontaneously and unexpectedly projected light from their hands. This surprising feature of lucid dreaming—the appearance of light when one intends to heal something—suggests that an underlying commonality exists in aspects of lucid experience. Where does this connection come from? A deeper layer of the Self? The fact of the commonality may, perhaps, give evidentiary support to an underlying order or principle in the dream realm, supportive of the concept of the collective unconscious suggested by Jung.

In various colors and in various forms, this inner light is a common feature for many in lucid healing, which makes one wonder, does the light heal? Or does it *represent* healing? Or something else, such as awareness, perhaps? And why various colors—why not just one color?

Let's consider a few cases in which lucid dreamers either used light or experienced a healing light. This first example is from a series of fascinating lucid dream healings recounted by Ed Kellogg. He received this account from a woman he refers to as "AH," who had gone to bed one night barely able to walk from the pain of six plantar warts on her feet. As a lucid dreamer, she reported the following dream:

> I walk through what appears to be a museum; it seems dark, like the lights are very low. [I see] small lamps attached to the walls, illuminating alcoves where religious objects sit on display. I weave in and out of the chamber in the flickering light. . . . Something about the light seems strange. I think of my feet because they are hurting me as I walk. So I sit down on a cube, like a wooden cube. Then I remember I can heal my feet [in a lucid dream]. At that moment, all of the surrounding room drops away to a black void where I sit. I recall using a ball of white light as I had been visualizing [before going to sleep]. Sure enough it appears around my hands. I put my hands on my feet—first, the right one. The light enters the foot and glows golden from within. I hold it there for several seconds and then move to the left foot. Same process. I put both feet down and realize I had done what I had incubated. It seems amazing and terrifying. That feeling is so intense I woke up. The feeling makes my heart pound.[6]

Ed comments: "The night before AH could hardly walk because of the pain from 6 plantar warts, 3 on each foot, each about one centimeter across. Before retiring she had checked their appearance, and did a visualization for healing (as on previous nights), but this time also a lucid dream incubation. In the morning she felt surprised when she felt absolutely no pain on walking. She checked on the warts—they had all uniformly turned black overnight. All of them fell off within ten days."[7]

In private conversation, Ed shared with me that AH had tried waking visualization techniques for many months, trying to achieve this same goal, with little or no success. Yet after just this one lucid dream attempt at healing, immediate changes occurred as the warts turned black and fell off.

AH's story, and others like it, remind me of the Buddhist claim that suggestions made in the lucid dream become nine times more effective than those made in the waking state. By acting "closer to the source" of creativity and deeper in the subconscious, we spur the healing energies to perform much more quickly and profoundly.

This next healing lucid dream example took place while I was a member of the Lucidity Project, in the 1980s (as I described in chapter 5). One of our group members had a knee injury and asked the group to try to assist in healing it lucidly. Though I had mixed feelings about the idea, I felt curious about the possibility of healing another in a lucid dream. How would I approach it? What would happen? Later that month, I had the following lucid dream:

> I continue in the lucid dream and see a hunting lodge on a hillside with large pine trees around. I suddenly recall about LG's knee and remember our goal to help heal her knee. I wonder about how to do this, when suddenly a "cameo image" appears in the dream—showing a woman's knee! The oval-shaped image seems projected about midway up on my visual field and takes up perhaps five percent of the visual field—like an oval television's picture in a picture.
>
> I assume this cameo image is LG's knee and mentally project healing energy to it—which suddenly appears as light hovering around the knee area. As I recall, it was a deep pink or light red light. I wondered where it came from, since I didn't consciously intend it. Then I wondered, do I have the correct knee? This looks like the right knee, but did she say it was the left? I think about projecting healing energy on the left knee as well.

As I recall, another person in the group also reported a reddish healing light when she tried to assist LG's knees. LG reported some modest improvement, but not a full healing.

Ed Kellogg reports another case of a lucid dreamer, referred to as "TLP," who experienced light along with an electrical-type energy in this lucid dream:

> I was in a standing position, leaning up against something that felt warm, buzzing, electric. It felt very good and I completely relaxed. I then felt the presence of three guides. . . . [One guide] told me that I was not caring for my physical body the way I should of late and that, combined with my emotional state, had left me vulnerable to sickness. I remembered then that I had gone to bed with a terrible sore throat and a fever [101F]. They began working on my energy field, or aura. I could see crystalline energy emanating from the mid section of their

bodies. This was happening simultaneously. I felt the energy hit me and I felt as if I was caught in an electrical storm. . . . I then felt something pop in my head, and it was as if very warm liquid oozed down my body and I felt as if I were going to melt into the ground. . . . Then I felt energy being directed into the throat area, into my third eye area, and into the solar plexus area. I completely "let go" at this time and merged with the sensations that I was feeling. The next thing I knew was [the guide] saying to me, "Sleep now, rest in your comfortable darkness. You will awaken well."[8]

Ed comments: "Indeed TLP did not remember a thing until she awoke next morning. She immediately got up and looked at her throat in the mirror. All of the dark streaks of red were gone—her throat felt completely normal. Her fever had gone and her temperature now measured almost 3 degrees below normal, a drop of 5 degrees from her temperature the night before. Although she has not had a major illness, TLP reports having had a number of dramatic results from lucid dream healings on illnesses such as colds, flus, back problems, and intense muscle stiffness."[9]

Interesting how the lucid dreamer sees "crystalline energy" and feels something like electrical energy hit her body in various places. She hears diagnostic comments from what she senses as "the presence of three guides." Something seems to "pop" in her head, and she finally "lets go" to accept the sensations. One guide concludes by advising her, "Sleep now, rest in your comfortable darkness. You will awaken well." For some lucid dreamers, dream figures occasionally appear as helpers or guides in such healing situations and conduct healing actions. From experience, I know that being "hit" by light or energy can be both a powerful and unusual sensation, so it seems necessary to open up to the experience and trust in it as you seek healing.

HEALING THROUGH THE POWER OF SOUND, CHANTS, AND AFFIRMATIONS

Could sound play a role in lucid dream healing? Various religious and spiritual practices have felt that sound innately contains creative energy and can be used for healing intent. Whether in the form of a mantra, powerful word, or chant, lucid dreamers can consciously experiment with sound in healing.

In addition to being a talented lucid dreamer, Ed Kellogg has long held an interest in the mystical practices of kabbalah and has used words, sounds, and chants to experiment in a number of lucid dream settings. To a large degree, he feels that these verbal expressions both focus his intent more powerfully and directly and may tap into other sources of energy as well.

Ed tells the story of his own experience in lucid dream healing. He explains, "On September 23, 1994, I had severely injured my big toe in an accident, dislocating it and splitting the upper skin of the toe from side to side in the process. After relocating the toe myself, I received 4 stitches but no other medical treatment. In December the joint began to ache, and I would feel twinges of pain 10–20 times per day."[10] The following is his account of the lucid dreams he experienced:

> December 10: [R]ealizing I dream, I decide to try healing my big toe after trying unsuccessfully to use dream computers. I try a healing chant with no effect. My toe looks bluish-purple, some red. I chant again while massaging my toe, seems to help.

> December 20: In a sort of college dormitory, I realize that I dream. It looks a bit like Duke University at night. I decide to go flying but remember I wanted to heal my toe. I use the energy beam chant, which works really well, blue and gold sparks emanate from my hand onto my toe—terrific visual effect—my toe absorbs them. I go downstairs to go flying . . .[11]

Ed reported the following results: "After the first lucid dream healing on 12/10 aching in the toe decreased 99%. I only felt one slight twinge from that time until Jan 1, 1995. I felt another twinge on Jan 11 after running for twenty minutes, but since then the toe has remained healthy and pain free."[12]

Privately, I asked Ed about why he undertook a second lucid dream healing of his toe, since the first decreased the pain by ninety-nine percent. He explained that the lack of visual effects in the first lucid dream left him feeling "unsatisfied"; thus, he sought another lucid dream experience with "great special effects" to make certain that the toe's health would be complete and ongoing. After this, he conducted a final lucid dream healing for the scar in which a "yellow laser beam" of light shot from his fingers. A week later, the scar had largely disappeared.

I also questioned Ed about what he meant by "energy beam chant." He explained that he devised a chant to help him recall his intent and focus it. The chant normally went like this: "From my hand shoots an energy beam, to heal my (blank) with Power Supreme!" In his experience, he found that certain wordings resulted in a more energetic and noticeable response.

During one of his first attempts at lucid healing, in 1984, Ed used healing affirmations. Prior to the dream, he had punctured a right tonsil with a wooden skewer while enthusiastically eating a shish kabob. His tonsil had become "horribly infected and swollen, looking about 3 times normal size, bright red, and w/ yellow lines of pus decorating the exterior." Using a "sensory awareness relaxation technique," he sought to have an OBE but had a lucid dream instead:

> . . . walking through a house I wake to the lucid dream state, decide to try healing my throat. I look in a mirror and my throat looks healthy, but the tonsils look more like the middle section [uvula] than like tonsils. So in my dream body my throat looks healthy, but different. I program for healing to occur [using affirmations], and my throat does feel much better on awakening.[13]

Ed comments: "Subjectively I would estimate that less than an hour had passed between waking and sleeping, and the pain had almost entirely disappeared. The next morning my right tonsil looked and felt almost normal, only slightly red and swollen. At least 95% of the infection had disappeared in less than 12 hours."[14]

POWER OF SUGGESTION: IMAGES OF HEALING AND HEALTH

A number of lucid dreamers have used the conscious creation of symbolic healing images and environments to promote their greater health. To some degree, this practice parallels visualization techniques commonly used to promote health. Lucid dream researchers Jayne Gackenbach and Jane Bosveld report of one woman who created an environment in a lucid dream to accomplish several different healings:

> [The lucid dreamer] has used lucid dreaming to quit smoking, stop biting her nails, lose weight, and rid herself of hives and menstrual cramps. Although she has never seen a doctor for her hives, she is often bothered by them and has controlled them by suggesting to herself as she falls asleep that she needs to calm down. Then when she turns lucid, she creates a cool meadow environment in which she continues to tell herself to be calm. Repeatedly, after this dream experience, her hives will disappear.[15]

When considering healing imagery in a lucid dream, lucid dreamers seem to take two paths. One group predetermines what constitutes a healing image or setting and then projects it into the lucid dream. The other group of lucid dreamers asks the dream to create the most appropriate healing imagery at that time and then enters into it aware. In this second approach, the lucid dreamer relies on the greater understanding of the unconscious to manifest.

In either case, we shouldn't assume that the healing imagery or setting contains the same healing potential for everyone. Healing imagery will naturally vary from person to person, depending on his or her background and culture, as well as from situation to situation, depending upon the disease. I recall one night, during a severe sinus cold, dreaming of myself as an underwater diver with a bell helmet that pumped in pure oxygen. When I awoke, the congestion had finally cleared, and I could breathe easily again. Consciously, however, I would have never selected that particular image as being symbolically powerful for me.

SEEKING INFORMATION ABOUT THE ILLNESS; FACING THE ILLNESS

For some lucid dreamers, the desire to understand the meaning of the illness (their own or another's) is paramount. In their lucid dream, they seek information about the illness or ask to see the illness's meaning. Can understanding heal? Can greater awareness trigger new actions toward health? Beverly Kedzierski Heart D'Urso, Ph.D., a long-time lucid dreamer and one of Stephen LaBerge's colleagues and first lucid research subjects, had a fascinating healing experience. In waking life, she visited her medical doctor and, after some tests, he told her that she had an "expanded uterus" with "both a large cyst and a mass that looked like it might be a tumor."[16] Concerned about the situation, one week later, Beverly had several lucid dreams including the following:

> I ask [the dream figures], "What does my condition mean and what should I do about it?" They do not give me clear answers, so I decide to ask the "Source" to show me answers on the wall structure in front of us . . . I say out loud, "What does my condition want me to know and what should I do?"
>
> I immediately see these projected images. The first one shows skeletons similar to the ones we had hanging on Halloween. I think

they might represent death. Next, I see a traffic scene. An ambulance and fire truck appear. Finally, an airplane comes smashing down from the sky onto a freeway.[17]

[In my next dream, I see] huge geometric figures in five different colors hovering and circling over us in the sky. They seem as large as ocean liners. A turquoise colored one comes closest to me . . . They all seemed to shoot a kind of energy on me, which I experience as a healing. I become very relaxed and open to taking in this invisible energy. I would best describe it as a type of heat. [I notice that the dream figure of my son] seems scared, but I tell him not to worry. I explain, "They came to heal me!" [18]

Later that same day, Beverly went back to see her doctor. "He did another ultrasound test searching for the cyst and the mass," she reports, "but they did not exist anymore. He found my uterus 'no longer expanded, but completely normal and healthy.'"[19] Amazingly, the situation had changed significantly, and she remains healthy years later.

Notice how Beverly initially asks the dream figures for answers but they fail to respond with helpful information. Then she decides to ask the "Source" of the dream for a response. She ignores the dream figures around her and addresses herself to the awareness behind the dreaming. When she does ask the Source, she suddenly sees new imagery projected on the wall that provides a symbolic answer to her question. Then the lucid dream is followed by a semi-lucid dream of geometric colored shapes that shoot healing energy on to her, which she recognizes as a healing act.

As I will discuss in greater detail in chapter 15, it may be possible to access unknown information, including medical information, while lucid. I once had a lucid dream in which I see the child of a friend. In the dream, I remember that this child has a rare, nonvisible physical condition. Even though he is only three or four physically, I ask him in the lucid dream, "Why do you have this condition?" He replies, "For my mother." This response stuns me, and I decide to wake.

Years after telling the child's mother about this lucid dream, she brought it up and told me that I had uncovered a family secret. For many centuries, the women of their family had given birth, on occasion, to children with this nonvisible physical problem. She said, "I don't know how you came up with that answer, since nobody knows this family secret. But you were right."

SEARCHING FOR HEALTH:
THE HEALING ROOM, THE HEALING
LIQUID, THE HEALING DOCTOR

In the waking world, healing often appears to come from others—from a doctor or a prescription or a machine in a hospital. Some lucid dreamers use this same approach as they seek healing help in dealing with their illnesses. Can a lucid dream doctor cure a physical disease? Do dream-created healing liquids work? Keelin, the experienced lucid dreamer I introduced earlier in the chapter, decided to find out in this next lucid dream example:

> A friend is dressed in brown tones, but the second time I see her, the same clothes are blue. While thinking that this is odd, they change once again right in front of my eyes and I realize I'm dreaming. In the next instant, she disappears completely. The sensation of mild, chilly vibes begins and I quickly shift focus to address my goal of attempting to heal the spot on my lip that still concerns me. I rub my hands until I sense they're glowing. The scene is now in my kitchen, the timing is midnight, with appropriate moonlight coming in through the windows. I rub my right index finger over my lip, strongly intending for healing to take place.
>
> After a couple of moments, I wake, then return to the same scene with lucidity intact. I hold my right hand in front of me and willfully conjure a drinking glass. At first it looks empty and I think: This will not do! Immediately it is filled with a clear liquid. I intend this to be a magic healing potion and drink it right down, making certain the liquid wets my entire upper lip.[20]

Keelin comments: "Although it's impossible to say precisely what physical effect this dream may have had on the actual condition of my lip, I felt tremendously empowered by assuming responsibility for the healing of my body and greatly comforted by the vivid imagery. The final biopsy diagnosis was benign. Nothing like the fear of surgery to provide great incentive for lucid dreaming!"[21]

Notice that Keelin actually uses two approaches in her set of lucid dreams. In the first one, she places her right index finger on her lip "strongly intending for healing to take place." Then in the second one, she decides to create a "magic healing potion" that, once consumed and touched to her lip, will then contain the healing intent. The first approach suggests a direct intent, while the second suggests an indirect intent, since she projects healing intent into the "healing potion."

When psychology investigates lucid dream healing, researchers may notice differences between the cases in which the healing intent is suggested directly and the cases in which the lucid dreamer projects the healing intent into an external agent such as a liquid or "magic healing potion." Lucid dream reports suggest that direct healing intent may offer the shortest path to physical fulfillment.

In another case, a long-time lucid dreamer repeatedly sought assistance from either a healing room or healing doctor. In this instance, she finds both. She recounts, "I'm outside so I concentrate on the Healing Room, go through a wall and find myself in a doctor's office." She now finds a nurse-like young girl who offers her chocolate cake, but she refuses it, saying, "It looks too good." The lucid dreamer continues and eventually finds a doctor, asking him, "How can you help me?" The doctor replies, "I don't know." She responds, "Well, try." He complains, "I'm tired. It's late and you always come here on Fridays."[22]

She continues to follow the doctor, who provides her some soup in a bowl. Discovering it's tomato soup, the lucid dreamer concludes, it "always disagrees with me." As the doctor walks away, she shouts, "This is my dream; you are as I'm creating you. . . . At least tell me something simple." The lucid dreamer wakes up.

In this particular case, the lucid dreamer doesn't note any improvement in health. Curiously, we can note some passivity in her action. While Keelin manifested healing liquid and directly applied healing intent, this lucid dreamer seems to seek healing outside of herself, in the actions of the dream doctor. Notice how she initiates the encounter by asking the doctor, "How can you help me?"

Also of interest, the doctor recognizes her pattern of coming late, on Friday, when he feels tired, suggesting perhaps that she seeks inner assistance at the wrong time, or in the wrong manner. Here again, she refuses his comments and his offer of tomato soup, because it "disagrees" with her. One wonders if the offering of chocolate and tomato soup functioned as possible literal or symbolic suggestions for better health. Or perhaps the whole interaction indicates a difficulty accepting health suggestions?

While it seems nearly impossible to know the symbolic meaning of an individual's lucid dream, another lucid dreamer tries the same projective technique in a search for greater health. "After I become lucid," the lucid dreamer recounts, "I recall I was going to try [Ed Kellogg's] challenge and ask what are the next steps for deep healing for myself." She decides that she will go to a building and inside it will discover the answer. "I get to a group of houses in the distance, but they are all boarded up," she says. "I figure they are empty so don't bother to go inside." She goes to a store and states that at the end of the escalator, she'll find what she needs for health. She discovers a "couple of pillowcase sets [which] feature tiny 'mojo bags' of the same material—commercial magic? [She assumes] the person fills the bag with healing items or protective materials and sleeps with it around his/her neck." She ignores these and grabs a teddy bear instead and then, twice, she ignores a black woman who seems to keep following her. She finds herself entering houses with a "not very neat" bathroom. She begins to tease a cat and suddenly realizes, "[I have on] white furry gloves, like the cat. I've lost the teddy bear. At that point, I wake up."[23]

As in the previous case, in which the lucid dreamer asked assistance from the doctor, this lucid dreamer did not experience any significant improvement in her health situation. She decides to find "the next steps for deep healing for myself," but where she intends to find the answer looks "all boarded up." While lucid, she could easily walk through the wall and go inside but instead surmises, "I figure they are empty so don't bother to go inside."

As she progresses, at each point at which she intends to discover an answer, she finds something only to discard it—apparently because it doesn't seem of any value to her. She twice ignores the black woman; the black woman continues to follow her. And the dream persists in showing her a "not very neat" bathroom.

By the end of the dream, she teases a cat, only to find that she herself has white furry gloves "like the cat." In a sense, the dream may represent a tease of sorts, between the lucid dreamer's desire for "deep healing" and her apparent refusal to accept any of the answers or any of the help provided by her dreaming self. One wonders if the lucid dream symbolism suggests the dreamer's conflicting desires about the usefulness of lucid dreaming for healing.

Of course, health challenges occur from many causes and may serve other purposes. One therapist, for example, taught a sufferer of post-traumatic stress disorder to become lucid to deal with recurrent nightmares. The therapist was shocked when the client said he would never use lucid dreaming to help himself with severe nightmares. When asked why, the gentleman explained that he needed the disability benefits!

Even when a person sincerely desires perfect health, he or she may not believe it's possible or achievable. When lucid, our beliefs and expectations exist as powerful factors that influence the lucid dream's direction and our response to the dream information. By looking back at ineffective lucid dream attempts at healing, we may gain insight into our limiting beliefs or expectations.

HEALING OTHERS WHILE LUCID DREAMING

As the examples in this chapter illustrate, healing oneself in a lucid dream has been repeatedly shown to be possible. A person aware in the subconscious (or unconscious) seems in an innately powerful place to direct effective suggestions of healing intent and energy. Lucid in the unconscious, constructive healing intent appears to quicken one's natural healing ability.

Could it also be possible, then, beyond self healing in lucid dreams, to influence a friend's health when lucid? Could a trained lucid dreamer use the lucid state to impact another's health? Though relatively rare, a few lucid dreamers have attempted this. It's important to note here that, for ethical reasons, lucid dreamers should always receive the other person's consent before attempting any healing in a lucid dream. In doing so, they remove any concerns about the other person's acceptance of the lucid attempt. Also, they don't end up in a lucid dream wondering whether they have the right to attempt such a thing and potentially lose some of their focus as they lucidly deal with an inner dilemma.

In some cases in which lucid dreamers have attempted to direct healing energy onto another, the dream interaction resulted in a subsequent improvement in the other person's health. In other attempts, however, lucid dreamers have seen their lucid dream healing energy rebuffed by the person's dream image, suggesting the healing energy or intent was unwelcome. As one would expect, in those cases, no improvement in health occurred.

In the following examples, each conducted with the consent of the ill person involved, Ed Kellogg recalls his efforts to assist another's healing process while lucidly aware.

> Fully lucid . . . [While staying at S's house in waking physical reality], I go into [S's and D's bedroom] and announce that we "dream." I ask [S], which knee needs healing, [S] says the right, but I want to see for myself. I have him pull up his pants to make sure. The left knee has a sort of metal plate, and on top of it a bump that [S] says needed healing [note left knee in waking physical reality needed healing not the right].

I place my hand over the bump, and my left hand under the knee, I do HC chant for S's left knee, and both blue and green energy [bright, laser-like] comes out of my right hand. After 10 seconds or so, S says, "That's it" but light still comes out of my hands for a minute or so. I take my hands off and try applying this energy to myself, but I hear a phone ringing and return to waking physical reality.[24]

Ed comments: "S. noticed marked improvement in the mobility and strength of his physical knee, and a marked decrease in pain associated with the movement, on the day following the healing. S. rated his knee for the week before the healing at about 4 out of a possible 10 (10= the healthy knee), and for the week after the healing as 8 out of 10. The functional improvement has persisted, with continued physical therapy and exercise, S. currently rates his left knee, now over 8 months later, at 9 out of 10."[25] Now, seven years later, Ed tells me, in a personal conversation, that the knee continues at this level of health.

In the next example, Ed seeks to assist someone with severe emphysema:

I try to fly to D., end up in a cloud, visualize their house and boom, end up on their front porch. They look much younger in Dream Reality, G. looks in her thirties, D. in his forties. . . . Inside I try a healing of D. . . . D. keeps interrupting, asking me what I do. I tell him I'll explain later in Waking Physical Reality. *I use a healing chant* (Now let the healing energy shine / To cure the lungs with power divine). A *green energy-liquid, like dark chlorophyll comes out of my fingers into D's chest* [emphasis added], where it seeps out again. I leave him to recover, but when I return I find him pale and frail in a wheel chair. I create a white light chi energy ball with rotating hand motions and try to charge him up. This technique really impresses the guests, but D., desperate for energy, keeps touching me, and grounding the energy into himself before I can build up a good charge.[26]

Ed comments: "Within a day or so following this lucid dream healing, D. showed a remarkable improvement. For the previous six months he had needed oxygen therapy twenty-four hours a day. Afterwards, he required oxygen supplementation only while sleeping at night. He continued in this improved state for over 5 years."[27]

These remarkable lucid dream experiences suggest a hidden dimension to lucid dreaming. The lucid dreamer's intent appears to engage a deep source of transpersonal healing energy with surprising effects. "In the future," Ed Kellogg says, "controlled studies may eventually confirm the effects seen in these anecdotal reports, and lucid dream healing may become one of the more accepted and practical applications of lucid dream research. But for the present, we will just have to let the dreams speak for themselves."[28]

Evidence so far suggests that lucid dreamers most likely to succeed with their lucid dream healing attempts display the following attitudes and behaviors: 1) a positive expectation or positive belief about possible success, 2) greater "surrendering" to the lucid dream and acceptance of its flow and intuited information, 3) the use of healing techniques that they can perform by their own actions, and 4) a willingness to call on inner energy.

Those less likely to succeed in their lucid dream healing attempts displayed some of the following attitudes and behaviors: 1) a neutral expectation or belief about their success; a possible expectation of failure, 2) greater rigidity to the lucid dream and its flow (for example, they refused advice, symbols, or items offered them in the lucid dream, seemingly because it conflicted with waking assumptions and beliefs), and 3) use of healing techniques they could not perform personally (they needed to "find" the healing place, the doctor, or the healing liquid); the healing seemed more external to them and could not be performed by their own action.

Ed Kellogg's considerable work on lucid dream healing has demonstrated convincingly the potential here to affect physical health positively. Through his decades of experience with lucid dreaming and use of focusing techniques to concentrate intent, he has gained deep insight into this practice.[29]

With lucid dreaming, we apparently have conscious access to the power of the unconscious. With more experience and more examples of lucid dream healing of self and others, we may begin to understand the interconnected nature of the unconscious, the physical body, and one's intent to heal. Lucid dreaming may become a primary tool to engage the conscious unconscious's vast creative powers to improve our mental, emotional, and physical health. As Patricia Garfield observed, "The potential for healing in lucid dreams is enormous."[30] We have only just begun to explore that potential, however. Through the attempts and discoveries of individual lucid dreamers, we have a chance to bring forth the profound creative and healing energies of the conscious unconscious and understand healing from the much larger perspective of the inner Self.

14

CONSCIOUSLY CONNECTING VIA TELEPATHY

EARLY IN HIS CAREER, PSYCHIATRIST AND INTERNATIONALLY RENOWNED dream expert Dr. Montague Ullman discovered something interesting while talking with his patients about their dreams. It seems they occasionally dreamt telepathically about his life. In some instances, the telepathic connections were small. For example, a distrustful patient dreamt of giving a chromium soap dish to someone building a home. Unknown to this patient, Ullman had recently been looking at a chromium soap dish he had mistakenly received when building his house and had held onto "in a spirit of belligerent dishonesty inspired by rising costs on the house . . ."[1] The patient seemingly homed in on this small incident via dream telepathy as a poignant symbolic expression for his distrust of therapists.

On other occasions, the patients seemed to pick up on larger issues that dovetailed with events or concerns in Ullman's life. Ullman found this repeated dream telepathy so fascinating that in the 1960s, he and psychologist Stanley Krippner, Ph.D., began formal dream-laboratory studies at the Maimonides Medical Center in Brooklyn, New York, to investigate dream telepathy scientifically. Over the course of almost ten years' research, they found considerable scientific evidence of dream telepathy and have reported the findings in their fascinating book, *Dream Telepathy: Experiments in Nocturnal ESP.*

Musing on why dream telepathy appeared initially in therapy sessions, Ullman and Krippner state: "The unique advantage of the psychoanalytic situation for discovering telepathic dreams resides mainly in the fact that dreams are regularly reported by the patient to the analyst. Nowhere else in our culture do dreams obtain such prominence. Ordinarily they are not discussed; people are not encouraged to remember them; nor are they encouraged to look for any inner meanings much less any paranormal correspondences with outer events."[2]

Simply by attending to dreams, we begin to realize that some dreams are tied to a larger sense of awareness that somehow goes beyond time and space and provides individuals with shared nonlocal information. In lucid dreaming, of course, we can take this further and consciously seek out such information.

Psychotherapist, author, and lucid dreamer Kenneth Kelzer works with clients to explore dreams and their meaning. Kelzer recounts one client's surprising lucid dream containing psychic telepathic information. "Suzanne" was an experienced lucid dreamer in her late fifties, trying to adjust to the forthcoming retirement of her executive husband and the positive and negative changes in lifestyle that might result. Kelzer describes her lucid dream:

> Suzanne is floating down a river to the ocean. As she reaches the ocean she realizes she is dreaming, and becomes lucid. As she swims out into the ocean she sees a gigantic male arm and hand reaching out to her, and someone calling and beckoning to her. It speaks to her silently and symbolically saying, "Come and help me." She feels the power of the gargantuan hand and is determined not to get caught in its grip, so she swims around it repeatedly sending it a vibration of love and peace until finally the hand and arm shrink down to a manageable size. Now she takes the hand in her hand and goes down with it into the ocean. They go down, down and she comes to the bottom of the sea and she sees a nude male body lying on the ocean floor and approaches it. The man looks similar to her husband, though also dissimilar in certain ways. She feels a great deal of compassion for him. She approaches him and tries to send him a message of consolation. . . . She peacefully floats up to the surface of the ocean and as the dream ends she feels very good.[3]

After hearing the dream, the group worked with it using a Gestalt therapy process in which Suzanne acted various roles in the lucid dream to obtain additional insight. You can imagine her hand reaching up, implying the feeling of, "Come and help me." Or see her acting as a figure on the floor, needing compassion and consolation. That evening, Suzanne's husband came home from work, entered the kitchen, and had a very unusual request. Approaching her, he asked, "Would you mind just hugging me?" She does so, and another unexpected dream-like element develops, which Kelzer relates: "[Suzanne's husband] suddenly lay down on the floor of the kitchen, and reaching up with one arm, said: 'Would you just mind lying here on the floor with me and putting your arms around me?' Again she complied. But now her mind was racing with all of the power of this event, which she recognized at once as both psychic and synchronistic."[4]

In Suzanne's lucid dream and physical-world reenactment, one glimpses the curious place where dream life intersects with waking life. Her husband's arm reaches up from the floor of the kitchen, just as it had from the floor of the ocean in her lucid dream; and, as in the dream, she comforts her husband. Powerful psychic events like these, Kelzer concludes, have the potential to "burst our old models of the universe."[5]

EVEN FREUD HAD AN INTEREST

Occasional telepathic or clairvoyant information appearing in dreams seems natural to those who monitor their own dreams or work with the dreams of others. Though reluctant to embrace the idea of dream telepathy, Sigmund Freud, the father of psychoanalysis, could not entirely escape an interest in it. According to Peter Gay, author of *Freud: A Life for Our Time*:

> In 1926 [Freud] reminded Ernest Jones that he had long since harbored a 'favorable prejudice in favor of telepathy' and had held back only to protect psychoanalysis from too close a proximity to occultism. But recently 'the experiments that I have undertaken with Ferenczi and my daughter have gained such a persuasive power for me, that diplomatic considerations had to take a back seat.' He found telepathy fascinating, he added, because his preoccupation with it reminded him, though on a reduced scale, of 'the great experiment of my life' when he stood up against public obloquy as the discoverer of psychoanalysis.[6]

One of Freud's disciples, Dr. Sandor Ferenczi, had an interest in psychic phenomena and apparently conducted informal experiments on "thought transference" with Freud and his daughter and life-long companion, Anna. Further, Montague Ullman and Stanley Krippner, in their book *Dream Telepathy*, have commented, "The tracing of telepathic elements in dreams led Freud to the view that it was an 'incontestable fact that sleep creates favorable conditions for telepathy' . . . Freud later conjectured that telepathy 'may be the original archaic method by which individuals understood one another, and which has been pushed into the background in the course of phylogenetic [evolutionary] development. . . .'"[7]

Freud's interest never led to clear support for telepathy, since his main focus was psychoanalysis, but intrigued by dream telepathy, he remained an interested agnostic, so to speak, and occasionally complained of the difficulty of creating a psychological structure or model to explain telepathic and similar phenomena.[8]

The French neurologist and hypnotist Jean Martin Charcot, whom Freud observed working on psychiatric patients during his time in Paris, made a remark that Freud often quoted: Theory is all very well, but that does not prevent facts from existing. Some lucid dreamers are beginning to feel the same way about their experiences with psychic lucid phenomena. The facts of these psychic lucid dream experiences are emerging, in spite of there being no acceptable theory to explain them. For lucid dreamers, conscious awareness in the dream state allows for the active exploration of psychic phenomena like telepathy, clairvoyance, and precognition. Aware in the dream, lucid dreamers can seek out unknown but verifiable information and see for themselves whether the dream state is conducive, as Freud said, to "favorable conditions for telepathy."

Though physicists have provided various theories that might allow for the incidence of telepathy and psi, no widely accepted theory exists to explain it. However, as Charcot observed, the innovator's experience often runs ahead of the theory and the slow wheels of science. In this and coming chapters, I hope to encourage lucid dreamers to explore psi phenomena in lucid dreams. Already, experiences exist to suggest lucid dreaming's potential to investigate and possibly prove this persistent facet of dreaming.

A LUCID DREAMER SEEKS UNKNOWN INFORMATION

As coeditor of *The Lucid Dream Exchange*, I read the various lucid dreams submitted to our quarterly publication. One university student in particular, Ian Koslow, struck me as having a natural talent for lucid dreaming. After having sent in several lucid dreams, Ian sent me an email one day with a simple, straightforward question. It appeared to him, he said, that I believed lucid dreaming could provide verifiable, unknown information. How could I be sure? he asked.

I knew enough to avoid a "battle of beliefs" and responded to Ian with a few observations and one simple request. I explained that nothing I could say would convince him that lucid dreaming provides verifiable and unknown information. "But you're a talented lucid dreamer," I said, "so you can try this: Devise an experiment that will prove or disprove the ability to get unknown, verifiable information in the lucid dream state—then do it for yourself in your next lucid dream."

A month later, Ian surprised me by submitting a lucid dream. With the help of a friend in his college dormitory, he had devised an experiment to obtain unknown information. As you will see, he became lucid and succeeded in his task.

> This is an interesting story that I want to share . . . I am still trying to figure out exactly what it means . . .
>
> I was talking to a girl in my dorm about lucid dreaming, and we were discussing whether or not the people you see in the dream are actually real, or just imaginations. To test this out, we decided to do a little experiment.
>
> She told me that somewhere on her back she had an awkward looking freckle and she wanted me to find her in my lucid dream, and see if I could locate her freckle.
>
> Well, it took me about a week, but I finally found her in my lucid dream and searched her back until I saw a dark freckle on her lower back, dead center, right above her ass. I remember thinking during the lucid dream that there was no way this could be the right spot, because I thought I remembered her hinting to me that it was on the side of her back.
>
> When I woke up I went to her room and told her that I was ready to guess where her freckle was. I went up to her back and pointed my finger at the spot that I saw it in the dream, and to both of our surprise, she lifted up her shirt and my finger was directly covering her freckle. Now, I have no idea what this means, but I don't think it's just a coincidence that I happened to guess exactly where the lone freckle on her back was. All I could think is that the power of lucid dreaming might be more than I imagined.[9]

Notice how the freckle doesn't appear on the side of her back where he thought she hinted it might be; instead, he found it deep down on her lower center back. Notice, too, how in the lucid dream he thinks "there was no way this could be the right spot" because it runs counter to the suspected hint that he already considered.

In effect, Ian's hint of an expectation seems overruled by the events in the dream, and he wakes with a bit of curiosity tinged with self-doubt. Thankfully, when he visits the young woman, he points to the exact place indicated in his lucid dream. He follows the lucid dream information faithfully.[10]

About a year later, I interviewed Ian for *The Lucid Dream Exchange* and learned that his successful lucid dream had been preceded by a failed attempt in which he appears to struggle symbolically with self-doubt.

> A few nights later [after setting up the experiment with the young woman] I became lucid, and the first thing that came to my mind was finding my friend and looking for the freckle. I left my dorm room and began walking toward hers, but as I got closer, it became harder for me to move. It was as if there was some type of force preventing me from moving any further. Then a different friend of mine who also lived on my floor came out of his room to yell and wake me up from the dream. It's interesting to point out that the person who yelled for me to wake up is someone who didn't believe in the concept of lucid dreaming and accused me of making it all up.[11]

Notice how it took Ian two lucid dreaming attempts to accomplish this task. In his first attempt, he experiences an inability to move, and a bothersome dream figure appears who possibly represents Ian's disbelief. Ian calls these doubting figures "Distracters." After a few nights, he lucidly tries again. This time, he lucidly intends the young woman to come into his room, and she does, whereupon they perform the wakingly conceived experimental task successfully.

In an experience like this, we begin to see the possible experimental capacity of lucid dreaming as a tool to explore the potential of the mind for unconscious information. The lucid dreamer doesn't have to wait for a clairvoyant or telepathic dream; he or she can help create one and awaken with the information. Such an ability could lead the fields of psychology and parapsychology to a whole new means to study psi phenomena.

Does this prove anything? No, one personal experiment like this, of course not. But as lucid dreamers, we can try experiments like this over and over until, at some point, the result of all that replication will provide us with our own experiences and, thus, our own set of evidentiary data and conclusions.

USING LUCID AWARENESS TO
WIN A DREAM TELEPATHY CONTEST

A small yet fascinating event at the IASD conference each year is the Dream Telepathy Contest. The contest is an outgrowth of the dream telepathy experiments conducted at the Maimonides Medical Center in Brooklyn, New York, in the 1960s and '70s. While not conducted as a scientific experiment, the contest is simply held for its educational value. The rules are simple. A telepathic sender is chosen. On the night of the telepathic sending, the sender chooses one envelope from a group of four sealed envelopes, all of which contain different images of a painting or photo. The sender retreats to his or her room, opens the envelope, and attempts to transmit telepathically the image of the painting or photo. The sender does so by looking at the image, talking about the image, imagining himself or herself involved in the image in some way, and so on. That night, the interested conference attendees try to dream about the image being transmitted

The next morning, the contest organizers get the image from the telepathic sender, open the other three envelopes with their images, and place all four images on a table where attendees can later view them. Attendees are then asked to write down their night's dream that most closely matches one of the four images. Of course, only one of the images is the target image.

Some conference attendees have become lucid on the night of the contest and sought out the target image while consciously aware, sometimes with incredible results. Lucid dreamer Clare Johnson, Ph.D., reported this amazing experience:

> I conjure up a strong visual memory of [the telepathic sender] Beverly standing in the auditorium a few hours earlier, clutching the sealed envelope with the dream telepathy image in it and inviting us to dream of her. "Okay, Beverly" I think. "I'm listening." Then I drop straight into an exhausted sleep.
>
> Green begins to seep into my dreams. It hangs in translucent blocks of color as a backdrop to the dream action. It reflects off people's faces. Soon I am surrounded by it and the scene morphs into a spacious park full of big old trees. The air is fresh and I feel happy. I am wandering around with IASD members, commenting on the greenness. In the distance, a woman's voice is shouting "Tree! Tree!" as if she has just discovered the answer to some fundamental question. I glance in the direction of the shouts but see no one. I hesitate, looking

into the woods, but I'm not lucid at this point and I'm caught up in the pleasant social interaction with the other dream characters. I feel it would be rude to leave them.

Later [in the dream], we are all at the conference site in a high-ceilinged room, discussing the dream telepathy contest. I see Beverly across the room and know that I'm dreaming this. Beverly looks cheerful but I think she's got to be tired since she must be having a sleepless night trying to transmit the image. I ask her how she is feeling. She flings her arms out, grinning, and says, "I've just been shouting the word inside my head!"

"That's interesting," I say, "because in my last dream, people were shouting about trees." I want to ask her outright if tree is the image she is projecting, but think this might be cheating. A woman across the room says excitedly, "I've been getting that, too. Tree shouting." We get into a discussion about the nature of greenness. Is green a positive or negative color? We agree that it is both dark and light. Deep and beautiful. . . . Then, very slowly, I wake up. I am smiling in the dark. "The telepathy picture really might be a tree," I think.

[When Clare wakens and arrives at the conference, she sees Beverly, the telepathic sender, and begins to relate her lucid dream. Beverly encourages her to go look at the four images and enter the contest officially.]

When I get to Registration with the slip of paper upon which I scribbled down my dream, there are three images which don't resonate with me at all, and on the end is a picture of the tree I tried to draw in my dream. I return to the workshop and can't concentrate on anything the presenter is saying.

As I had to fly home that day, I missed the dream ball and so only discovered a few days later that I'd won the contest. I was intrigued to learn that Beverly did actually shout about trees inside her head while attempting to communicate the image. This experience has given me food for thought concerning receptiveness in lucid dreams.[12]

PERSONAL EXPERIMENTS
WITH LUCID DREAM TELEPATHY

Although the Dream Telepathy Contest took place in an organized group setting, anyone can conduct a dream telepathy experiment. All you need is another interested person. On a predetermined night, one person acting as the sender simply selects a vivid and unusual image to send telepathically, while the dream receiver seeks to dream of the image being sent. On the following morning, the dreamer emails all of his or her dreams to the sender. (The dreams don't need to be lucid; dream telepathy appears to work in all dream states.) Then, the sender reveals the image and determines if the reported dreams connect to the image.

Often, both the sender and the dreamer feel shocked by the correspondences. Normally, the image dreamt about is not an exact reproduction; rather, elements of the image enter into the other's dreams. For example, if the target image is a pagoda in Tokyo, the dream receiver may dream of something similar, such as Mt. Fuji or meeting people from Japan. "Very rarely does a receiver, or percipient, report a dream that exactly duplicates the stimulus the sender, or agent, was trying to transmit," Robert Van de Castle writes in *Our Dreaming Mind*. Often, Van de Castle notes, the receiver will pick up the dominant color, action, form, or texture of the image.[13]

A friend and I conducted a series of dream telepathy exchanges with excellent results. After several attempts, I finally became lucidly aware (October 2006):

> I seem to be in the lobby of a building. People come and go. I go near the elevator and notice that the shine on the metal seems unusual. "Oh, this is a dream!" I realize.
>
> I get on the elevator, looking at the others who get on. I get off the elevator and consciously walk around. I ask about the place where I find myself, and someone seems to indicate it is a place for people who "misperceive reality."
>
> We turn to the balcony area and I see a magazine or child's book. I think, "Oh, I can use this to find out the telepathic image." So I decide to open it and see the telepathic image. When I do so, I notice on the page's right side, the profile of a man's face looks out straight ahead. It is an illustration, not a photo. The lines are flesh colored, maybe a bit darker. He seems to look out over a valley or "vista" (a nice view). . . . I wake.

In my dream journal, I drew a round, bald head with a funny, triangular eye area, looking out over a valley. I sent the dream to my friend and she, the telepathic sender, provided me with the image that she had transmitted. The image was of a hot air balloon hanging over a valley. (Although I was unable to locate the original, the photo you see here is very similar to the photo used in the experiment.) The balloon had an interesting triangular eye shape on it, much like the triangular eye shape that I saw in the lucid dream. Though not a perfect translation, I easily picked up the valley perspective. However, I seemed to translate the shape of the hot air balloon and transpose it into a round, bald, flesh-colored head.

(Courtesy of Continental Tours, Cairo)

From my own experience and in talking with other lucid dreamers, I have noticed that verbal messages are sometimes more precisely and accurately transmitted than visual images. Often the images get morphed into look-alike structures (a balloon becomes a bald head, for example), while the verbal messages come through more clearly. It may be that words have stricter communication values in telepathy—the word stands for itself—while imagery has to be interpreted by the dreamer and thus opens itself to a symbolic reworking.

One of my more interesting lucid dream experiences incorporates both symbolic and verbal information. And, similar to the experience of Suzanne in Ken Kelzer's dream group, this lucid dream made its way out of the dream world and into the waking world (November 24, 1998):

> My wife and I are driving a pickup or SUV. The roads are dark, and suddenly I see a blue truck come into our lane, passing another truck. I pull over and it passes us. I feel relieved we weren't hurt. We pull up to a restaurant or bar, and I realize, "This is a dream!"
>
> I'm inside enjoying a feeling of lucid euphoria, when I see my friend Moe come inside. She's wearing a white T-shirt and black pants. I ask her if she realizes this is a dream. She seems just a little bit alert, so I walk her around a bit. Then I decide to hold her and levitate (to convince her we dream). I keep saying, "See, we're floating! This is a dream."
>
> Trying to make some impact on her, I get the idea to make a peace sign with my fingers. Putting them in front of her face, I say, "Look, Moe, do you see this peace sign? Every time you see it, it can make you become lucid—you'll know you're dreaming." Again, I put the peace sign right in front of her face. I wake.

Four months later, I'm traveling on business on the West Coast and call Moe to see about having lunch. We make plans to meet.

Arriving early, I wait outside the restaurant and, at last, I see Moe coming down the sidewalk. As she walks up to me, she gives me a curious look—then suddenly reaches up and puts a big peace sign right in front of my face!

I am completely stunned—I had recalled the lucid dream earlier in the day, but had not mentioned it to her. "Why did you do that?" I asked. She just shrugged her shoulders and said nonchalantly, "I don't know. Just felt like it." Later over lunch, I told her about my lucid dream of meeting her and showing her the peace sign and how shocking it felt to see her mimic my lucid dream behavior.

Driving away that afternoon, I wondered, had I telepathically encouraged her to put the peace sign in my face? Or, did this response emerge as an impulse from her subconscious self's participation in the dream? Or maybe from her inner ego? In the dream, did I interact with a dream figure representation or the dreaming person?

Unlike some examples that we might write off as mere coincidence, this event was truly profound and shocking. Not only had information been exchanged, but my dream action appeared to influence Moe's waking action. Suddenly, the two worlds of dreaming and waking didn't seem so separate. For a moment, on a sunny suburban street corner, lucid dreaming merged with lucid waking.

TESTING YOUR TELEPATHY TALENT

To see if you have a talent for receiving telepathic information, I encourage you to find a friend, perhaps online, and play with sending and receiving images in the dream state. Try it once a week, on a predetermined night. Decide which role each of you will play, sender or receiver, and give it a try. By approaching it in a spirit of fun and adventure, you can learn a lot about this simple yet fascinating experience.

Across cultures and social classes, dream telepathy is a commonly reported dream experience. Whether the dream reports the coming illness or passing of a loved one, announces the birth of a child, or just provides general news for the dreamer, an inner system of communication seems to exist. By paying attention to dreams, we gain access to the occasional telepathic message and can learn how to differentiate telepathic news from other dream information. When we become consciously aware in the dream state, we have the capacity to deliberately seek out our own telepathic information. Whether we find a hidden freckle on a friend's back, learn about a new acquaintance, or seek contest information, those actions have the power to reshape our view of the world and direct us to the mysterious depths of mankind's muse: intuited knowledge.

Beneath the surface layer of communication apparently lies another layer, ancient and unappreciated. Perhaps, as Freud pondered, this inner telepathy is the "original archaic method" of communication that we still carry in the unconscious, a vestige from the past. To become aware of those invisible strings of communication, conceivably all we need to do is believe in their existence, practice old forms of listening, and pay attention to dreams and our inner life.

After years of experimental work, the authors of *Dream Telepathy* state, "Our main surmise is that the psyche of man possesses a latent ESP capacity that is most likely to be deployed during sleep, in the dreaming phase. Psi is no longer the exclusive gift of rare beings known as 'psychic sensitives,' but is a normal part of human existence, capable of being experienced by nearly everyone under the right conditions."[14]

As Charcot suggested and Freud often repeated, theory is all very well, but that doesn't prevent facts from existing. Dream communication, or dream telepathy, appears to be one of those "facts," if we would only investigate it seriously.

15

FORWARD-LOOKING PRECOGNITIVE LUCID DREAMS

FOR MILLENNIA, RELIGIOUS TEXTS, HISTORICAL NOTES, AND PERSONAL memoirs have recorded fascinating accounts of dreams that seemed to contain precognitive information. From pharaohs to presidents to common men and women, precognitive dreams have ignored status, rank, culture, and belief and transfigured the unquestioning acceptance of linear time and local perception for those who have experienced them. In many ways, precognitive dreaming remains a persistent mystery in search of an acceptable explanation.

In his book (with coauthor Letitia Sweitzer) *Dreams That Come True*, psychologist David Ryback, Ph.D., recounts his movement from skeptic to believer. A survey of his college class showed sixty-six percent felt they had experienced a precognitive dream. When half of the class provided examples, his rigorous analytical criteria found that eight percent of the class had dream experiences that suggested paranormal future-sensing as the most likely explanation. His subsequent explorations supported his contention that one out of twelve individuals has evidentiary precognitive dreams.

Though precognitive dreaming has been dismissed by many, lucid dreaming may offer a new means to acquire precognitive information and counter critics who frequently claim:

1. Much precognitive dream information is announced retro-cognitively, or after the fact. *Lucid dreamers could seek out possible future information about a specific topic, wake up with it,*

label it "precognitive," provide it to a fair witness, and wait for the event.

2. Much precognitive dream information seems too general or too symbolic. *Lucid dreamers could set up experiments to require a non-symbolic response, such as yes, no, a number, a letter, and so on. Then the response is both specific and basically literal.*

3. The supposed precognitive information is actually subtle cues, subliminally sensed information, a type of anticipatory guesswork or self-fulfilling prophecy, and so on. *Lucid dreamers or scientists could devise experiments that exclude these possibilities and point to the dreamer's receipt of nonlocal information outside of linear time.*

Conscious in the dream state, we can finally begin to experiment with the true limits of dream awareness.

Possibly the first lucid dreamer to write about apparent precognitive information in a lucid dream is the Dutch psychiatrist, Frederick van Eeden, who coined the term *lucid dreams*. In a paper titled, "A Study of Dreams," van Eeden discussed a lucid dream experience with an apparent forward-looking warning:

In May 1903 I dreamed that I was in a little provincial Dutch town and at once encountered my brother-in-law, who had died some time before. I was absolutely sure that it was he, and I knew that he was dead. He told me that he had much intercourse with my "controller," as he expressed it—my guiding spirit. I was glad, and our conversation was very cordial, more intimate than ever in common life. He told me that a financial catastrophe was impending for me. Somebody was going to rob me of a sum of 10,000 guilders. I said that I understood him, though after waking up I was utterly puzzled by it and could make nothing of it.

As events came to pass, van Eeden discovered that the warning carried apparently valid information. In his report ten years after the lucid dream, he continues:

I wish to point out that this was the only prediction I ever received in a lucid dream in such an impressive way. And it came only too true, with this difference, that the sum I lost was twenty times greater. At the time of the dream there seemed not to be the slightest probability of such a catastrophe. I was not even in possession of the money I lost afterwards. Yet it was just the time when the first events took place—the railway strikes of 1903—that led up to my financial ruin.[1]

As with many a lucid dreamer's first experience with forward-looking information, van Eeden did not seek out the information;

instead it came to him. Conscious in the dream state, van Eeden sees the dream figure of his deceased brother-in-law, who suggests that van Eeden's "guiding spirit" had mentioned an impending "financial catastrophe." With hindsight, van Eeden sees that the time of the lucid dream, May 1903, coincided with the "first events" that would ultimately lead to the financial loss.

Warning dreams appear throughout history. Whether symbolized in the words or actions of deceased loved ones, the gods, or some perplexing dream symbol, the dream's emotional impact haunts the dreamer. The book of Genesis 41:14–36 contains a classic warning dream. There, the Egyptian pharaoh has a troubling dream of seven fat cattle, followed by seven thin cattle. Dissatisfied with his counsel's interpretation, he turns to Joseph, who interprets the dream to mean seven years of abundant food will be followed by seven years of famine. Feeling the interpretation's correctness, the pharaoh makes appropriate plans and prepares to store extra food stocks in the good years.

Crucial to warning dreams is the issue of proper interpretation. Though van Eeden clearly received a financial warning, the exact nature remained unclear to him. Lucid dreamers should investigate such warnings and try to interpret the offered advice properly.

A similar warning lucid dream occurred to a professor friend of mine, who sent it for publication in *The Lucid Dream Exchange*:

> I am outside by a building with others near me when I realize this is a dream. I decide to fly . . . I fly quickly to several hundred feet and I repeat three times, "I seek my highest." I remember this was my goal when I become lucid. After flying upward, I'm somewhat surprised by running into a ceiling and I remember that sometimes this happens when I fly upward in dreams. I try to push my body through the wall near the roofline and it morphs a bit into the wall, but I can't go through easily, so I go back . . .
>
> I see a very tall house with no side wall—so I can see a woman on the top floor doing something. I fly over to her and see she is using two large smudge sticks. She lights one and tells me to use it. I realize that I had been incorrect when I thought she was Asian and that she's really Native American. The smudge stick is mostly out and not smoking very much. Her child is here. I know that I've been at other smudge ceremonies, but that I don't really believe in this cause-and-effect view of smudging. [Smudging is often used as a means to clean or purify negative energy.] She says something about food or what she or I am eating. I say that I believe that what you "think" about what you eat is much more important than what you actually eat. I feel very confident

about my experiential understanding of this comment . . . Suddenly, I mostly lose lucidity when I see a man across the hall . . .[2]

Flying in his lucid dream, he "seeks the highest" but strangely hits an invisible ceiling. Noticing a Native American woman, he consciously decides to fly over to investigate. There, the woman lights a smudge stick for him (a symbol of cleansing or purifying) and encourages him to consider his diet. The lucid dreamer disagrees with the woman, stating his view that belief about diet seems more important. A nearby event distracts the lucid dreamer, who soon wakens.

Reading this exchange, I felt extremely concerned for the lucid dreamer and almost called him on the phone to encourage him to take this warning seriously. Seeing that his lucid attempt to seek "the highest" resulted in meeting a Native American woman suggested a detour of considerable importance. When she offers him a smudge stick and mentions a proper diet, I noticed my friend seemed to ignore her advice. I recall saying a silent prayer for him that something "constructive" would occur.

When I met my friend later in the year at an IASD conference, I asked about his health. He looked at me with a curious expression, "Why do you ask?" I explained that it was because of the lucid dream of the Native American woman. He expressed complete surprise, since he had not discerned the health warning that I sensed in the lucid dream.

About six months after the lucid dream, he had an extremely painful digestive problem late at night, so severe that he began to feel that he actually might die. As he stumbled around his rural home in extreme abdominal pain, he spotted a publication about the Cascara tree, which Native Americans used as a purgative. Seeing this as his only hope, he hobbled outside in the dark and rain until he found the Cascara tree—a relatively rare tree he had once identified on his isolated acreage. Stripping some branches from the young tree, he began to chew them until, finally, they acted to remedy his dire situation.

After telling me the story, he marveled that I saw an actual warning in his lucid dream, which he totally ignored and resisted. But as he repeated again that he truly felt that he might die that night, suddenly the intertwined symbolic connection between the Native American woman, her comments, and the natural remedy became clear to him.

Jung notes that the unconscious seems to possess an anticipatory knowledge of certain events: "Thus, dreams may sometimes announce certain situations long before they actually happen. This is not necessarily a miracle or a form of precognition. Many crises in our lives have a long unconscious history. We move toward them step by step, unaware of the dangers that are accumulating. But what we consciously fail to see is frequently perceived by our unconscious, which can pass the information on through dreams."[3]

Even though in lucid dreams we receive the anticipatory information with more conscious awareness than in regular dreams, we may not perceive it as such or can refuse to hear it, deny it or misunderstand. What lessons in lucidity could one take from this? Three come to mind:

1. If a positive-seeming dream figure delivers a warning to you, seriously consider heeding it. By positive-seeming, I mean dream figures for whom you have a personal and positive regard.

2. If you feel confused by the symbolism or fail to understand the message, seek to have a clarifying lucid dream in which you actively search for more information about the possible warning and possible steps to avoid it.

3. If you have few or rare lucid dreams, then before going to sleep, simply ask for or incubate a dream of clarification in which information about the troubling dream will be made clear to you. Often, this results in a traditional dream that makes evident the issue at hand.

One imagines that had van Eeden more clearly understood or taken the warning seriously, he could have taken action that would have resulted in the events not happening. Similarly, my friend who needed the purgative may have subconsciously aided himself by placing the publication about the Cascara tree's medicinal quality in a place he would see it when needed. Warning lucid dreams seem to suggest probable events, not predestined ones.[4]

ACTIVE AND AMBIENT PRECOGNITIVE LUCID DREAMS

Like van Eeden, most lucid dreamers never conceive of the idea of actively obtaining forward-looking information in the lucid dream state. Rather, lucid dreamers seem more likely to notice precognitive information after the fact, either as a warning from a dream figure or simply embedded in the dream space.

In his book, *The Lucid Dream Manifesto*, early lucid dream researcher Daniel Oldis mentions an odd experience of apparently obtaining future information in a lucid dream. Interestingly, he did not intend to discover future information; rather, he simply noticed it in the dream state. Aware in a lucid dream, he writes:

> Decided to walk downtown and see what adventures awaited me in my dream state. I decided to enter a gift shop that I had never been inside of during waking life as it had just recently opened; went in and looked around. On the wall in the back of the store something caught my attention—a sack of a specific type of plastic cowboys and horses that I had played with as a child but had never seen since in any toy shop.
>
> I awoke soon after and forgot about the dream in the days that followed. About a week later, I had occasion to be in the store with a friend, and *upon looking on the back wall noticed a plastic bag of toy cowboys and horses identical to those I had seen in my dream* [emphasis added].

Oldis points out, "This, of course, brought back the memory of the lucid experience and strengthened my interest in the psychic nature of lucidity. . . ." He concludes that the connection between his lucid dream and the later waking event seems to "challenge scientific explanation."[5]

When a lucid dreamer happens upon unknown or future-oriented information without intending it, I consider these "ambient" precognitive lucid dreams. Amazingly, the to-be-discovered information simply happens to exist in the dream space. You amble onto it. You don't seek it out so much as simply note it. The future information occupies "the space."

My realization that some lucid dream experiences appear to contain future information occurred much like Oldis's. I had the lucid dream and later visited the location of the dream event while waking, only to discover that the waking location had now changed and existed as I had lucidly dreamt! Here are my two examples of ambient lucid precognitive dreams. The first occurred to me in a dream in which I was being chased by gangsters in a car in my old hometown. When I passed 17th and Plum, I drove behind the old Vickers gas station to hide, but became lucid when I saw a large car wash there. In waking physical reality, there was no car wash there—at least at that time. Probably five years later, a car wash was built in the exact location as in my lucid dream. Since I had not lived in that town for almost a decade, I felt shocked when I saw the car wash in the same spot as my earlier lucid dream.

My second ambient lucid precognitive dream occurred, again, in my old hometown. In the dream, I rode with my father and oldest brother in a small station wagon, when it dawned on me that we did not have such a car. With that realization, I became lucid. We stopped in a parking lot of a local Methodist church, where I noticed the parking lot was much too large since, from waking experience, I knew a house sat on the exact spot where we had parked. Years later, when I passed this church again, I saw that the church had torn down the adjacent house and expanded the church's parking lot to include that very spot! The parking lot looked exactly like my memory from this lucid dream.

An interesting aspect of both of these dreams, as well as that of Oldis, is the "information" exists literally. The toy soldiers, the car wash, and the parking lot all appear as later seen. Unlike most precognitive dreams that rely on symbolism (the pharaoh's fat and thin cattle, for example), these ambient precognitive lucid dreams seem noteworthy for their direct relation to the later materialization.

Some have suggested that the landscape may contain the energy pattern of past and future events. Since lucid dreaming often results in the lucid dreamer existing in a mental model of an actual waking environment, one can wonder if these ambient lucid dreams provide hints of probable-world models that preexist their physical manifestation, along the lines of Rupert Sheldrake's morphic fields.[6] Does the heightened awareness of lucid dreamers make them more likely to recall the dream environment and later similarities?

From a scientific perspective, some would argue that this unsought, ambient, lucid dream precognitive information suffers from the same "retro-cognitive" or after-the-fact awareness attributed to many reported precognitive dreams. Many critics of apparent precognitive dreams suggest that since the dreamer sees the connection to the dream only after the fact, sometimes, weeks, months, or years later, the dreamer may, knowingly or unknowingly, shape the dream recall to conform to the waking situation. Lucid dreaming, however, offers a means to counteract these criticisms and more thoughtfully approach the age-old question of dream precognition. By seeking out possible future information in the conscious dream state, lucid dreamers can provide prenotifications of the results. That is, they can register a prediction before the event occurs.

Just such a possibility is explored in the book, *Extraordinary Dreams and How to Work with Them*.[7] A long-time lucid dreamer and artist happened to attend a baby shower for a friend who was expecting her first child. At the party, many wondered whether it might be a boy or girl. On the way home from the party, the lucid dreamer thought about this, too, and thought about it again before going to sleep. That night, near the end of a long dream, he dreamt:

> The next thing I became consciously aware of was standing in front of a door covered with a heavy drape. All at once the drape is pulled back and I see Suzanne with her newborn baby. I am now completely lucid and am amazed at the reality of what I see. She holds the baby in her arms and I see that it is a boy with reddish skin. I see the shape of the face and the color of the eyes. I look at him exactly as I would if I were going to try and remember each detail for a painting.[8]

Feeling the lucid dream might be precognitive, the lucid dreamer woke and "decided to type out his dream, date it, and seal it in an envelope." Weeks later, he learned Suzanne had delivered a healthy baby boy. When the lucid dreamer visits her with the sealed envelope, he discovers: "The experience was like a déjà vu. I walked into a darkened room, just as I had in the dream. Suzanne was sitting in the same position holding the boy and he was exactly the same person I had seen in the dream, even the shape of his head and color of skin. Suzanne read what I had written and agreed that it described her baby."[9]

Besides correctly identifying the baby's sex, the lucid dreamer noted in his written record many additional details of the baby's features such as skin color, head shape, and eye color. Also, the lucid dream included many details of the setting where he ultimately saw the mother and child for the first time—the darkened room and the mother's position, for example. And finally, note how the lucid dreamer becomes curious about the sex of the expected baby and then that night dreams lucidly about it. Curiosity shows up repeatedly as a precursor to lucid dreams. When we become curious, we seem to engage inner forces of intent that focus on the subject of our curiosity and may assist us in becoming lucidly aware.

When we explore consciously for unknown, future-oriented information, lucid dreaming's revolutionary potential to toss aside the constraints of linear time becomes apparent. If we can use that potential to engage the dream actively for forward-looking information, we demonstrate the malleable nature of time and the apparent time-less aspects of the dreaming dimension in which the inner awareness resides.

ACTIVELY SEEKING FUTURE INFORMATION

The first time I tried to have a precognitive lucid dream came in response to a challenge many years ago by Linda Lane Magallón, author of *Mutual Dreaming*. Before receiving the letter containing her challenge, the idea of seeking forward-looking information in a lucid dream had never occurred to me. I decided to give it a try. Curious myself, I had to wonder, "Could a lucid dreamer actively receive precognitive information?"

That weekend, I became lucidly aware (August 1994):

> I find myself in something like a big stage area for a band with a dance floor. There are instruments all around, a drummer behind his drums, chairs, etc. I think, "What should I do? Should I send energy to people I know?" No, I decide, that doesn't interest me. Then I recall, Linda wants people to precognate in dreams. But as I consider it—I can't think of how to precognate! It seems absurd. I begin to think, "How am I supposed to precognate when I am cognating now (in this dream)?"

When I woke, a bit upset at this miniphilosophical crisis, it quickly became evident that I needed to project the precognitive information outward from myself as if from another source. For example, when lucid, I might ask a dream figure for the information or intend to discover it when I open the door to a room. By intending to discover the information "out there" or "apart from me" in the lucid dream, I could then realize the response.

As far back as 1986, Ed Kellogg wrote in the *Dream Network Bulletin* about developing a method he calls the Lucid Dream Information Technique (LDIT), which would be useful for finding answers to all types of questions. In the following lucid dream, Ed performs the basic technique:

> In a lucid dream I demonstrate an incubation technique using a silver bowl to a group of other dreamers. Basically the technique consisted of the following. First the lucid dreamer decides on a question, in which he or she asks for the information most needed at the present time. After deciding on a specific question, the dreamer inverts the silver bowl and consciously focuses on the question. After waiting a few seconds for the answer to materialize, the dreamer then turns over the bowl to find a materialized note with the answer written on it.
>
> For myself I asked for a message from an official in a government agency about the possibilities of future research grants, and received

the answer, "Goodbye!" which I clearly understood meant that I would receive no further funding from this agency (note: which incidentally, has proved quite true).[10]

When lucid, one might use this technique "as an oracle of one's unconscious information," Ed suggests. In an updated commentary, he calls the technique "a dreamtime search engine to successfully access information of all kinds."[11]

In his own experience, Ed found the resulting information "of a very high quality." However, like the oracles of Ancient Greece, the information provided in response to his lucid request did not always seem exceptionally clear or useful. "In one case, where I had requested investment information, I got my answer on a clay tablet in what looked like cuneiform!" he reports. Sometimes his students would use the technique but not understand the symbolic answer and ask Ed for help. "I told them to get the meaning from their own unconscious that materialized the answer, and not to ask me!" he says.

Ed concludes: "The essential principle behind this technique involves first finding a medium for the materialization of the answer (such as a bowl, or closed drawer) asking the question, waiting a few seconds, and then reading the materialized answer (after turning over the bowl, or opening the drawer, etc.). I have found it most important to pick an appropriate medium in each dream for the LDIT [response]. . ."[12]

The issue of "an appropriate medium" in the lucid dream is significant. In the earlier example of the college student who lucidly sought the young woman's odd freckle on her back, she (or a dream figure representation) appeared in the lucid dream, turned around, and showed the lucid dreamer the exact place. But what if this same lucid dreamer had become aware, remembered the task to find the freckle's location, yet not seen the young woman? How should he have proceeded? As Ed suggests, he would have to create an appropriate medium for the answer. Perhaps the lucid dreamer would ask a nearby dream figure to show "where" on its body the woman's odd freckle could be found. Or perhaps the lucid dreamer would suggest that a diagram of the body appear on a nearby wall with a mark showing the location of the odd freckle.

The appropriate medium may depend upon the individual lucid dreamer. For example, some lucid dreamers find dream figures differ in their cooperativeness. Dream figures also vary in apparent awareness; one may need to consider the most seemingly aware dream figure. Otherwise, one should seek answers from dream objects (inside a drawer or on a paper in an overturned bowl, for example, as Ed suggested). Or conversely, simply shout out the question to the aware unconscious for a response.

When lucidly experimenting, we must be prepared for an answer's creative expression. Sometimes the answer comes in a simple yes or no form, while other times it may be expressed in a visual or symbolic form. I recall one talented lucid dreamer who yelled a question to her inner awareness; in response, a famous painting appeared in the sky.

Some visual images in dreams may contain common or even universal meanings. For example, as many dreamers have discovered, the telephone often symbolizes a communication medium. Not surprisingly therefore, studies of extrasensory perception (ESP) "cite frequent examples of information that is received over long distances in dreams about receiving a phone call," as Patricia Garfield has noted.[13]

In the following dream-conceived precognitive experiment, I decide to use the telephone as a medium for getting future information:

> While traveling on business in Detroit, I become lucidly aware in the dream. Remembering my interest in obtaining future information, I spontaneously create a precognitive dream task. In the lucid dream, I announce out loud, "When I pick up this telephone in the dream, I will hear from the most important person to talk to me on the next day." Feeling good about this plan and lucidly aware, I pick up the phone, expecting to hear the most important person to talk to me on the next day. Putting the phone to my ear, I hear my wife talking to me very happily. I decide to wake up and write the lucid dream down.

Upon waking, I felt a bit disappointed that I had not thought of a more convincing precognitive task. The next day, as I went to my meetings, made phone calls, and traveled, I considered the lucid dream. That evening, when I called my wife, as is my habit, she announced that she had great news. As I recall, she was offered some exciting task by the university to chair a search committee for a faculty position.

Though the experiment seemed a success in one way—I did hear on the dream phone from the most important person to talk to me during the coming day—from an experimental design perspective it had many flaws. For example, how does one define "most important person"? And when I said "to talk to me," the underlying unspoken intent involved over the telephone instead of face to face; however, I didn't clearly make it part of the experiment.

Experience has taught me the importance of creating an experimental task in advance, while awake. Whenever I devised a wakingly conceived predetermined task, the lucid dream experiment contained structural elements that made for stronger waking world verification. Also, the lucid dream seemed primed to pre-incorporate my intent and provide the proper dream conditions (symbols and setting) conducive to the experiment.

The strength of the lucid dreaming mind (creativity, associations, and so on) is not the strength of the waking mind (logic, reasoning, and so on). When lucid, reasoning may be secondary to other mental processes such as expectation. Essentially, the lucid dreaming mind may need the waking mind to develop convincing experiments suitable for the waking viewpoint. The lucid dreaming mind may not see the need to investigate the malleable nature of time and space (in the same way as the waking mind), especially if the lucid mind takes the malleable nature of time and space for granted.

The following four accounts (the first of which I related earlier) illustrate my actively sought lucid dream attempts to obtain unknown or future information. In some cases, I have changed the identity of those involved for the sake of privacy:

1. As a preface to this lucid dream (May 1996), I had become quite enamored of looking into eyes in the lucid state, a characteristic reported by other lucid dreamers. Even in lucid dreams, eyes seem to have a particularly fascinating and powerful aspect to them.[14]

Lucidly aware in the dream, I see the eye of a friend's child. A bit of a red line floats on the child's eye. Seeing this, I recall that in the waking world this child has a rare but nonvisible physical condition. Lucid and now curious, I go up to the child and ask, "Why do you have this physical condition?" The child succinctly responds in a matter-of-fact tone, "For my mother." This completely shocks me because it's totally unexpected. I decide to wake up and write the lucid dream down. What could that possibly mean—"For my mother"?

I told my wife about this odd lucid dream but otherwise kept it to myself. As it happens, I had a number of dreams about this family. Finally, I had a dream in which a dream voice suggested that I share my series of dreams with them. I woke and, later, over dinner with them, asked them if it would be okay to share my many dreams with them. They happily agreed.

I had made a list of the dreams beforehand and started to tell them about them. They enjoyed the series of dreams about themselves, making comments like, "Oh, you don't know this about me, but I used to dress just like that," until, finally, I came to the lucid dream in which

I asked their child about the medical condition. I told the dream and how I asked, "Why do you have this condition?" and that the child responded, "For my mother." This was met by stony silence. They didn't seem angry, more stunned than anything, and I quickly went on to the next dream.

Years later, my friend returned to this lucid dream and told me that I had uncovered a family secret. In their family, for many centuries, the women had given birth on occasion to children with this nonvisible physical problem. In some cases, the children had died quickly and suddenly. "I don't know how you came up with that answer," she said, "since nobody knows this family secret. But you were right."

2. In one of three lucid dreams in one night, I eventually had a spontaneous desire to experiment with precognitive lucid dreaming (January 2000):

> I am in our family house, which has big rooms and a sunken living room. As I walk around, I realize, "This isn't our house! This is a dream!" Lucidly, I talk to some of the people there and admire one young woman in particular.
>
> After a while, I see DJ and wonder what to do in this lucid dream. Recalling some precognitive lucid dreams, I step up and ask him, "When I hear from you next, what will be the first words out of your mouth to me?" He looks me square in the face and replies, "Robert, you . . ." I make a mental note to remember that.
>
> Then once again, I have this incredible surge of sound energy within me—like an inner explosion that makes all my cells feel altered and tingle. For a moment, I worry that I am waking up my wife and wonder if my body is flopping around in bed. I wake up tingling and a bit shocked by this sound explosion, since it came unexpectedly.

Nearly five weeks later, the phone rings and my wife answers. She calls out, "Robert, it's DJ." I instantly recall the lucid dream and take the phone. I say "Hello" and DJ responds with "Robert, you are finally there!"—confirming my earlier lucid dream that predicted the first two words as "Robert, you."

Potentially, perhaps, one could monitor hundreds of DJ's common greetings and see if "Robert, you" ever appears on the list. An open-ended response from the pool of verbal possibilities might make this verbal pairing, "Robert, you," a one in one thousand or even rarer combination.

3. In this next lucid dream, I have various lucid dreaming adventures and run into some friends (April 1996):

We go out into a courtyard, where a banquet is going on, and people are sitting about. I start to wonder what interesting thing I could do in my lucid state, and I think I should ask someone to predict something. I see JD sitting by the door and ask him some questions. I ask, "A year from now, where will you be living?" He calmly responds, "In Boston" (which is where he is living at the time of the dream). Then recalling his apparently serious relationship, I ask, "A year from now, will you be married?" Again, he calmly responds, "No." At this point, I realize that another JD has appeared, sitting about five feet away from the first one, and he's looking at me skeptically. I wonder about two images of the same person and decide to wake.

Though this experiment required that I wait a year, the responses given to both lucid dream questions were eventually confirmed as correct. At the time of the lucid dream, JD had already told me of plans to move to a new city but ultimately did not. Also his serious relationship did not lead to marriage, confirming the other question's response.

The appearance of the second JD surprised me and made me wonder if the second dream figure was the person's telepathic response to his or her subconscious awareness or concern regarding my questions. Looking back, I wish I had had the presence of mind to ask the second figure, "Who are you? What do you represent?" and listen for the response.

4. After writing about these experiences for *The Lucid Dream Exchange*, a reader called me and asked if I had ever tried to dream lucidly of lottery numbers. I had to admit that I had never even considered such a thing. The caller then told me that he had attempted this. I asked what happened. As I recall, he said that he had gained lucidity and recalled his task to get all six pairs of numbers for the Big Lotto. He looked around and decided for the numbers to appear before him. He then began to see pairs of numbers appear on a white notepad. Quickly he tried to remember them all and felt that he had succeeded. He decided to awaken before he forgot them. The caller told me that remembering six pairs of numbers exactly from the lucid dream state to the waking state was harder than anticipated. Upon waking, he quickly wrote down the pairs, but only felt confident about the first three pairs; he was not confident about the final three pairs.

When the Big Lotto numbers appeared in the newspaper, this lucid dreamer reported getting the first three pairs exactly right. In the final three sets, he had recalled various numbers, but not the proper combination of pairs. It simply seemed too big a task to memorize, and then take from the dreaming state to the waking state, a set of six paired numbers. Because of his success at recalling the first three pairs, however, he felt that it must be possible. He urged me to give it a try but suggested I select a lotto that had fewer numbers. Thinking that all I had to lose was a night's dreaming and a dollar, I decided to attempt to discover precognitively the numbers of the Pick Three lottery game for the upcoming Saturday. Unfortunately, my attempts to find the exact rules of the game (before the lucid dream) failed, so basically all I knew about the game was that it involved the selection of three numbers (May 31, 2000):

> I'm walking along with a radio, listening to something. I seem to be on the sidewalk near my old elementary school. It's nighttime. As I go along, something seems "odd"—I realize that this is a dream. I put my hands out in front of me and run down the sidewalk yelling, "This is a dream, this is a dream!" I can see my hands go out of focus after about five seconds—and I think that I need to be careful not to lose my visuals.
>
> The stars are very bright and seem more numerous than in waking reality. I think about flying up to the stars but don't think it would amount to anything. I put my hands up again and repeat, "This is a dream." I turn right, toward my childhood home, when I see a car with headlights on in our neighbor, Mr. Major's, garage. Even though this looks different than in waking reality, I run over there. The car turns off its headlights.
>
> It occurs to me that I could ask Mr. Major what the Pick Three numbers are for the next lottery, as another lucid dreamer had mentioned as a precognitive test. I can't quite recall the name of the lottery game. As I mentally try to formulate this and prepare to ask the question, I suddenly see a circular item in my hand—like the Wheel of Fortune on the TV show, and in color. I think, "Is this providing the answers?"
>
> Looking down, my vision seems to fall on the only number visible, number 8. I look away, and then back down at the wheel, but this time, I see no numbers, just the wheel—blank. I looked away again and then see an 8. Then finally I see a 1. I think, "Is it 8-3-1?" falsely reasoning that I didn't see a second 8 because that would be repetitious and therefore it must have been a 3. I look again—but the wheel of numbers has changed. For some reason, 831 seems like the number of something familiar (reminding me of an old lock number on a post office box in college that was circular shaped like the wheel). Mr. Major is now out of his car, but he is about 40 years old (instead of the 80-year-old man that I knew) and so is his wife. I can't get greater lucidity, feel a bit frustrated, and decide to wake up.

When I woke up, I felt strongly that 8 was one of the numbers. But I wasn't very pleased with how the numbers showed up one at a time and before I even asked the question formally. Then I realized that in the dream when I thought the "next lottery," I meant that it would be the Saturday weekend lottery. So I felt a bit awkward about the whole thing, since I didn't verbalize my exact intent; rather, the dreaming kept giving me answers as if, somehow, it already knew my intent and the correct answer.

Symbolically, I enjoyed the dreaming's creative insertion of Mr. Major, who lived in my old neighborhood. In waking life, he had the good fortune of discovering oil on his farmland, so I assumed he had considerable wealth even though he lived very modestly. By the time of this dream, I believe that he had passed away a decade earlier.

In any case, that Saturday's Iowa Pick Three lottery numbers were announced: 8-0-8.

Having never played the Pick Three, I hadn't realized that zero was a possible choice. I wondered, too, whether my lucid dreaming mind even considers zero to be a number. Is that why I saw no numbers on the wheel? And to make matters even more confusing, one number—8—showed up twice.

As my dream report shows, I looked at the wheel the first time and saw an 8. Then I saw no numbers, which could possibly be considered zero, or nil, nothing. Also, when lucid, it didn't occur to me that the same number could show up twice, which explains my doubting the number 8's reappearance and deciding 3 seemed more appropriate. A liberal interpretation of the experience might say that I saw an 8 on my first look, "nothing, but the circular wheel"—which also happened to be shaped like a big 0—on my second look, and another 8 on my third look. But because I didn't know the exact rules of the game, I misinterpreted the numbers.

If another lucid dreamer were to try this experiment, my advice would be to go for a simple lottery situation, learn all the rules, and have an exact goal date in mind. Then, after your lucid dream, buy a ticket and before the winning lottery is drawn, send your lucid dream report to a friend or friends for verification purposes. Lucid dreamers should realize that the dream's response may come in a manner that requires interpretation, as it seemed to do in my case. If the lucid dream provides an unclear response, keep your cool and ask the dream for clarification. (If sufficiently lucid, you may have the presence of mind to question the response by announcing to your inner awareness, "Show me this more simply because I don't understand." In most cases, a new response will result with clearer information.) Since any information that needs deciphering can be misinterpreted, be certain of your interpretation.

OTHER DREAM STATES: DREAMS OF CLARITY

As one progresses more deeply into dreaming and lucid dreaming, certain sets of experience distinguish themselves as being unlike typical dreams. In my experience, a type of dream exists in which there's a relative lack of symbolism, action, or movement; instead, the visual field contains perhaps one or two figures or objects in a dark void or expanse but is otherwise empty. This dream setting appears to be a place to communicate precise information or have direct conversations, hence its symbolic sparseness and lack of movement.

In Western dream literature, I have never seen this type of dream mentioned. When reading *The Tibetan Yogas of Dream and Sleep* by Tenzin Wangyal Rinpoche, however, I immediately recognized something that sounded similar.

Tenzin Wangyal Rinpoche, the Buddhist monk from the Bon tradition, suggests that one may experience dreams of clarity, "which arise when the mind and the prana [or vital energy] are balanced and the dreamer has developed the capacity to remain in non-personal presence." Unlike normal dreams where the dreamer gets swept back and forth, "in the dream of clarity the dreamer is stable." And unlike normal dreams, in which the dreamer's interests and habits seem projected onto the dreaming, "[i]n the dream of clarity it is as if something is given to or found by the dreamer. . . ."[15]

In my case, I simply noticed a set of rare dreams in which I existed in the dream state with perhaps one other person or one other object. Otherwise, the visual field was a glistening darkness, like a darkened, empty theater stage. Normally, very little action occurred there; instead, I was shown direct information or I was involved in a conversation with one or more dream figures. The following exemplifies one of my experiences:

> In an expansive empty gray space, I see JA, a postdoctoral student from a foreign country. He tells me that he would like to introduce me to his wife, whom in waking reality I have never met or seen. From behind him, she now steps forward and does a little spin.

I look at her and feel very surprised, since she looks nothing like what I had expected. They both smile at me, and the dream concludes.

A week later at a dinner party, some graduate students tell me that they had finally met JA's wife. I stop them and say, "Before you say anything, I want to tell you what she looks like. I met her in a dream." I begin to describe her, just as I saw her in the strange dream state—her face, her skin tone, her hair, and all the details I could recall. One of the grad students replies that I have obviously met her in the waking state. Another says that she probably weighs 130 pounds, not 125 pounds, as I estimated. The other concludes that this is simply impossible, and I must be making it up.

A month later, I happen to meet this woman at a gathering to hear a new band in town. When I meet her in waking reality, she wears the same dress—same color, same design as in the dream. Also, I recall that in the dream she performs a little spin, and now, with this band playing, I see her spin on the dance floor.

I have had a number of these dreams of simple and clear communications. Normally, I have a feeling of semi-lucidity, because I recognize "Oh, another one of these"; however, sometimes I become fully lucid. One of the oddest experiences of this type involved me and a geometric figure composed of light (May 2003):

> This dream begins in the empty dream space. As I stand in the glistening darkness, I notice something odd to my upper right. There hangs a shaft of glowing light—it seems a hexagonal (six-sided) shaft of intense, pale greenish, glowing light about six to eight inches across and four feet long. Semi-lucid now, I simply know this shaft of light is "precognitive information." Suddenly the shaft of light comes slamming into my right temple. Like a painfully sweet energy being plunged into my mind, it comes pushing deeper and deeper. At this point—*bam, bam, bam, bam*—I experience four or five precognitive dreams, seemingly in microseconds.

I wake and begin to write them down as fast as possible. The first involves a professor friend who had moved away. She tells me about the man she plans to marry. The second involves a brief, interesting encounter at a shop with a rarely seen acquaintance. And the third involves talking to someone unusual while kids play in the background. By the time I recalled the third dream, the additional dreams had faded. The dreams entered my mind in microseconds, yet each took several minutes to write down.

In the morning, I told my wife about this odd shaft of light containing precognitive information slamming into my right temple and how it seemed our longtime friend had an upcoming marriage. I mentioned what I had learned about the man she planned to wed. Still, I had to wonder what this all meant.

About three months later, I found out.

On an ordinary day in the middle of the afternoon, all three dreams played out in the course of about twenty minutes. The sequence began as I walked out of the grocery store, saw the "rarely seen acquaintance" from the second dream, and felt the same feelings as in the dream. A bit of dream déjà vu, I mused to myself. After driving home, I pulled the mail from the mailbox and then responded to a business phone call from an unusual person as kids played in the background, a virtual replay of the third dream. Now, that's odd! As I looked through the mail, I opened a letter from our professor friend, telling us of her marriage plans with many of the same details from my first dream. Incredible!

When I realized the dream series had suddenly all come to pass, my mind reeled. How could three seemingly unrelated dream events come packaged in a shaft of light and then all come to pass months later within a twenty-minute period?

As I watched the dreaming realm overlie the waking realm, or perhaps the waking copy the dreaming, I began to wonder about this distinct dream state—dreams of clarity—in which information is presented more directly and without symbolic overlay. It seems as we go deeper into dreaming and lucid dreaming, we discover distinct levels or layers of subconscious awareness. With greater depth comes greater clarity.

SOME SUGGESTIONS FOR ACTIVELY SEEKING UNKNOWN INFORMATION

Some lucid dreamers may have the desire to experiment with obtaining unknown or future-oriented information in the lucid dreaming state. Although I encourage such efforts, I wish to reiterate three points. First, remember the probabilistic nature of future events. I don't believe future events are predestined; they may, however, exist in a range of higher probability. Second, prepare your experiments in the waking state. And third, keep in mind the interpretation effect. As the person experiencing and interpreting the dream's response, your interpretation is an important part of the equation; so while the information may be correct, your interpretation may not be. It may be best to see the results of your experiment on a continuum of accuracy. Why? Because some experiments will lead to yes or no answers, and you either get it right or you don't, but others will be less clear-cut. Let's say, for example, you ask in the lucid dream, "What kind of car will Ashley's parents get her for graduating from college?" and suddenly you see a white Mustang convertible. Months later, without telling Ashley, it comes to pass that she gets a car from her parents (just as she expected), but it's a blue Mustang, and it's not a convertible, it's a hardtop (though Ashley tells you they thought about getting her a convertible). What then? Was this an experimental success or a failure? Using a continuum of accuracy, you can assess the lucid dream information to the actual event better.

Because lucid dreaming allows the conscious dreamer to actively seek a specific goal or task, it is valuable for scientific precognitive experimentation. Lucid dreaming allows for "before the fact" reports and information with less overt symbolic content. Though the nature of reality might be inherently probabilistic, lucid dreaming provides a means to explore this and thus provide a huge leap forward for scientific investigation.

In dreams, the nature of time seems much looser; people and objects from your past, present, and possible future intermingle in an associative mélange. In dreams, time seems naturally nonlinear. Could that be because time *is* naturally nonlinear? Or is that simply the nature of dreams? Lucid, you can investigate the truer reality of "time" in the dream state.

For those who wish to try your own personal experiments, I offer a few suggestions:

1. Agree to be completely honest with yourself about the lucid event and the results.

2. Treat the experiment with sincere curiosity. Open up to it. Avoid making this dead serious work because, in the mentally responsive environment of lucid dreaming, it can become too charged with emotion or mental heaviness.

3. Make specific notes upon waking and avoid making assumptions. It seems better to describe the dream figure, "a fifty-ish, slender woman in a blue dress," rather than conclude it was "Aunt Jo," unless you know with certainty it was a specific person.[16]

4. Prepare a thoughtful experimental task before lucid dreaming. First timers would be best not to compose a complex experiment or one that involves a lot of memorization. Also, don't compose one that may require years to come about or has poorly defined terms such as "Dream, tell me, who will be the next person in my family to become seriously ill?" (What do you mean by "seriously"?)

5. If working with a partner to seek some secret about the partner, make sure that they are willing to give you an honest answer. Some people will simply refuse to confirm (or deny) the veracity of hidden information.

6. If you seem to have a predisposition to certain types of predictions, construct your experiment around that. You may have an easier time working with things that interest you than with something seen as impersonal and uninteresting.

7. Develop a track record before betting on conclusions. If your first experiment comes to pass, avoid the assumption that all future ones will be equally correct. Wait until you have a history of experimental results before calculating your overall level of accuracy. Many results are validated by comparing their accuracy to chance.

8. Realize that carrying information from the lucid dreaming state to the waking state can be problematic. You may experience, among other things, a false awakening, memory overload, errant assumptions, or symbolic misinterpretations. With practice, you will develop techniques that assist you in perfecting these experiments.

16

MUTUAL LUCID DREAMING

MUTUAL DREAMING, THAT IS, DREAMS IN WHICH TWO OR MORE PEOPLE share the same dream, remains a fascinating yet profoundly disturbing idea. Fascinating in its implications, disturbing in that it invalidates the idea that dreaming is an exclusively private activity. Mutual dreaming indicates that some dreams may possess elements of a consensus reality. In effect, any evidence for mutual dreaming advances the idea of the dream state as an alternate reality, albeit a mental one.

Though rare, some dreamers have claimed to have experienced this phenomenon. Linda Lane Magallón, in her book *Mutual Dreaming*, includes this account from a lucid dreamer who requested to remain anonymous:

> In the spring of 1978, I was attending a small Midwestern college. I was friends with a group of five young women who occupied a dormitory suite at the other end of our co-ed dorm. We were friends only, and I never felt any romantic interest in any of them.
>
> One night I dreamt that I was in their suite, and I went from room to room and made love to each one. It wasn't passionate/lustful lovemaking; it was more like sharing a soulful experience, and communicating with each other our deepest thoughts and emotions.
>
> In fact, I clearly remember one of the women of the dream telling me how extremely unlovable she felt, while I reassured her. Later, I learned that this woman had a very unhappy home life.
>
> The next day I remembered the dream because it was so vivid. As I was walking to class that afternoon, someone in the dorm came up

to me and said, "Hey, I heard you were quite a Romeo last night." I asked her what she meant by that. Then she told me that Nadine and Sheila both dreamt that I made love to them in their dorm rooms the night before. I was amazed! Three of us apparently recalled the same dream incident!

I was too shy to talk to them about it, and I was also concerned that they would interpret the dream on a physical level, instead of the deep emotional level that it was to me. Now I wish I had talked to them and gotten the details of their dream experience.[1]

Normally, I might doubt a story like this. After all, it was submitted anonymously and, therefore, the person may have simply made it up. In this case, however, I have reason to believe the account. You see, I was the author. Yes, it happened to me as a college sophomore. I submitted the story and asked for anonymity, more out of embarrassment than anything else.

Even now, I remember my friend shouting across campus, "Hey Romeo!" At first, I didn't get it and asked "What?" Then I proceeded to hear how I had been quite a Romeo the night before in the dream world. If it hadn't involved sex, I likely would have been able to talk to the others involved—but since it did, it felt far too embarrassing to bring up—even though I saw it as a symbolic event. Most touching for me was the young woman who felt so unloved. In waking reality, she was the one always dressed to the nines with perfect makeup, but in the clarity of dreaming, I sensed her secret despair in feeling completely unlovable. I just couldn't face trying to talk to these young women about this mutual dream experience.

Underlying my reticence was the larger issue of discovering real consensus in a dream event. After all, science and society say that our dreams are mere symbolic reflections within our private minds. Yet here, three people were agreeing about an event that occurred in the privacy of three separate, individual minds. How could I counter society's belief and suggest to them that we were evidence of private minds meeting in the dream state?

MEETING DREAMS AND MESHING DREAMS

In *Mutual Dreaming*, Linda Lane Magallón proposes that mutual dream reports often come in two forms: meeting dreams and meshing dreams. Meeting dreams involve a "personal recognition and interrelationship in a shared dream space,"[2] meaning both dreamers (or three in the preceding case) report seeing each other and agree upon elements of the dream space environment. In meshing dreams, the focus moves to "information interchange," when both dreamers become aware of the same basic information. In their dream reports, they may not see the other dreamer, but their dreams express a very similar idea, emotion, symbol, or event. [3]

An example of a meshing mutual dream happened to my niece and me. We both dreamt that her recently deceased grandfather (my deceased father) wanted us to get something out of the closet. In my dreams, I understood the item to be in one of his suit coat pockets there. After realizing that we had both dreamt the same request, I assumed the dream had a literal meaning and called my mother. At first, she feared that she had given my father's clothes to charity, but then recalled that a couple of suits had been saved. When she checked the suit coat pockets, she was shocked to discover meaningful family photos that my father had placed in one pocket. In this example, my niece and I didn't see the other in the dream state, but we had the same basic information and experience, the information meshed and proved true.

Lucid dreamers have recounted a number of likely mutual encounters in the dream state. Sometimes by design, sometimes by happenstance, and sometimes by deep longing intent, mutual dreaming occurs, as we see in this story by an experienced lucid dreamer, artist, and professor, Fariba Bogzaran, as recounted in *Extraordinary Dreams and How to Work with Them:*

> In her exploration in lucid dreaming, Bogzaran constantly incubated lucid dreams of being in her home country and visiting an old friend whom she had not seen for eighteen years. One night she had the following lucid dream:
>
> "I am walking in my old neighborhood where I grew up. Suddenly I ask myself, 'How did I get here?' I do not remember taking a plane. At that point I become lucid. I continue walking and have a strong intention to see Yalda my old childhood friend (she has moved and I have never been in her new house). I find the street where she lives and walk towards her house. The color of the door is pale blue. I ring the bell and she opens the door. I am overjoyed to see her. We cry and hug each other with overwhelming emotion. Embracing her feels absolutely real. The intensity of the experience wakes me up."
>
> Bogzaran recorded the dream and in the morning she wrote her friend a letter enclosing the dream. In her letter, she detailed what she saw in her dream and described the location of her friend's new house. A week later she received a letter from her friend. In this letter,

dated the day after the dream, her friend described the same dream. In Yalda's dream, Bogzaran came back home for a visit. Her friend described the same scene that Bogzaran had experienced, where Bogzaran knocked at the door and Yalda opened the door. Surprised to see each other, they embraced with great excitement. At that moment Yalda also became lucid in her dream."[4]

The criss-crossing letters of two friends separated by thousands of miles and many long years provides clear evidence that this mutual lucid dream touched both of them deeply. Thankfully, each took the time, independently of each other, to write about the dream, the similar dream setting, and the events. A rare blend of deep interest and focused intent may have propelled this reunion experience into the inner space of lucid dreaming.

Another fascinating example of an apparent mutual lucid dream occurred to Dale Graff, a former director of project STARGATE, the government program that investigated remote viewing phenomena. From my association with Dale, I know he has a deep interest in dreaming and uses dreaming as a targeted means to collect unknown, verifiable information.

In his book *River Dreams: The Case of the Missing General and Other Adventures in Psychic Research*, Dale relates a story of working with a woman named Diane on their first long-distance remote viewing project. In the course of the experimental process, Diane reports "a crazy dream" in which she becomes lucidly aware on a Saturday night. Remembering that he had a lucid dream on the same night, Dale asks for the details. Diane pulls out her typewritten sheet with her lucid dream:

> Suddenly I am aware that I am high in the sky! Nothing is holding me up and I begin falling toward the ground. I look down and see a huge mountain. I can see gullies and slopes. I look up and see something like a parachute, but I am not attached to it. The parachute has many colors. Someone else is nearby, but I cannot see who it is. Then I am falling faster and see the mountain approaching. I stop the dream.[5]

Transfixed by her account, Dale provides his lucid dream from the same night:

> I am in a large airplane that is open at the back. I walk toward the opening and fall out. As I am falling toward the ground, I clearly see a mountain below that is sparsely covered with small trees. I look above and see a large multicolored shape that looks like a parachute.

Someone is nearby, also falling, but I do not recognize the person. I continue falling. The mountain zooms toward me. I know I am dreaming and decide to leave the dream. [6]

Though unplanned, Diane and Dale both report remarkably similar lucid dreams on the same night with a high level of corresponding details. While the lucid dreamers don't actually identify the other person as they fall toward the mountains, they both remark that someone seems to be falling with them.

With the enhanced awareness of lucid dreaming, tantalizing possibilities for mutual dream exploration arise. Two or more lucid dreamers should be able to connect consciously in the dream state, notice similar dream environments, exchange information, and reemerge into waking life with the information intact. Although challenges exist on various levels, it certainly appears that mutual lucid dreaming has occurred.

DUAL-PERSON-LUCID AND ONE-PERSON-LUCID MUTUAL DREAMS

Lucid mutual dreams come in two forms: dual-person-lucid dreams and one-person-lucid dreams. A dual-person-lucid mutual dream occurs when both parties achieve lucid awareness and meet in the dream state. The example by Bogzaran of lucidly seeking her friend, meeting her, and then the friend becoming lucid shows dual-person-lucid awareness in a common dream environment. Both parties achieved lucid awareness together in the dream state.

A one-person-lucid mutual dream occurs when a lucid dreamer interacts with a non-lucid dreamer in the dream state and then both report a very similar meeting or meshing experience. Normally, the lucid dreamer provides a much more descriptive and active dream report than the non-lucid dreamer.

I played the role of the non-lucid dreamer, meeting up with a lucid Ed Kellogg in the dream state in a mutual dream in July 1998. In my dream journal I wrote, "I see a beach scene; it seems like a four-sided rectangular island with a beach and a big sand dune hill. The interior is somewhat empty, lagoon-like. Odd." I recall flying down to this island, seeing it from above, and mostly staying on the interior lagoon side.

That same night, about fifteen hundred miles away, a lucidly aware Ed Kellogg dreams:

. . . in a tropical setting, white sandy beach, palm trees, near a clear body of water like a lake or lagoon. I see Robert and suggest that we go swimming. Robert comments that he came back unexpectedly and did not bring any trunks. I tell him he does not need them, as he has not come here physically, but in his dream body. If he wants, he can materialize a pair. I look at [Robert] and see he has already material- ized a pair of light turquoise blue and white patterned trunks, boxer style, with irregular large rounded splotches of color. At this point I really wake up to the fact that I dream also. I assume that he at least seems minimally lucid, although he has a sort of vague look in his eyes, unlike his usual focused and energetic expression. Curious about consensus, I ask him how he sees them—he tells me he wears a pair of black and white patterned trunks, rather than blue and white. I look at him again, and now he has on a pair of bright turquoise blue Speedo style. . . . I feel annoyed that this possible lucid mutual dream follows so closely on the one two days ago, when I have still not set up a detailed protocol [for our formal experiments]. Still, I've done the best I could with this, carefully noting details and exchanging code words. Nevertheless, in a fit of pique I go over to a wall/rock and punch a hole through it, rock dust flies everywhere.[7]

The next day Ed emailed me to ask that I send my dreams to a fair witness (impartial person) while he does the same. After I sent my dream report, Ed revealed his lucid dream to me. As questions for greater de- scriptive detail went back and forth, I suggested that we simply draw our individually recalled scene, thinking a picture would be worth a thousand words. Here are the results:

As you can see, both environments share common elements—col- ors, objects, and shapes—suggesting a mutual dream definitely oc- curred. But although we experienced a strikingly similar environment, my lack of awareness allowed me to recall only: 1) the environment, and 2) my basic actions. Lucidly aware, however, Ed was able to recall: 1) the environment, 2) his actions, 3) many of my actions, including a match for my movements in the dream, 4) my demeanor and lack of lucid awareness, 5) his thoughts, and 6) his emotions. The variations in our accounts illustrate how the lucid dreamer plays with a full deck, while the non-lucid dreamer can barely hold his cards.

Often, lucid dreamers feel frustrated by the non-lucid person's poor recollection of dream details that could verify the mutual encounter. Many discover their non-lucid friend or associate's dream recall may pro- duce nothing, or just a few basic details. Sometimes as the lucid dreamer begins to describe what took place, the non-lucid dreamer's memory

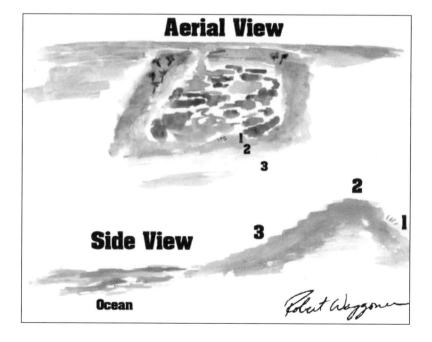

returns, and they blurt out just-remembered details that the lucid dreamer has yet to mention. Very rarely does the non-lucid dreamer recognize definitively the lucid dreamer's presence or involvement. At best, the non-lucid dreamer may recall "someone else" in the dream environment and provide a basic description of gender, height, and hair color.

In such a situation, questioning the non-lucid dreamer about *unstated* elements can help to bring up details. Was it daytime or nighttime? Indoors or outdoors? How many people approximately? What colors were prominent? Can you describe the landscape? Any actions or feelings? As a result, the non-lucid person may recall more than originally thought and thereby verify many aspects of a lucid experience.

Ed once phoned and questioned me about my dreams of the previous night. As I recounted them, he focused in on one dream in particular. As we discovered the basic corresponding elements, he began to identify the people's gender and seating placement at the table I sat at in the dream. "How do you know that?" I asked in surprise. He quietly replied, "Because I sat to your left, lucidly aware."

DUAL LUCID MUTUAL DREAMS

Dual-person-lucid mutual dreams, those in which two lucid dreamers share the dream space, are relatively rare in dream reports. This doesn't seem surprising inasmuch as lucid dreaming occurs much less frequently than regular dreaming and, thus, the statistical probability of both you and a friend being lucid on the same night becomes less likely. Add to that the idea of you and your friend both being lucid *in the same dream space* on the same night, and you can see the inherent rarity of dual lucid mutual dreams.

In my research, I have uncovered only a handful of dual-person-lucid mutual dream reports. Here, once again, I rely on Ed Kellogg because he is one of the few lucid dreamers to investigate mutual lucid dreaming seriously. In the following lengthy excerpts, all taken from Ed's paper, "Mutual Lucid Dream Event,"[8] and used by his permission, Ed describes his and and his friend Harvey Grady's mutual dream experience and discusses the complex, practical, and theoretical issues involved in mutual dream interactions and reporting.

Ed Kellogg's dream of December 10, 1994:

In a sort of archeological dig—in Mexico—I see people digging for gold, peasants, in a sandy Sonoran type desert. We find huge old wagons on the side of the road, from a circus or something, which had bones of elephants and/or lions, etc. I go with the group—realize that I dream, but don't know if they realize it—a sort of virtual reality field trip. I talk with the leaders and they respond. I see [Harvey Grady], and tell him to give me a collect call on waking up to WPR (waking physical reality), if he recalls this dream, and to let me know if he really does participate in a WPR tour at this time. [Harvey] looks like he just shaved off his beard. He shows me some old airplanes in a museum, and I look forward to virtually flying them, although I wonder what would happen to my physical body if I crash . . . (my lucid dream continues, but I leave [Harvey] behind).

[Ed comments:] I finally talked with him on the phone, carefully avoiding questions that might "lead the witness." Harvey gave me a brief account of his dream. . . . At this point I confirmed that his dream seemed very similar to mine, and asked if he had participated in an archeological expedition (the only detail I shared from my dream), and he said he did not recall this. I asked him to *please* write the dream down in detail, which he finally did on Feb. 11, 1995.

Harvey Grady's Lucid Dream, February 11, 1995:

I remember Ed and three or four other men, whom I knew in the dream but not in daytime, talking about an expedition to explore for probable archeological records, then traveling to an arid desert area with desiccated hills and twisted arroyos, where we split up to search the surface soil for possible artifacts. We also watched for caves. We were dressed appropriately with hats for shade, a little reminiscent of Indiana Jones.

The land in the dream was similar to Israel hill country, or arid portions of Arizona, Nevada, or New Mexico. We were searching for ancient artifacts, like [from] Atlantis or Mu. I recognized that the dream dealt only with one part of an ongoing series of the search for evidence of ancient civilizations.

In the dream, I felt that we were going through the motions of the search in the astral plane in order to establish energetic templates for the persons who would conduct the search on the physical plane. The energetic templates created from our experiences would guide the search of some physical explorers. Therefore, we went through the motions of the search like actors playing out roles, in order to generate thoughts, emotions, and desires for the template . . . This double level of awareness made the dream more interesting to me.

Ed's analysis:

Our dreams display a number of interesting congruencies:

1. Harvey and I appeared in each other's dreams (on the same night, at about the same time).

2. We dealt with multiple levels of awareness in ourselves, including lucidity.

3. Desert locale.

4. An organized group effort of a small group of men.

5. We both saw the dream as a "rehearsal" for a physical reality event.

6. Bones or other evidence of ancient existence.

7. Digging or searching for something hidden in the earth.

Of course, aside from the similarities, many differences also exist in the two dream reports. In my experience, the dreamscape functions like a sort of Rorschach, in which dreamers selectively notice, perceive, and idiosyncratically identify some elements while ignoring others. Selective, or fragmentary, recall of the dreams afterwards further compounds the difficulties involved in making valid comparisons. Given the inconsistent nature of human observation documented in accident reports, one can no more expect an exact agreement in description for two participants in a dream event than one could expect it for a physical event which involves far fewer confounding variables. This makes the similarities shown in the two dream reports even more significant. Also, although Harvey had not shaved his beard physically, I wonder whether he in this case dreamed of himself as clean-shaven like Indiana Jones. The appearance of my dream body often differs markedly from my physical body.

Ed reports that realizing "the possibility of contamination of one dream account with the other," he intentionally "tried to keep such contamination to a minimum, by withholding details from [his] dream until [he] had heard them independently from Harvey." Further he notes that "our appearance in dreams can differ markedly from our physical appearance, [and thus] makes a confusing situation even more confusing. In the physical world we habitually use appearance to determine identity. In the dream world this habit serves us poorly, as one's appearance can change, from moment to moment, and from dream to dream."

Moreover, "the dreaming mind often shows very poor discrimination by identifying unfamiliar dream people, or things, with familiar and somewhat similar physical reality counterparts." He explains:

In 1974, I had a lucid dream that led to my personal discovery of this tendency, which I called "the substitution phenomenon." Lucid dreamers have experienced at least one blatant example of the "substitution phenomenon," when they realized while dreaming that they had mistakenly identified (substituted) dream reality as physical reality. But the discovery of this misidentification only begins the process of unmasking the pervasive nature of "substitution phenomena" in even the most lucid of dreams.

For example, I dream of my brother, but when I wake up to a more critical awareness in a lucid dream, I usually find that my dream [brother] does not really look like, or "feel" like, my physical reality brother, and I encounter instead a substitute whom I had misidentified as my brother in the dream. Similarly, I often dream of my home, yet on attaining lucidity I notice that my dream [home] differs in many ways from my physical home. . . . My dreaming mind seems to take the path of least resistance by identifying unfamiliar people, objects, or locales with familiar ones, quite often fitting square pegs into round holes."

To understand the dream experience better, Ed notes:

In my experience, dreams, like plays, occur on at least three qualitatively different levels. First, the *structural level*, that consists of the stage settings and props, the raw dreamscape before we project meaning onto it. This level makes up the substratum of the dream, dream phenomena *qua* phenomena. Second, the *meaning level*, in which symbols, feelings, and the relationships of the dream characters and objects predominates. And finally, and most superficially, the *labeling level*, where we verbally interpret and identify what happens during a dream.

Written and oral accounts usually focus on describing the *labeling level* of dreams, where we often boil down a multilevel experience into a few simplistic identifications. Many dreamworkers probe deeper and focus on the underlying *meaning level* of the dream. The *structural level* of the dream, the substratum, usually remains either unnoticed or ignored, but it may prove the least idiosyncratic level of them all. As such it may hold the key to providing the best evidence for dream mutuality. For example, although both Harvey and I dreamed of ourselves in almost identical desert dreamscapes, I identified it as Mexico, whereas Harvey first identified it as the Holy Land in Israel. Those who wish to investigate the possibility of mutual dreaming may need to pay more attention to descriptions of the *structural level* of dreams, rather than to the identifications made by the dreamers on the *labeling level*. A similar effect exists in "remote-viewing" experiments, where researchers find that when subjects focus on the structural content of their perceptions, as opposed to the verbal identifications made from that content, that the probability of their achieving a "hit" on a remote-viewing target improves markedly.

AN EXPERIMENT IN INTENTIONAL MUTUAL LUCID DREAMING

In one set of experiments Ed Kellogg, Linda Lane Magallón, and I conducted, we set aside certain nights to become lucidly aware, meet in dreaming, and then pass on a preselected secret word and special gesture, both selected from a list by the toss of dice. In the morning, all dream reports would be first sent to an impartial third party (fair witness) before being shared.

On our first night's attempt, Ed and I came close to a lucid mutual exchange. Because of the length of our lucid dreams, I have selected parts of the dream report (as quoted from the dream reports we sent to the third party) to show certain similarities in progression:

Ed Kellogg	Robert Waggoner
"Seems like New England"	"Feels like Pennsylvania or New England or England"
"Seems like my hometown"	"I am driving through a city"
"I am in a large house"	"I am in a car"
"Outside I see a panel van"	"We drive by a small truck or panel van"
"I see Robert"	"I turn and see Ed"
"It's daytime"	"It's daytime"
"At first he doesn't seem lucid"	"Suddenly I become lucid"
"Robert tells me his code words"	"I look at Ed and say my code word, "Screwdriver! Screwdriver!"
"Robert leaves quickly"	"I feel like the lucid dream is ending"

At this point, three unfortunate things happened. First, I had selected my code word, screwdriver, from the wrong list of code words. So on waking, when Ed looked at the list of possible code words, none of them seemed to match. Stymied, he chose a three-syllable code word that began with S, structurally similar to screwdriver. Second, I lost lucidity before Ed could pass on his code word and gesture. And third, Ed continued in his lucid dream, trying to meet up with Linda; the time and effort involved in doing so made it hard for him to recall exactly what my code word had been upon waking, since in long lucid dreams, most lucid dreamers have difficulty remembering earlier details exactly.

From my list of similarities in the dream report, one can see a number of correspondences that suggest an interaction occurred in a similar environment: general location, time of day, objects, dream figures, feeling/affect, movement, progression of action/events, and verbal exchange.

Throughout our experimental period, many examples of dream telepathy occurred. On one experimental night, Ed lucidly arrived, apparently, in my living room (because his description seemed to match nicely), where I greeted him and made a show of pouring him a glass of red wine, while he passed on his code word and gesture. In the morning, he correctly guessed my code word of "grapes" (from a list of 100 labeled objects, ten of fruit, one of a cluster of red grapes) and noted my lack of lucid awareness. He also noted details of my living room, which he had never seen in waking life.

However, our collective desire for a platinum-quality mutual lucid dream meeting never materialized in these attempts. At times, we came close, with remarkable telepathic hits or one-person-lucid mutual dreams. I believe that experienced lucid dreamers with the proper scientific protocol and circumstance will achieve, eventually, a valid, verifiable dual-lucid mutual lucid dream within the structure of a scientific experiment.

On April 9, 2005, as members of a panel presentation on extraordinary lucid dreams, four lucid dreamers, Lucy Gillis, Ed Kellogg, Beverly D'Urso, and I sought to attempt mutual lucid dreaming. Because of the volume of dream reports, all of which appear in a lengthy article I wrote for *The Lucid Dream Exchange*, titled "Meeting Dreamers in the Dream State: A Lucid Quest," I will present here just a few of the coincidental occurrences.[9]

In my first dream of the night:

> I seem to be at a college like Michigan State, where I seem to be taking two courses, one on "forms" and one on "philosophy." After talking with others about the classes, I say, "It's not like I actually have to weld anything together, like a rhombus and an octahedron . . ." Then they all pipe up, telling me that the test involves exactly that—welding things together!

Unbeknownst to me, Ed (who attended Michigan State) had woken about this time to read a book, *The Number Devil*, about a boy named Robert who in a lucid dream learns about mathematics and shapes by cutting out and pasting together figures, including an "octahedron." Already, telepathic influence seems apparent in the first dream of the night!

A couple of dreams later, Ed becomes lucidly aware and begins to chant my name, then begins flying. After minutes of flying, he smells the "salty rotting" smell of the ocean, but wakes. My room that night was the Sheraton Hotel near the San Francisco airport and yards away from the salty San Francisco Bay.

In Ed's next dream, he lucidly finds himself near a large staircase and calls my name. Meanwhile, I, semi-lucid, dream of hearing Ed's voice calling as I stand near a staircase.

In my final night's dream, I do become lucid, and see Beverly about fifty feet in front of me.

> I see Beverly looking left and right, walking down the street toward my direction surrounded by seven to ten others. She wears black, and a black hat! I can scarcely believe it. . . . I go down to her and say something like, "Beverly, wow, this is amazing!" I decide to make a gesture, and put my hands straight up, like a "goal." She says something back and has a fairly typical look, but not as animated as mine. I tell her about becoming lucid . . . she looks at me, but does not make a gesture in reply.

Miles away, Beverly's brief dream record reads: "5:01 A.M. Women come together in a locker room wearing all black, hooded gowns so no one could recognize them."

Once again, we came very close to having two lucid dreamers simultaneously aware. When I saw Beverly coming down the street in a group of women all wearing black, I had to modulate my emotions so that I wouldn't end the dream. Mutual dreaming history seemed to be in the making! However, as I interacted with her, I came to suspect that she had not achieved lucid awareness; rather, she seemed semi-lucid.

As should be clear by this point, it seems very likely that given the opportunity, lucid dreamers will objectively prove the reality of mutual lucid dream interactions. When demonstrated, such experiences could begin to revolutionize traditional views of dreaming and the dreaming state. Like Alice in Wonderland, lucid dreamers could open the door to investigating a world made "curiouser and curiouser" by the appearance of an alternate reality, a mental one or, if you prefer, an alternate maya.

COAXING THE NON-LUCID
TO LUCID AWARENESS

You might ask, "Has a lucid dreamer ever prompted another dreamer into achieving awareness?" The answer is yes, lucid dreamers have tried with apparent success. I can recall one night meeting a non-lucid Ed and trying to coax him into lucid awareness. In the morning, I called him, and he did become lucidly aware that night, but in a different general environment without my presence. His response didn't surprise me, since in my lucid dream I didn't hang around him waiting for him to "come to."

After about twenty years of lucid dreaming, I found that dream figures sometimes assisted me in becoming lucid. Certain actions seemed intended, purposeful, and directed toward my realization of consciously aware dreaming. How did they do it? Normally in one of four ways:

Repetition: Seeing the same dream figure twice jogs your memory. It makes you stop and wonder, "Where did I see that person before?" which often calls up lucid awareness. I recall that once, a group of dream figures entered my visual field in a revolving door three times before I "got it" and became lucid.

Odd Creations: Watching a dream figure do something totally odd can call up that critical mindset and make you think "Odd. Could this be a dream?" Odd things might include the dream figure disappearing and then reappearing, changing the color of clothing repeatedly, and so forth.

Persistent Attention: On some rare occasions, the dream figure or figures may continue interacting with you to prompt your lucidity. I recall once, a whole group of twenty or more dream figures sang songs for me, told jokes, and so on until finally I became lucidly aware and they began to applaud! Suddenly, I recalled they had tried this same thing the night before!

Questions: At least once, I have become lucid when a dream figure asked me a question. Having to think about the question and my response made me realize that I existed in a dream. Questioning seems a potent way to elicit lucid awareness.

As a lucid dreamer engaging a non-lucid friend, you might use the same strategy of repetition, making odd creations, persistent attention, and asking questions to elicit your friend's lucid awareness. Some lucid dreamers have also reported success by touching their non-lucid friend to prompt awareness.

DIFFERENTIATING DREAM FIGURES AND MEETING UNKNOWN LUCID DREAMERS

Once you've become lucid in the dream state and encounter a friend you would like to bring to lucidness, how can you tell if you have encountered an actual dreamer or some other type of dream figure? In my early years of lucid dreaming, sometimes I would try to get one or two of my brothers to join me on a lucid dreaming adventure—like a group fly-in—but they acted so goofy, I could never seem to get their cooperation. Eventually, I gave up. When I finally met experienced lucid dreamers at the Association for the Study of Dreams conference, this question of the actual nature of dream figures came up. Ed Kellogg responded that in some valid encounters, the non-lucid person's figure often behaved as if semi-drunk. Their eyes and head shifted almost randomly. They moved disjointedly or with little coordination. They seemed "there" but largely unfocused. When they looked at you in the dream, no hint (or very little) of recognition crossed their face. If you talked to them or pointed out features of the dream environment, they seemed barely to register it. Maintaining a connection with them was a constant challenge.

I totally agreed with Ed's comments and realized that we both recognized a common feature of valid encounters with other dreamers whom we met while lucidly aware. Sometimes, the persons show semi-lucidity or a bit more awareness in the dream. In these cases, they follow your comments, move with you, and act somewhat appropriately, but their inability to initiate actions toward you, the lucid dreamer, gives them away. Formulating a response or acting purposefully seems to require a higher order of awareness and would be considered evidence of the other's lucidity.

Of course, if a lucid dreamer met another aware lucid dreamer, then one would expect to find a look of recognition and awareness, decisive movement and action, a general sense of rapport with appropriate responses to questions, an ability to focus on the other's issue or concern, and so forth. In effect, two lucidly aware individuals should demonstrate something similar to a common waking-world give and take between two aware viewpoints.

Yet other questions persist. How does one tell whether he or she has simply met a dream symbol or thought form who just "looks like" a friend? Of course, a lucid dreamer could request that "All thought forms must now disappear!" and see what results. Barring this, the average thought form would appear disengaged in the setting. Unless "expected" into action by the lucid dreamer, a thought form simply exists. Like a potted plant in the corner, the thought form appears in the dreaming space as an appropriate item but with no greater purpose or motive.

As previously mentioned (in chapter 11 and elsewhere), however, you may meet, while lucid, a class of consciously aware dream figures who engage in reasoned discourse, appear to have memory, display a greater understanding of the dream environment, and possess knowledge. These same dream figures may reappear and show some permanence in the dream realm. Since they seem to carry their own "identity," it seems hard to imagine they would assume a friend's appearance in your lucid dream, though it remains a possibility. More probable may be the lucid dreamer's unconscious expectation that they look like an associate and then see them as such.

Complicating all this, one could take the theoretical position that all meetings—real, imagined, dreamt—occur in one's mind, so all figures exist as thought-forms. Or, in such a case, one could say that any exchange of information has occurred at other levels, possibly telepathically. If so, the apparent meeting place and action were only a symbolic production of the mind's receipt of mental information. Thus, the information exists, but the meeting in a dream space does not; the dream space is only an illusionary projection of the mind.

Many experienced lucid dreamers can provide examples of meeting another lucid dreamer in the dream space, conversing and interacting, yet the other lucid dreamer comes from outside their circle of acquaintance. When I first had this kind of experience, I began to tell the other lucid dreamer to contact me. I gave my name, phone number, and address—a lot to recall, even for a waking person. In one memorable example, the other lucid dreamer, a librarian in a town in (she informed me) Moldova, took me to her simple walk-up apartment. Upon waking, I thought the meeting imaginary, since the woman told me her town sat on the river across from the Ukraine—and I felt confident that Moldova did not share a border with Ukraine. Since this dream occurred only a few years after the breakup of the Soviet Union, I decided to investigate Moldova's location and was stunned to discover that Moldova bordered the Ukraine and shared a river. I even found the likely town of the librarian from her pronunciation. (Isn't it strange that the name of the city was in Moldovan or Russian, while our conversation seemed in English except for the name of the town?) If this person exists in waking reality, I would recognize her by a distinctive facial mole near her nose.

In another lucid dream, I encountered a lucid dreaming artist in central Europe. I could see the canvases behind him, his paintings, and the whole layout of the studio. After giving him my name and all the other pertinent contact information, he told me that he wouldn't be able to recall it. Realizing that even if I wrote it out, the lucid dream writing would not be there for him upon waking, I decided to let it go.

So, do lucid dreamers occasionally stumble into each other's dreams? Or does some joint interest, purpose, or similarity draw lucid dreamers into a mental meeting? Perhaps someday—or maybe it has already happened unbeknownst to me—two lucid dreamers, unacquainted in the waking world, will consciously exchange enough information when lucid to make contact later in waking reality.

DREAM SPACE: OPENINGS AND CLOSINGS

The words "Space, the final frontier" opened each episode of the *Star Trek* series as Captain Kirk, Spock, and the rest of the crew ventured across the galaxy to new worlds.

For some lucid dreamers, creating a mutual lucid dream involves making a new world by either entering another dreamer's dream space or calling another dreamer into your dream space. Here again, certain common features seem to exist that show some structural elements to the lucid dream environment.

For example, when lucid dreamers independently report moving toward another's dream, many experience leaving their dream imagery behind, moving through a darkness or gray state, before entering another's dream. Also, lucid dreamers independently mention entering the dream or having others enter their dream by creating a vertical or horizontal "slit" in the dream screen. Just as one might cut through a theater screen to get backstage and then "step through." In one example of my own (January 1999):

> I have a ripped up notecard in my hands that I had pulled out of my pocket, and as I look at it, I have the feeling that I can put it all back together. All of a sudden, as I try to do so, it makes me realize this is a lucid dream! I look around and think "I'm lucid. I'm lucid. What did I want to do? Oh yeah, I want to get Ed here." So though I get some odd looks from the other dream figures, I start walking around calling out every ten seconds, "Ed Kellogg! Ed Kellogg come here!" I have a big grin at the thought of it, and keep looking to see if he will come through a door or what.
>
> Within thirty to forty seconds, as if stepping through a curtain tear in the air, out steps Ed Kellogg! He's just six feet away! I'm shocked to see him, particularly in the manner in which he appeared. Ed looks very strong and vibrant, almost exactly as he does in waking

life except stronger, no gray in his hair, and a bit more filled out and taller. Actually when he stepped out, it was as if he was about four inches above the floor. He is wearing a short sleeve T-shirt of medium frosted green, brand new jeans that are quite dark blue and casual brown shoes and glasses. He has a very alert look on his face of awareness—he seems to realize this is a lucid dream. He steps to a point about three feet in front of me.

A FEW OTHER CONSIDERATIONS

Various questions arise whenever a mutual dream or mutual lucid dream is reported. Does it primarily involve dream telepathy, or do two dream selves actually interact in a dreaming space? If a dreaming space, then who creates the dreaming space—the first person there, the most energetic person, or a combination of both dreamers? Does the exact clock time matter, or do these interactions occur in a dimension outside of waking time and space? How could one ascertain whether two dreamers meet in the same dream space or if two dreamers simply share telepathic information about a space?

In my experiments with Ed Kellogg and Linda Lane Magallón described earlier, we felt that an exchange of unknown information, like a code word or gesture, needed to be made between two lucid dreamers and recorded by both to demonstrate mutual lucid awareness. Stephen LaBerge alternatively suggests that one could place lucid dreamers in the lab with the agreement that they would make a special signal when they met. If these two signals occurred simultaneously from the two lucid dreamers, then it might suggest a meeting in a shared dream realm. However, if the signals were not close to being simultaneous, then LaBerge felt that at best, one could suggest they possibly shared dream plots.[10]

Although more experiments need to be performed to begin to answer those questions, I suggest considering the following when attempting a mutual lucid dream:

1. Select partners with strong lucid skills, excellent dream recall, and high integrity.

2. Set up a protocol or set of procedures to follow, requiring detailed dream reports.

3. Don't contaminate other dream reports by sending your possible mutual lucid dream to other dreamers. Have everyone send their

dream reports to an uninvolved third party who will wait to release the dreams once everyone has reported.

4. When you read over the dream reports, try to be objective. Often you will notice areas of dream telepathy that indicate a dream meeting or meshing; but to show a lucid meeting took place, did the two lucid dreamers exchange any information with each other and then correctly report it in their separate waking reports?

5. Don't be surprised if the other party did not achieve lucid awareness on the same night as you. It may take a few attempts. Keep the spirit of the experiment light and carefree.

You may be surprised at the amount of time it takes to set up an experiment, report, read, and analyze one night's dreaming, but having a strong experimental design increases the impact of your results.[11]

It may be that mutual lucid dreaming, just like precognitive lucid dreams, serves to provide evidence that space, like time, is fundamentally not as we perceive it. Reaching back to the original Sanskrit term, maya, we may literally help create, emit, and form the dream space that we then experience. Using our beliefs, expectations, focus, intent, and will, we may assist in the reality-cocreating efforts of our larger Self as we interact with changing ideas, emotions, and information and spark the apparent world into its constant, ever-changing projected mental space to which we then react in a perpetual, ever changing Now.

In one sense, there may be no "space" where this occurs, except in the dynamic, larger awareness of the Mind. Similarly, there may be no inherent separation between selves except as the selves cling to their self constructs. The apparent distance between any awareness may have more to do with the belief in our selves as separate and apart instead of part of a larger whole.

17

INTERACTING WITH THE DECEASED

WHILE I TRAVELED ON A BUSINESS TRIP, MY WIFE CALLED ME WITH SAD news. A colleague's wife had passed away after a short, severe illness. Sorry to hear this, I asked how the husband was handling the loss. I felt bad about being on the road and missing the funeral, even though I didn't know his wife very well.

Within the next few nights, I found myself in a dream walking down a white staircase:

> As I turn the corner to go down the next flight of stairs, I discover the deceased woman, Dorothy, and her husband, Larry, coming up the stairs. At this point, realizing that Dorothy has passed, I become basically lucid.
>
> Remembering that I haven't expressed my condolences yet, I step closer to them. Turning to Larry, I somberly say, "I'm so sorry to hear about Dorothy's passing." They look at me confused, and mutter, "What?" Now looking at them both to make myself perfectly clear, I announce a bit more vigorously, "I am so sorry to hear about Dorothy's passing."
>
> Suddenly their faces register complete shock. Looking at me, then at each other, they immediately turn and rush back down the stairwell. For a moment, I consider following them to try and explain but then realize I have already provided quite enough information for one night!

Apparently, my assessment of Larry and Dorothy's situation differed remarkably from their own. Perhaps I should have been more circumspect and expressed my sorrow for the passing of "Dorothy's physical body." Or I could have asked them a simple question to see if they understood the situation. But in that moment, the finer points of lucid dream etiquette eluded me.

Dream encounters with the deceased seem fairly common. Throughout history, the deceased have frightened, comforted, warned, and advised dreamers. While the interactions range from the profound to the simple, the commonality of the occurrence seems notable. Theoretically, meeting with the deceased in dreams may stand as a major impetus behind the formation of religions across cultures because dreaming of the deceased calls into question the apparent finality of death.

In her wonderful book, *The Dream Messenger: How Dreams of the Departed Bring Healing Gifts,* Patricia Garfield provides many fascinating examples of dreamers interacting with deceased dream figures. Common themes arise from these communications, including messages of comfort and assurance that the departed is "okay."

On some occasions, Garfield discovered, the departed bring concerns or warnings to the dreamer, suggestive that they might continue awareness in a nonphysical form. In other instances, however, interactions between the dreamer and the deceased seem to be part of the dreamer's grieving process, and involve symbolic and emotional healing. In a variety of dream settings, the dreamer continues to resolve his or her grief, loss, and unspoken concerns.

Because lucid dreams contain considerable symbolic content, dreamers have to take care when dealing with the symbolic imagery of dying. Some dreams of death refer only to a symbolic death of the old, followed by the birth of the new, a lesson I learned in this humorous lucid dream (July 1998):

> I find myself in a small town in Kansas, looking for a phone booth to contact one of my brothers. Wandering around, I see something odd—a church with its doors wide open, the lights on, and finely dressed people in the pews.
>
> As I walk toward the church, I see what appears to be the beginning of a funeral, as I can see a coffin up by the altar. I walk down the aisle, curious about the odd shaped coffin—shaped like a body. I become fully lucid now at the strangeness of this whole situation. Sizing it all up I decide, "What the heck, this is a dream. I'll open the coffin." As I reach to pull the coffin door back, I am quite shocked to see a good friend lying inside! He opens his eyes and smiles.

Confused by this sudden turn of events, I try to fathom the meaning of this. I ask, "Does this mean you'll pass away in the next couple of years?" He looks up and says, "No." I ask, "Does it mean that you'll live for the next few years?" He says, "Maybe."

I wake, comforted by our lucid conversation but still wondering why my healthy thirty-something friend would be in church lying in a coffin. About two days later, the mystery was solved. My friend called me to tell me the big news: He was engaged! Suddenly, it became clear—my friend the single man had died, but my friend the engaged and soon-to-be married man was alive. The church setting fit in nicely because it hosts the life passages of both death and marriage.

I chuckled at my symbolic depiction of the "death" of the single man. The lucid dream conversation had hinted that the imagery was symbolic and didn't suggest a physical passing. My friend's phone call provided the missing pieces of the puzzle for this bit of lucid dream telepathy.

THE QUESTION OF THE DECEASED

Seeing the deceased in a dream often serves as a prompt to initiate lucid awareness. Noticing Grandmother, you may suddenly realize, "Wait a second, Grandmother is dead. This must be a dream!" Thus, deceased dream figures help increase the likelihood of lucid awareness and provide lucid dreamers with a rare opportunity to interact consciously with them. In the world of dreams, dreamers can lucidly converse, question, challenge, or be challenged by the deceased dream figure.

The unsettling question for all dreamers concerns the actual nature of deceased dream figures. Does one see merely a personal dream symbol? Or does one see the actual deceased but in a nonphysical form? Or something else?

When meeting a deceased dream figure, lucid dreamers normally follow one of three paths: 1) they view it through their assumptions about lucid dreaming, such as, "it's all in my head, one sees what one expects," 2) they experience it according to their beliefs about the after death state, such as, "Grandmother is in heaven, or Grandmother does not exist," or 3) feeling uncertain, they try to reason it out with a proactive approach of curious questioning and investigations leading toward evidence.

Undoubtedly, a fully lucid dreamer can engage the deceased dream figure quite deeply with questions. However, for many lucid dreamers, their assumptions or beliefs determine their approach to the deceased. Either they immediately assume the deceased exists and happily reunite, or they immediately assume that the deceased doesn't exist and ignore or rebuff the dream figure as nothing more than a "dream character."

There are several ways lucid dreamers could go beyond their beliefs and try to reasonably ascertain whether they interact with a mere symbol or the actual deceased. One approach involves seeking information indicative of a valid interaction, such as information unknown to the lucid dreamer. If information provided by the deceased dream figure proves correct, the lucid dreamer could reasonably assume he or she has experienced an interaction. If the information proves incorrect, the lucid dreamer could assume he or she has dealt with a symbol or thought-form and not the deceased.

For example, lucid dreamer Sylvia Wilson wrote of seeing her former pastor in a dream and becoming lucid as she realized he was deceased:

> I was dreaming of an old dead Pentecostal preacher that I knew as a child. I loved him a great deal. . . . Suddenly I realized that I was talking to a dead person . . . [lucid] I realize I don't have much more time with him and I ask him quickly, "What message do you want me to give to your wife?" He says, "Tell her, if she has the big picture of me, it is not me!"
>
> Then he absolutely disappears and I awaken in a shock. I feel absolutely certain I have talked to my old dead preacher. So the next morning . . . I finally get her [the widow] on the phone, I tell her she may not believe it, but I believe that I talked with her dead husband. Then I tell her what the message was to her. This starts a huge bit of crying and she explains. She said that she had a huge old picture of her husband [hanging in her home] that used to hang in the church, and she had been crying and trying to pull him from the picture. So I guess the message to her was: that's not him anymore.[1]

Thankfully, Sylvia had both the presence of mind to ask what the deceased dream figure might want to say and the capacity to remember it upon waking. In this case, the lucid dreamer had no knowledge of the widow's behavior toward the picture of her deceased husband. By calling the widow, Sylvia's lucid information was verified. After talking with the widow, the strange response—"Tell her, if she has the big picture of me, it is not me!"—makes perfect sense and suggests an actual interaction with the pastor's awareness.

Another method to determine whether one interacts with a dream symbol or the deceased involves noticing the objects and memorabilia around the deceased. Occasionally, these dream details provide clues to a real encounter. For example, lucid in a dream with a deceased person, the lucid dreamer may see a collection of brass telescopes lying on a table. Upon mentioning this to the deceased's relatives, they may reply that the deceased had a serious interest in astronomy as a teenager, back when brass telescopes were common. Unknown details like this suggest an actual encounter happened.

The third approach involves the lucid dreamer receiving a helpful warning or valuable advice from the deceased dream figure. As I recounted earlier (in chapter 15), Frederik van Eeden, who coined the term "lucid dream," consciously dreamt of his deceased brother-in-law who warned him of an impending financial loss. Upon waking, van Eeden failed to understand the warning but later noted that around that same time, events occurred that led to a considerable financial blow. The deceased dream figure's warning, while misunderstood, was valid.

Finally, a valid interaction may occur when a lucid dreamer and another dreamer independently report of interacting with the deceased in dreams. Lucy Gillis, coeditor of *The Lucid Dream Exchange*, reports such an event. When seeing her deceased mother in a lucid dream, Lucy asks the figure of her mother, "What would Gramma want for her birthday?" Her deceased mother smiles and says, "The usual." Later, when Lucy spoke with her Gramma, she learned that her deceased mother had visited Gramma in a dream around the same time. Incredibly, as they compared notes, the dream figure wore the same outfit (not one she owned while alive) and looked the same age in both dreams. Lucy later realized that her grandmother's deepest wish was to be visited by her daughter in dreaming. This event indicated she got her wish.[2]

COMPLICATING FACTORS

Getting past our beliefs and assumptions about lucid dreams and the nature of dream figures seems quite a challenge in itself; the emotional weight of seeing the departed only adds to the complexity. Our emotional closeness to the deceased and issues of our own grief and loss often become the primary focus, even for lucid dreamers. It may take many encounters before the lucid dreamer feels ready to consider the actual nature of the deceased dream figure.

Beverly D'Urso, the extremely talented lucid dreamer who played a major role in Stephen LaBerge's early experiments, recalls frequent dreams about a close friend, Patrice, who died in a car accident at age nineteen:

> At first, I'd see her, and we would continue as we would have when she was still alive. One time, I remembered that she had died. It scared me so much that I woke up. Afterwards, I learned to stay in the dream and talk to her. It took me time to get accustomed to hearing her voice, but I was finally able to ask her questions, and, eventually, listen to her answers. I felt very relieved to connect with her this way.[3]

When I asked Beverly privately about how she understood the figure of Patrice in her lucid dreams, she replied, "At that time, I'd say that I saw her as my representation of 'Patrice.' I figured that her character would act according to my expectations." But now, Beverly considers other possibilities. "I do feel open to the possibility that I can connect to what people might call the 'essence' of someone else in my dreams," she says, "including someone who died. However, I do not think that I do so every time I dream of someone whom I interpret as another person I know."

Finally, religious and spiritual beliefs may collide in our encounters with deceased dream figures. Those with a rigid belief system may be unable to see the need to investigate this question, since their strong belief or lack of belief has already finalized the issue for them. Moreover, a resolution of the question of deceased dream figures raises new problems that we may wish to avoid. If we allow ourselves to view the encounter as valid, we may have to deal with a whole host of conflicting religious and scientific ideas. If we view the encounter as invalid, we suggest our own mortality and annihilation. Some may resist even considering the idea on any level because of the implications of either result.

A lucid dreamer who strongly believed that the dead no longer exist in any form wrote to *The Lucid Dream Exchange* of being followed by the dream figure of his deceased mother on almost a nightly basis. One night, he became lucidly aware and, seeing the dream figure of his mother once again, asked sharply, "Let's cut to the chase, this isn't really you. So who are you?" She replied, "I'm the image of your mother that's in your head. You need me, so why do you fight me?"[4]

Whether from emotional reasons or scientific and spiritual ones, general reluctance exists in lucidly exploring the issue of the deceased. Clearing the tangled brush of beliefs around the topic requires a certain fearlessness. One must let go of the false stability of assumptions, while holding tight to the vapors of uncertainty. Approaching the issue with curiosity and an open mind may open up a constructive pathway.

In lucid dreaming, we have a skeleton key to resolving the perennial question of life after death. Whether it can provide evidence to unlock the door, we shall see.

ALLOWING LUCID INTERACTIONS WITH THE DECEASED

In my view, we often repress dream knowledge about a coming death or misfortune and make it clear that we don't wish any foreknowledge, preferring the "bliss" of ignorance instead. I feel this censoring of dreams occurs at a basically conscious level. Our beliefs, expectations, and focus collaborate to shape much of our dream recall, and we often remember dreams that align with those factors and fail to recall those that don't. The common observation that "Freudians have Freudian dreams, and Jungians have Jungian dreams" suggests the active impact our beliefs and expectations have in our dream formation, recollection, and interpretation. As such, we both censor and shape what dreams we recall.

As the long-time keeper of a dream journal, I believe my dreaming self would not ignore the approach of any significant event, even the death of a parent, unless I knowingly or unknowingly decided to remain unaware of it. In fact, I clearly told my dreaming self that I wanted to know about the eventual passing of my aged father. Unlike most people, I opened up to and consciously allowed the information.

Actively believing that my dreaming self would keep me informed, I felt fortunate to receive many forward-looking dreams about his passing. I recall one that occurred exactly a year before he passed, which contained a number of details to be later experienced. As the date of his passing drew closer, the dreams about the event seemed to multiply until, finally, on the night of August 12–13, 1997, I had this lucid dream:

> It is dark and cold, and I am driving with my dad across the North Dakota prairie in the winter. Outside there is snow and ice on the ground. We come to a motel and park there. I stand outside and talk to the office clerk as he sits at a window. I seem to have some complaint that there is only a room for my father and none for me, but the clerk doesn't seem to care.

I walk back to the room but get confused about where to go in the dark. I decide to go investigate a large building that I see, thinking it may have room. As I get to the front of it, I realize it is a large, empty, deserted church. There are no lights on; it looks pitch black inside. The outside marquee sits empty, without names. I can hardly imagine such a large church deserted like this. Something seems odd about that, and I realize that I'm dreaming.

Lucid, I jump up in the night air, thinking, "What do I want to do?" I decide to fly deep into outer space. As I look up, I see an older man, hovering about twenty feet off the ground. Incredibly he seems to glow from within, as if he contains light within him. He doesn't wear any clothes. He looks at me, then his face registers surprise as I fly right past him, higher and higher into the night sky and beyond to the gray dark outer space.

After a while of flying deeper and deeper into the darkness, I stop and ask the dream to show me something important to see . . .

A day later, at 4 A.M. on August 14, our small cat uncharacteristically jumped right on my stomach and woke me up. I played with the cat for a moment and tried to get it to lie down and sleep, but it refused to lie down and kept rubbing me. A few minutes later, the bedside phone rang, and I thought, "Dad has died." My wife handed me the phone; my sister told me Dad just passed away, minutes earlier.

Recalling my lucid dream, the symbolism felt quite obvious and extraordinary—the dead of winter, the dark of night, the empty church, a room for my father but none for me—all symbolic suggestions of death, journey, and passing over. Most fascinating was seeing this man who glowed from within—like some golden light illuminated his being. He looked very much like one of my uncles, a favored brother of my father's, who had passed away earlier. Of my hundreds of lucid dreams, I cannot recall ever meeting a personage who glowed like this. Unfortunately, I didn't stop to ask him his purpose there in the dream, something I deeply regret now.

My father passed over very peacefully. Thankfully, in the hours between my lucid dream and the next night of his passing, the nurses called the family, having noticed that his blood pressure and other vital signs had dropped significantly. Our family had time to spend precious hours talking with him and wishing him well.

After my father passed, I had a short series of dreams in which we always met at the TWA gate. Normally, he just sat there, like someone waiting for a plane. Finally, I wondered, "Why do we keep meeting at the TWA gate?" Then, I got the dream pun. People like us two, the living and the dead, always meet at the "Trans World" gate.

In these dreams, I assumed my father was a dream symbol. When deceased dream figures display little initiative, awareness, or activity (like my father at the TWA gate), I normally conclude they exist as thought-forms or symbols. On the other hand, when deceased dream figures display considerable initiative, awareness, or activity, their status seems less certain. They may exist as thought-forms, aspects of self, archetypal energies, or something else. The figure's degree of awareness, knowledge, and initiative seem the determining factor.

After the passing of a loved one, dreamers should expect to have a number of dreams in which they sort through their own feelings, ideas, and realizations. In these dreams, one likely deals with his or her own personal issues and symbolic figures. It may be, too, that the deceased have their own issues to contend with.

Though in retrospect it appeared quite impatient of me, only a month after my father's passing, I decided to take matters into my own hand. I would lucidly go in search of him. Consciously aware, I sought to push my way through the trans-world gate and visit the other side (September 1997):

> I drive to an old part of town and push through some construction— finally get out and walk. I go to an area that is kind of like a church. In talking to a young woman, something very minor occurs, which makes me realize this is a dream.
>
> I fly around the area and up past a gold and blue onion dome on the building. I feel great and fully lucid. I notice ten people standing in one area apparently watching me, so I fly over to them. I decide to ask questions about what the symbols in the dream represent. They are very talkative and give answers quickly. I ask "What does that dome represent?" They grin, and one says something like "The dome is on top—as a symbol of your spiritual growth, it is where you want to be." I ask about other symbols and receive responses.
>
> I then decide to ask to see my dad. After I ask, they all politely demur, as if it is not a good idea or not possible. I try various alternate suggestions, but all are met with this same disinclination . . . A woman dressed in blue announces that she is always watching over him (or us), and she is there to help at all times, perhaps trying to alleviate my concern.

I then ask if they can tell me the future, for say, the next week. They respond that sure they could tell me what is "likely" to happen, but that my own thoughts, beliefs, and expectations determine what finally happens. So they could tell me, but what would be the point? I concede to their explanation.

The dream continues with another long conversation, about reincarnation; then I decide to wake up.

In this lucid dream, it appears that interaction between the lucid dreamer and the deceased does not always happen "on demand." In other lucid dreamers' reports, I have noticed that when the deceased has recently departed, the lucid dreamer's ability to contact them seems similarly compromised. Whether this occurs as a function of the dreamer's emotional state, the deceased's situation, or some other factor seems a matter of conjecture.

After this incident, I decide not to pursue my father in the dream state anymore but to let him contact me if he wishes. A year and a half later, my father appears in a dream (a dream of clarity, it seems). Not knowing if I speak to merely a dream figure representation or something more real, I decide to ask him questions. Perhaps if the answers have validity, I can discover whether the dream figure has validity as well (April 1999):

The dream scene begins basically like a dark stage. Now I see a golden wood ladder right in front of me, hanging in the air. I can see the polished wood gleaming and the narrow grain on the wood. Suddenly I see a foot and then another and look up—I recognize my dad is coming down the gold wood ladder. I realize, "Hey, Dad's dead" and think, "Well, then this is a lucid dream." I'm a bit surprised by his bad haircut and grin at the absurdity of not getting a good haircut in the after-death state! He looks about sixty years old and very healthy, even though he passed on at eighty-two.

At this point, I begin to wonder if I'm meeting a symbolic thought-form or my deceased father. Reasoning that if he comes from the "land of the dead," he should be able to answer questions about death, I decide to ask him some tough questions.

He looks bright and alert as we exchange greetings, and he tells me that he is doing fine. Then, I pull out my first question, "Dad, tell me, when do you think Mom will die?" He looks at me and says, "Oh, Mom will probably die in two to six years." I then ask, "Of what?" [In my notes, I wrote "heart," but I can't recall if he said Mom would have heart problems. To the best of my knowledge, my mother's medical record had never shown heart problems.]

I ask him some other questions, but finally he remarks that he came to tell me certain things. He says that the coming months may be challenging, but that the family can make it. I get the feeling that August will be the most difficult. He also tells me that I need to be more compassionate and understanding of one family member, saying something like, "You don't understand the circumstance of her life, so it isn't for you to judge her now." He has some other advice, but I don't recall it. I feel very pleased to see him.

Immediately upon awakening, I realized there were several striking pieces of information in this dream encounter. The Old Testament symbolism of the Golden Ladder was particularly appropriate, since my father was a minister's son. And seeing the bad haircut was a priceless detail. I was a bit surprised that he would ask me to be more compassionate to this particular family member but agreed that he had a point and changed my perspective. As for major challenges in the months following the lucid dream, the only issue I recall is that a tornado damaged a family member's house in the following month; at the time, it was hard to know whether this was the "major challenge."

What struck me most in this lucid dream encounter, though, was my father's answers to my questions about my mother's possible future passing. My reasoning in asking him about my mother was that since he was in "the land of the dead," he might have some special insight. At the time, there was no indication that my mother had any heart issues, but two years after this lucid dream, my mother went to the hospital in March 2001, complaining of shortness of breath; the doctors diagnosed that she had developed a heart problem. While the veins and arteries were very healthy, she required medication to help the heart function. Two years later, she went to the hospital again, this time with additional heart problems, which the doctors later realized were the result of a common prescription drug she had been taking. So in the end, my father's warnings of heart issues did play out.

LUCIDLY SEEKING THE DECEASED

Curious about the possibility of contacting the deceased in the lucid state, Ed Kellogg used his lucidity to investigate. Roughly two months after an elderly acquaintance's passing, Ed performed a lucid dream incubation to visit him and had the following lucid dream:

I come to myself in a room setting, sitting at a table with three old men. I realize that I dream, and remember my task—to find Bruno. First I decide to look over the men. We sit at a circular table, the men look in their 70s and 80s, old white-haired, one balding another fat, all look feeble and flabby. None of them looks like Bruno even when he died, and I expect him to look much younger and healthier now, as several months have passed since then. The old men try to talk to me, but I excuse myself, getting up, saying "Sorry to break this [dream scene] up, but I really need to look for Bruno."

I stand up and call "Bruno L." a few times, and look over in a corner to see [Bruno] sitting in a chair. He looks in his thirties or forties, very lean and self-possessed. He has on an elegant dark gray silk suit, a white shirt and a dark tie. He has a deep tan—very dark, and looks almost like an American Indian. He also has on a pair of glasses with black or very dark frames. Most odd of all he has a full head of white hair, although his eyebrows have dark hair. At first glance his hair looks straight, but when I look closely his hair looks frizzy, like that of a black man, it sticks up about two inches from his head and seems so unexpected it makes me question whether I've found Bruno.

I say "Hi Bruno! How do you do?" He replies "Good to see you! I haven't seen you around?" I look at him and say "Well Bruno, you died!" [Bruno] immediately replies "No I didn't! I was reborn on three planes." He looks cool and self-possessed. I tell him "Bruno, when I said you died I meant physically. For me the word death implies rebirth." [Bruno] nods and apologizes for "not being more demonstrative." I find it hard to hear him, realize I begin to wake up. I try to move around to prevent RWPR [return to waking physical reality—ed.], and ask Bruno to try to speak more loudly, as I can't hear him. Despite my efforts the whole scene fades into a sort of white light.[5]

Ed took the lucid dream to Bruno's son and asked whether it contained any verifiable details. Bruno's son mentions a number of points that Ed correctly identifies. Ed notes:

1. During the period I knew Bruno in waking physical reality (from about 1986), he had almost no hair, no tan, physically a bit flabby. He wore wire rimmed glasses—for presbyopia [age-related sight problems—ed.], I assumed. I do not recall ever seeing him in a suit and tie—almost always he wore a casual shirt and a bolo tie.

2. His family buried Bruno in a dark gray silk suit with a dark red tie (unknown to me).

3. Bruno wore glasses for most of his life, not just in later life—and in his 30's and 40's he wore *glasses with black frames* [a detail that Ed noted in his dream report].

4. For most of his adult life Bruno had a very dark tan—something I did not know and had not seen.

5. Although Bruno began losing his hair as a teenager, and certainly did not have a full head of hair in his 30's—he did have extremely curly/frizzy/kinky hair which he used to wear in a sort of afro style. I had absolutely no clue about this, as Bruno had lost all but a fringe of his hair when I met him, and his son had straight dark hair—which I'd assumed that Bruno did also—until I learned otherwise when I checked with his son after this dream.[6]

Interestingly, most of Ed's details correspond to Bruno's life between age thirty and forty, which appears to Ed as the age adopted by Bruno in the after-death state. Various sources have identified a tendency for the deceased to appear much younger in dreams than they actually are at the date of their passing, almost as if the deceased or dream version of the deceased reflects the physical description fitting their feeling about themselves at the time.

Almost three years later, Ed tries again to contact another deceased acquaintance, "D. B.," who had passed away ten weeks earlier. Five days before his successful lucid dream, Ed experiences a lucid dream in which he meets a dream figure who agrees to take him to meet the deceased. Before they arrive, however, Ed loses lucidity and wakes. Later, in the successful second attempt, Ed becomes lucid and, announcing his intent, meets the same dream figure who once again agrees to take him to meet the deceased. Ed's numbering, 1 through 7, in this long lucid dream corresponds with the numbering in his comments that follow:

Driving in the dark with my truck, I can hardly see—something that has happened to me in recent dreams. I believe that I probably dream this, so I stop the truck, and use the "With an eagle's sight I see" chant to see if my vision improves. Overhead lighting comes on after I've chanted, my vision improves markedly and I find myself in a parking lot. [Shazam]—my dog—rides with me in the truck. I get out to go exploring, and go into a nearby store that looks like it sells health foods. I check to see if I dream by testing to see if I can put my hand through a window without breaking it—and find that I can.

Now fully lucid, I remember my task to contact D. B. and call out his name: "D– B— ! D– B— !" a few times. I feel close to waking up, when the same man shows up from a previous attempt I'd made to contact D. B. in a lucid dream [five days earlier]—middle sized, non-descript, balding. He looks sort of like an assistant coach or hospital aide. I call out "D– B— !" one more time. The man greets me in a friendly fashion, and says that he recognizes me, "From when we met in heaven a few nights ago," he says. To justify my visit to D. B., I tell this man about my friendship with D. B. and of our work together. He smiles, but then tells me he has some important things to tell me about D. B. before I visit him—I believe him, but in trying to passively listen to him, I feel the pull of returning to physical reality again. I tell him I need to stay active so that I can remain in dream reality, so please, just take me to D. B.

He leads me through a series of corridors, into a sort of dingy gym-hospital like basement . . . (1) I hear [D. B.'s voice], but I can not see him. I tell the aide that I can't see [D. B.], and he says "Don't worry—you will." [D. B.] apparently dictates his memories and obser-vations into something that looks like an old dictation machine—suit-case sized and brown, resting on the floor. (2) He has either not noticed my arrival, or has chosen to ignore me. I listen to him as he talks about "the wonder of calligraphy" (I have to listen very carefully to make out the word) and how "people do not fully appreciate (or understand) the mystery of it." (3) I get a little tired of this—[D. B.] seems deliberately hiding from me and ignoring me.

I notice [Shazam] at my feet, who has apparently tagged along. As Shazam knew D. B., and as D. B. liked Shazam, I direct [Shazam] to "Find D— ! Find D— !" [Shazam] runs under the desk, a dark gray blanket flies up in the air (4), and [D. B.] suddenly appears—he looks about fifty or so. I humorously chide him a bit, saying, "You know in this place you can choose your body—and you can do better than that!" He replies something to the effect that "here I don't get to keep my body," implying that his current body has no value, precisely. because it does seem so impermanent, mental rather than physical, and that he misses his physical body very much and does not consider the one he has now as an acceptable substitute. However, he does change his appearance, and now looks about 35 or so. I would hardly have recognized him if I had not seen the picture of him in his early twen-ties. . . . He has thick, black hair, and although clean shaven, the hair on his head looks quite bushy. He looks much more built up than in the picture I'd seen of him in his twenties where he looked somewhat thin, but this [D. B.] body also looks pale, a bit out of shape, and has a sullen expression.(5)

[D. B.] tells me he has the task of recording all of his memories. I think he feels glad to see me, but that he also seems determined not to show it. The aide looks pleased that at least I've stimulated [D. B.] enough to get him to stand up, and to respond, moving out of his depression/brown study, and perhaps to take a break from his obsessive focus on recording his memories. (6) I try to cheer [D. B.] up, and talk with him about the work we shared, and of an interview I (falsely) remember having recently done with a yoga/Eastern philosophy magazine on the subject. (7) [D. B.] actually looks interested. I ask him if I can do anything for him—perhaps something he wants me to relate to someone in physical reality? I tell him that his wife E. B. does well, and ask him if he has any specific message he'd like me to relay to her. He looks like he might, but before he can answer, against my will I rapidly return to waking physical reality."

Of the corresponding points that follow, numbers 1 through 6 are based upon information Ed received from D. B.'s wife, E. B., "information unknown to [Ed], consciously, at the time of the dream."[7]:

1. D. B. died on Oct. 12, 2000. He spent time during his Navy days writing reports in cabins on ships, and even on a submarine, The Nautilus. Perhaps the dream environment that I saw seems a recreation of that environment—metal walls, metal doors, a dimly lit enclosed space with no windows. He very much enjoyed the time he served in the Navy, and had many fond memories of that period of his life.

2. D. B. did indeed enjoy having and using dictation machines—brown and suitcase sized. When he died, he had two machines like this in his bedroom. In fact, he not only liked using his dictation machines, he cherished them.

3. D. B. did indeed have a keen and ongoing interest in calligraphy that began in about 1995, would in fact buy books on calligraphy, every two years or so, as well as calligraphy equipment, although he never found the time to practice calligraphy himself.

4. In his later years D. B. routinely wrapped himself up in a favorite blue-gray blanket made of alpaca wool. Under dim lighting conditions, the blanket simply looked gray.

5. In his thirties, D. B. looked much as [D. B.] looked in the dream—pale, a bit out of shape, and unhappy, the result of a miserable marriage, smoking, and drinking too many martinis.

6. Apparently this seemed a habit of D. B.'s while still living—he would routinely make notes, or have his wife make notes of his thoughts and observations, filling many notebooks and pieces of scrap paper. Also, when D. B. focused on a task he would quite often do so to the exclusion of all else until he had finished it.

7. A false memory. In physical reality at least, I have not done any such interview.[8]

Displaying considerable talent at intending the lucid dream and maintaining lucid awareness, Ed discovers five or six previously unknown details about the deceased by carefully observing him in his dream environment. Each detail is confirmed later by the deceased's spouse. Also, as Ed talks to the deceased dream figure and chides him for his choice of bodies, the deceased dream figure adopts a younger body in response, but still in keeping with the deceased's physical-world body and attitude (which was unknown to Ed at the time). If we assume that the new body's appearance had been dictated by the lucid dreamer, we would expect the lucid dreamer to provide something more attractive than a younger-looking body that "looks pale, a bit out of shape, and has a sullen expression." If the lucid dreamer didn't change the deceased's appearance, we are left to wonder what or who did.

Similar reports of meeting deceased friends and family members have been mentioned to me by some other experienced lucid dreamers. Long conversations and the direct or indirect exchange of previously unknown information between the dreamer and deceased, the deceased's more youthful-appearing body and similar behavior to who they were when alive in the physical world—all of this suggests that lucid dreaming may contact or access a dimension where conscious interaction with the deceased seems possible and offers experiential proof.

Interestingly, Ed succeeds on his second try after he again meets the dream figure who guides him to the location of the deceased. The dream figure shows a degree of awareness as he recalls their previous meeting's approximate time and apparent place. Ed concludes by posing the perennial question:

> Do we really visit with those who have "passed on" in some of our dreams? For myself, from a factual perspective, just considering the unexpected correspondences that have showed up in my own psychopompic[9] dreams, I'd answer this question with an "I think so, but other explanations—such as telepathy, etc., might account for the unexpected, and accurate, information obtained." On the other hand, from an emotional perspective, judging the experiences based on the astonishing degree of emotional resolution that I experienced following each of these dreams, I feel obligated to say, despite my personal attachment to the phenomenological attitude, "Yes, almost certainly."[10]

Indeed, the world would be a tidier place if the deceased never appeared in dreams, never provided unknown information, and never passed on valid warnings, since then we could ignore any thoughts of a possible nonphysical life beyond death.

The world would be an even tidier place if dreamers couldn't become consciously aware in dreams and interact, explore, and experiment with deceased dream figures, since then we could maintain the blanket assumption that all dream figures exist as merely symbolic representations created by the dreamer.

In some lucid dream interactions with deceased dream figures, we confront likely evidence that one's awareness does continue after physical death. Whereas spiritual traditions have maintained that position for millennia, normally as an article of faith, many lucid dreamers are confronting the issue of awareness after death as a matter of personal experience when conscious in the dream state.

Across cultures, dreaming has operated as the one consistent place where figures of the deceased appear and interact with the living. Now with increasing numbers of dreamers capable of conscious awareness, these dream interactions will certainly become more numerous, varied, and curious. We finally have a means to provide convincing evidence that awareness can continue in some form after death.

Evidence of a nonphysical dimension, alongside the physical, may rewrite the human experience. We may discover, too, that the spiritual tradition has overplayed aspects of this nonphysical dimension, involving punishment and reward instead of education, continued growth, and fulfillment. Consciously aware in dreams, we may finally comprehend the existence of a mental realm hidden behind the physical.

18

THE UNIFIED SELF IN A CONNECTED UNIVERSE

BY ATTENDING TO OUR DREAMS, WE NATURALLY ATTEND TO OUR INNER life. Whether lucid or not, the nightly recognition of dreaming connects us to our inner psychological reality and subtly reminds us of the creativity, information, and life energy that lies deep within. Mindful of our dreams, we naturally assist in opening channels of communication between our waking self and our inner awareness.

As we develop our nightly listening skills, we begin to hear more clearly the daytime whispers of intuitions and impulses. Those quiet moments, when new thoughts and insights arise, remind us of our ever-present inner connection with a greater awareness. In letting go of our concerns, we more easily access a sense of natural grace and knowing.

Years ago, my wife and I joined a seven-day float trip down the Colorado River through the Grand Canyon. Within a day or two of being constantly in nature and totally out of touch with the world of work, meetings, phone calls, and national news, we felt ourselves readjust mentally and emotionally. Surrounded by nature, we became inwardly more natural, more alive, and more aware in each moment.

On the trip, I noticed that I had particularly interesting dreams and became lucid on two successive nights as I lay asleep outside on a tarp under the brilliant stars and moon. It felt good to be free of routine concerns and return to nature's simple rhythms.

On the fourth day in the Grand Canyon, the August sun blazed deep into the cliffs as our raft pulled to the rocky shore near Havasu Canyon—home of the famous, beautiful spring-fed waterfall and luscious, milky-blue creek waters. As we disembarked to explore, our guides told us to follow the trail across the rocks and up above the steep embankment alongside the creek for about a mile, and then the trail would drop down to the silky blue canyon water.

Watching our group scramble along the rock and wisp of a trail, I looked back to see my wife helping a woman, the oldest person in the group, negotiate the easiest route. There was no sense of hurry now. I hung back and helped my wife and the woman at various rocky points. Up ahead, the rest of the boat made quick progress along the trail.

Eventually, and with some effort, we helped the woman down the steep embankment of loose gravel and dirt to a quiet place in the creek where she could soak. "Aaahhh," I murmured as we started to cross the swift, cool waters of the creek; this silky water has some mineral in it, which made for its smooth feel and soft white stone formations underwater. Finding a spot, we eased ourselves into the delicious coolness. I relaxed and closed my eyes. This was heaven in the August sun; I literally soaked it all in.

A few minutes later, I took a quick glance around. Most everyone had gone farther upstream, to the waterfall, perhaps. My wife and a couple of others relaxed twenty feet away in a quiet pool. I closed my eyes again. Feeling at peace and playful, I mentally said, "So Canyon, what do you have to say to me?" Immediately, I mentally heard a voice clearly state, "Get out while you still can."

Now *that* was completely unexpected! I sat up and looked to see if I was hurting something, sitting on a plant or breaking a rock. Everything seemed fine. Still, I couldn't deny that I had clearly heard something suggest otherwise.

I closed my eyes again, feeling assured that I was not hurting the canyon. More relaxed now, I decided to ask one more time, "So Canyon, what do you have to say to me?" This time it sounded even more urgent, "Get out while you still can!" Hearing those words a second time, I knew something was really wrong. I still didn't know what, but the canyon knew.

Pulling myself out of the water, I called to my wife, "We have to go." Lazily, she asked why. "I don't know," I said, "but something's wrong."

Moments later, I looked to the sky and there, beyond the west canyon wall, I could see the dark front edge of a massive thunderhead coming into view. "Look over there," I pointed, "it's a thunderstorm headed this way. There's going to be a flash flood."

My wife's first concern was the elderly woman. "We've got to get her out of here," she said. We roused the others from their quiet relaxation in the stream and told them of the approaching storm. Together, we helped the elderly woman up the steep embankment and onto the trail above the creek bank. By then, the crew from the boat appeared, running up the trail, yelling, "Get out! Get back to the boat! A storm's coming. Hurry!"

Everyone made it back to the boat just as the heavens opened up with a thunderous downpour. As we pushed off into the river looking for a ledge to moor beneath and escape the torrent of rain, I thanked the canyon for letting us get out "while we still could," knowing that in moments a flash flood would be racing through Havasu Canyon.

THE FORCE OF AWARENESS

Jung recognized that each person's inner awareness can influence the conscious thought process. "So," he wrote, "by means of dreams (plus all sorts of intuitions, impulses and other spontaneous events), instinctive forces influence the activity of consciousness."[1] Not only dreams of the night, Jung noted, but also the intuitions, impulses, and other spontaneous events of each day appear to arise from this same deep, inner source. He qualifies his point, however. To hear from the unconscious clearly, he maintained, you must deal with any repressed or distorted aspects in your own consciousness. Otherwise, you will simply distort the inner communications with your personal overlay of repressed and distorted material. By consistently working with dreams, these personal fears and issues often become evident, moving us closer to acceptance and resolution as they loosen their distorting influence.

Much of the clarity of inner communication relates to the clarity within our own minds and our simple ability to listen. Since the information comes *through* our mental processes, we need to consider the contents of our minds. While Jung highlights repressed information as a major distorting aspect, I also feel that personally held limiting or erroneous beliefs and expectations serve to distort or inhibit information.

As I lay in the cool waters of Havasu Creek and playfully asked the canyon a question, I did so because I had taken seriously the idea announced to me in a lucid dream—that everything is sacred, conscious, and alive. I had come to believe that we all exist within an aware universe. Each item and each space is conscious and alive.

Though many believe that each individual possesses a conscious and an unconscious, with possibly a subconscious buffering between the two, it seems we also possess an intra-conscious function that goes beyond or transcends our private conscious awareness. Our intra-conscious connects us to the larger field of awareness beyond our waking selves. But if we don't believe in that possibility, or see no purpose in focusing inwardly for information, we will rarely experience this intra-conscious awareness.

In the language and terms of psychology, we are taught a presumption of isolated awareness in which our conscious, unconscious, and subconscious exist within our self alone. By virtue of that belief and teaching, the instances of telepathy, clairvoyance, intuition, and synchronicity seem inherently suspect, since these suggest a connectedness of awareness or intra-consciousness. Though Jung's view of the collective unconscious suggests common features within the individual's psyche, it falls short of suggesting an active connected awareness at an unconscious level—something I believe lucid dreaming provides evidence of.

In my first twenty years of lucid dreaming, as I came to seek an ultimate or base reality beyond symbols and appearance, beyond dreaming and lucid dreaming, something deep within allowed the awareness that enlivens me to experience the "clear light" of pure awareness (as described in chapter 7). After exiting that experience, I knew that each dot of awareness, each speck of aware light, existed equally with all others and equally connected to all others. The awareness of the collective could be accessed in the awareness of the tiniest speck.

From that moment, I sensed that behind all appearances an unparalleled, profound connection exists at a deep, deep level. Beneath each experience lies a connectedness. Behind each life, each object, each action, an awareness exists joined to all other life, objects, and actions. The inner working of all this awareness spills out into a reality formed and experienced and connects all in a massive symphony of individual creativity and fulfillment.

In certain moments, if you allow it, you can sense that the world around you is deeply interconnected: the sound of this bird is connected to a neighbor opening his door, the wind rustling the leaves announces the car appearing around the corner, your brief sudden thought of a friend lies in synchronicity with an action hundreds of miles away. The thought, the wind, the car, the bird, all connect at some deeper level where awareness resides, intersects, creates, and fulfills. Behind all appearances lies the movement of awareness.

The great Oglala Lakota Sioux medicine man and visionary, Black Elk, said:

> The first peace, which is the most important, is that which comes within the souls of men when they realize their relationship, their oneness, with the universe and all its powers, and when they realize that at the center of the universe dwells Wakan-Tanka, and that this center is really everywhere, it is within each of us. This is the real peace, and the others are but reflections of this. The second peace is that which is made between two individuals, and the third is that which is made between two nations. But above all you should understand that there can never be peace between nations until there is first known that true peace, which, as I have often said, is within the souls of men.[2]

PLAYING WITH THE CONNECTED UNIVERSE

Throughout this book, the examples of lucid dreamers who consciously sought out telepathic and clairvoyant information, assisted in the healing of others, and interacted within mutual lucid dreams, have pointed out the existence of an inner connectedness. As we enter into a deeper exploration of the so-called unconscious through techniques such as lucid dreaming, we will need to redefine many of our concepts about the nature of conscious awareness, developing new terms to express our discoveries. Granting each person a connected or intra-conscious awareness may be one of these developments.

Regardless of the term—unconscious, subconscious, or intra-conscious—the ability to explore inner aspects of awareness requires each individual to develop greater flexibility and reduce distorting personal influences. In lucid dreaming, we see how our experience largely follows our beliefs, expectation, and focus and how these factors create and influence the perception that we then perceive. As we venture inward, we must work through the constraints of the self as we seek to fathom the larger Self and the framework in which this larger Self naturally exists.

Our larger connectedness often appears most clearly when we learn to let go, refocus inward, and allow the sensing of inner experience. In our normal nightly dreams, we do this reactively; in lucid dreaming, however, we are provided an open gateway to experience deliberately and thoughtfully the waking self's connection to inner awareness. Through experimenting with lucid dreaming, we have an opportunity to see for ourselves the larger relationship that surrounds us—the inner Self in a connected universe.

Invariably, connections allow for possible influence in both directions. As I grew more certain that the so-called unconscious was actually very much conscious, alive, and listening, I began to play with this idea. One night, as a test, I announced to the inner Self that I no longer wished to experience dream imagery and symbols; I wanted only to remember the message of the dream. Curious about what might happen, I prepared for sleep and placed a pen on my dream journal. When I woke in the middle of the night, I found myself completely incapable of recalling a dream plot or images or symbols—I had only clear messages reverberating in my mind. They were like pithy statements from some esoteric text. I once received the message, "The One connects to the All," for example. And sometimes, the messages were much more mundane, reflecting concerns about a family member or friend. Once, the message involved a friend's concern for her daughter, for instance. As for dream imagery, nothing appeared; the maya-making projectionist had been asked to go away.

After about two weeks of waking with messages of the dream but no recall of dream imagery, I deeply missed the drama of dreaming. I felt nostalgic for the curious plots and interesting dream figures, the sudden juxtaposition of forgotten friends with new locales, the spectacular visual nature of never-before-seen creations. I missed the panorama of activated ideas and emotions vividly projected onto the theater of my mind. So, tired of pithy messages that now seemed as dry as dust, I asked my inner Self to resume the beautiful, engaging, and mysterious dream stories; immediately, the dreams resumed, reminding me, again, that the unconscious is always listening and responsive. Whether realized or not, we have a connected relationship with the conscious unconscious that goes both ways. When we believe this, individually and collectively, when we learn to speak and to listen to our inner awareness and its broader connectedness, we will begin to reap the benefits of our relationship with the conscious unconscious.

Perhaps, in emulating the conscious unconscious, our goal should be that as we engage the world, a portion of our self will remain listening. Whether chopping wood or carrying water, whether signing business documents or comforting a child, some part of us is allowed to listen to the inner awareness, to stay connected to the active unknown. One purpose of dreams may be to perform this important function at least once each day and thus keep us from becoming totally out of touch with our inner aware Self.

While falling asleep one night, I reminded myself that I needed to write an article for the next *Lucid Dream Exchange*. As sometimes happens when we fall asleep thinking of lucid dreams, I had the following lucid dream (February 2006):

> I talk to a friend at IASD and ask him about being busy and various projects. He responds about the amount of work and correspondence.
>
> As I walk away through a cafeteria-type setting, a tall man dressed in regal clothing (as if from another century or perhaps a religious order) comes from my left and asks me a question, "What book do you have in your hand?"
>
> I realize that I'm carrying a book and pull it up to look at the title. Seeing it clearly, I tell him, "It's *Dreams: God's Forgotten Language* by John Sanford." With that, I know I own the book but have never read it. That's odd. Suddenly I become aware that I am dreaming.
>
> I fly off, feeling ecstatic, and shout (something like), "I send out one hundred pieces of love to others!"

Upon waking, I went to my bookshelf and pulled out my unread copy of *Dreams: God's Forgotten Language*. (I later learned that the author had passed away a few months before this lucid dream.) John Sanford, an Episcopal priest and Jungian analyst, suggests listening to dreams and the psyche or larger Self to help us through life's trials. Using examples of dream work in his pastoral counseling, Sanford shows the creative power of dreaming as it points out resolutions to conflicts, suggests areas of individual growth and freedom, and provides information beyond normal space and time. Repeatedly, he shows the inspired and directive aspect of dreaming and wonders (as dreamers often do) at the power and intent of dreaming's source.

Of particular interest to dreamers is Sanford's reflection on dreaming's ability to show us our totality as humans—not only the brightest but also the darkest aspects of our being. He exposes our personal and cultural inclination to focus exclusively on the bright and good and positive while refusing to acknowledge darker and troubling portions of our own experience. Dreams, Sanford suggests, encourage us to acknowledge all aspects of our being and come into greater awareness of the seeming dark and light. By doing so, we improve our ability to hear clearly and not distort inner information.

In his final chapter, "The God Within," Sanford concludes:

> We are not only conscious; we are also unconscious. Unconscious psychic reality is as real and substantial as is our conscious life. It expresses its reality in a hundred ways, one of which is the dream. The center of our conscious life is the ego, the center of our total psyche is the self, which seeks to express through our consciousness the totality of our nature. The experience of the totality of our nature is not *just* a psychological experience, but also a religious one in the sense that it connects us with a meaning and purpose beyond our egos. Our dreams serve our psychic totality, and seek to bring the ego into relationship with the psychic center in order that our totality may be consciously known and lived.[3]

At its best, lucid dreaming offers the potential to use our conscious awareness within the dream state to explore and more actively "bring the ego into relationship with the psychic center." When lucid dreamers understand that something exists behind the dream, they can begin to engage the awareness that "connects us with a meaning and purpose beyond our egos," as Sanford suggests. Unfortunately, he points out, we often unthinkingly adopt cultural beliefs and expectations that can condition us to avoid engaging dreams and our inner realm. "Collective thinking consists of all those attitudes and prejudices we acquire from our parents, compatriots, teachers, and our present overly intellectual and material culture," Sanford writes. "It throttles our individuality and prevents us from hearing the creative voice within. . . . Nowhere is collective thinking more conspicuous than in the way it causes us to ignore, or distort, the meaning of our dreams."[4] To value and truly understand dreaming's significance, then, we have to uproot internalized, limiting cultural beliefs about dreaming.

When the regal-looking dream figure asked, "What book do you have in your hand?" he called to my attention not only an unread book on my bookshelf but another example of the vibrantly aware realm of the unconscious. In that moment, my dreaming self achieved lucid awareness, but even more important, my waking ego self experienced another instance of an apparently thoughtful, engaged, and constructive inner awareness.

If we could adopt Sanford's belief that all dreams "bring the ego into relationship with the psychic center," we could see that we possess a purposeful and unified Self. In a unified Self, there may be challenges and concerns to address, but underlying it all exists a constructive intent. Within a unified Self, we may symbolically meet our deepest fears, but we do so knowing that it leads to our greater fulfillment as we strive to grow beyond those self-adopted limitations.

When the waking ego learns of the constructive intent of inner portions of itself, it sees clearly that it lives as one portion of a unified Self. With that awareness, the waking ego can begin to let down its defenses, recognize its inner support, and accept its connection to a broader state of being. Recognizing the unified Self, the waking ego can hear more clearly the naturally constructive intuitions, impulses, and dreams as suggestions for personal growth, healing, and wholeness.

An Outline of the Connected Universe

As I have endeavored to illustrate throughout this book, the waking ego, the waking self, seems only a small portion of the totality of conscious and unconscious awareness. How can something with such a small and limited perspective understand the greater psychological reality in which it has its being? So too, how can the waking ego or waking self be the creator of the vast reality of our inner life? Even Freud concluded, "The Unconscious is the greater sphere that includes the smaller sphere of the Conscious. . . . The Unconscious is the true reality of the psyche, its inner nature just as unknown to us as the reality of the external world, and just as imperfectly revealed by the data of consciousness as the external world is by the information received from our sensory organs."[5] How, then, can our waking self ever expect to understand this more expansive "true reality" in which our psyche resides? I believe lucid dreaming provides one path to understanding because it has the capacity to show 1) the existence of an inner awareness, 2) the truer nature of the dream environment, 3) a hidden reservoir of unconscious information, and 4) the underlying source of awareness.

1. The Existence of an Inner Awareness

Through conscious dream explorations, we can experiment with the so-called conscious and unconscious frameworks; finally begin to perceive the inner awareness there; and understand its intent, purposefulness, and relation to the waking self. I believe science will confirm that once the lucid dreamer escapes the subconscious atmosphere of overt personal desires and fears and directs his or her attention to the nonvisible awareness behind the dream, the waking self will be shown to interconnect with an inner awareness. These interactions will show a responsive, helpful, constructive, even protective awareness and overturn many traditional assumptions about the nature of the unconscious.

This inner awareness or inner Self likely represents, as Jung supposed, the "ego" of an inner "psychic system." The experiences of lucid dreamers so far indicate that the inner Self's purpose or direction appears to be instructive, supportive, or educational. It does not seem intent on dominating or usurping the lucid dreamer's awareness; rather, it appears to support its further development.

The recognition of a second psychic system or inner realm with an accompanying director or inner Self is, as Jung stated, "of revolutionary significance." It naturally calls for a reconsideration of the nature of the waking self, its meaning and purpose, and for a further investigation of the inner Self and its relationship with the waking self. Like the Copernican revolution, the existence of an inner Self inherently reorders the place of the waking self in relation to the larger psyche and its doings.

Realizing that we possess a conscious unconscious seems the first step in developing a relationship with the largest portion of our psyche. Throughout this book, various lucid dream examples suggest the means for talented lucid dreamers to discover this for themselves.

Like all natural systems, when viewed from a larger perspective, the system of the Self seems best described as unified and naturally harmonious. I held this belief through innumerable unique lucid experiences, and like a mathematician who can sense infinity without ever having experienced the totality of it, I sensed and came to believe in a unified Self within a connected universe, far beyond my knowing. The trust and belief in a unified Self allowed me to let go and, in letting go, become more than I had been.

2. The Truer Nature of the Dream Environment

From the repeated experiences of lucid dreamers, the dream environment responds to and operates under common principles across dreamers. It does not seem *innately* primitive, chaotic, or irrational; instead, it normally reflects in part the qualities, concerns, and attributes of the dreamer (which, of course, may be primitive, instinctual, repressed, and so on). As a principled realm, dreaming naturally exists as an orderly mental space with many common features. Since we largely don't comprehend the principles and have mischaracterized the environment of dreaming as innately chaotic, we routinely fail to see the orderliness and principled nature of the dream realm. Experienced lucid dreamers, by contrast, learn of its principled and orderly nature as they consciously interact with the dream environment.

The dream environment appears to exist as a mental framework in which lucid dreamers consciously engage various types of their own mental and emotional representations along with other portions of the Self. The dream realm and dreaming, therefore, facilitates these interactions and partially serves as an exchange of information between layers of the Self and the awareness of the waking self. Dreaming also exists as a meeting ground between waking awareness, other portions of the Self, and additional unconscious information from other sources.

Though information and concerns may be exchanged and reacted to in the dream state (accompanied by various emotional and ideational reactions by the dreamer), the information, emotions, and reactions are not characteristics of the dream environment any more than an argument in your car is a characteristic of your car. A more thoughtful consideration of the dream space would show it as a largely neutral environment, constructively disposed to assisting the waking self and larger Self. By considering it thusly, we move away from attributing the events of the dream to a native aspect of the dream realm or a native aspect of the unconscious—and finally begin to observe the dream environment as it exists, apart from the action that occurs there.

Conscious in the dream state, most any lucid dreamer can see the reality creating principles of belief, expectation, focus, intent, and will. Additionally, most lucid dreamers can see the X—or the unknown Inner—involved in various aspects of the lucid dream's creation. Both lucid dreaming and dreaming exist as cocreated products involving more than the waking self's emotions or mentations.

3. A Hidden Reservoir of Unconscious Information

Lucid dreamers discover that a natural part of the aware unconscious appears to connect to a layer of accessible information outside of the realm or creation of the waking conscious. In many reported lucid dream experiences, this accessible information goes beyond mundane observations about the dream or dreamer to profound information, experiences, concepts, and ideas. Moreover, it appears that this layer of information supports the historic belief that forward-looking, clairvoyant, and telepathic information is occasionally accessed in the dream state. Already, lucid dreamers have reported success at receiving this type of nonlocal information, which indicates a new means to investigate scientifically the apparent nonlocal abilities of consciousness to obtain unknown but verifiable information.

Because lucid dreamers have discovered that requests for accessible information have been denied, either due to the errant nature of the request or the abilities of the lucid dreamer to handle the receipt of conceptual information, some limitations exist (beyond the lucid dreamer's level of expertise and clarity). Undoubtedly, lucid dreamers' ability to access unconscious information deserves further investigation. Though not without challenges in procuring and accurately reporting, the presence of an unconscious layer of information has the potential for a major reconsideration of the appearance of certain types of knowledge and the nature of the mind.

4. The Underlying Source of Awareness

Beyond the symbols, beyond the figures, beyond all appearances, beyond the dream, lies a realm of pure awareness. Through this base reality, one senses the structural unity of awareness. Though reflected outward in billions of manifest forms and activities and individual awarenesses, underneath, all are enlivened by the same light, the light of awareness.

While apparently apart from others and apparently separate from objects, nature, and space, this awareness connects us at a deeper level. In lucid dreaming, we can consciously access this knowing and begin to demonstrate the existence of this profoundly connected realm. Its truest expression occurs when we go beyond lucid dreaming, inwardly through our own mind beyond the materializations and symbolic representations and beyond the conceptualizations of self, letting go and returning to experience our animating essence, pure awareness.

THE ENORMOUS BEAUTY

Much of what I have presented in this book may seem almost unimaginable, but the paradox of lucid dreaming—being conscious in the unconscious—provides each person a tool to explore and experiment for themselves. Your own experience can offer you the proof you seek. As you make your way—if you allow yourself—you will likely find that your own intent, your own deep wonder, naturally creates your path and helps draw the necessary experience to you. In lucid dreams like this one, you find the portions of the self joining together to assist, and you realize the inner support available to you on your journey (December 1999):

On a neighborhood street, I seem to be playing and talking with some adults and kids. The kids really like me and possibly call me Uncle. It's a very friendly group—maybe twenty people total.

Someone keeps doing something repeatedly, like playing a song, over and over. Finally, I realize the oddness of this and become lucidly aware. Then I notice—everyone was waiting for me to become lucid! In particular, there are three dream figures—one is a tall blonde guy and the other two are shorter with dark hair—and as they recognize that I am lucid, they appear very pleased that I have made the mental shift. We all hug and then perform a spontaneous chant, like a team.

I feel very happy to see them. Part of me thinks, "This is a mutual lucid dream—the four of us are all lucid." There are a lot of jokes and verbal exchanges. They even joke with me about getting me to this lucid state. Then suddenly I recall a similar dream in which I did not become lucid—my god, these dream figures had tried this before! We talk some more and I look around, noticing the details and people.

To our left stand three Asian women dressed in traditional garments. They have box hats, veils, and outfits composed of gauzy, silky fabrics—one woman primarily dressed in ivory, one in light orange, and one in light blue. The one in ivory has an instrument and begins to play a beautiful piece. I jump up and say, "This is incredible!" Looking around, I find my dream journal and start to sketch her profile. I look down at my drawing and then up at her, again and again, working on this sketch. It's filling in nicely except for the mouth. I tell everyone, "This is simply wonderful—the whole thing!"

I remind myself every now and then that this is a lucid dream and start to think that it is becoming fairly long. We applaud these Asian women when they finish, and people get up. . . . A man has a guitar and starts singing songs. They sound like familiar tunes but the lyrics are new and funny. I try to write them down in the dream journal. . . . He performs another song. Everyone laughs.

At this point, I truly become overwhelmed by the beauty and love in this lucid dream. I stand up and everyone looks my way. I say, "When I awake in physical reality as Robert Waggoner born on

January 28 in Kansas, sometimes the cold and snow of physical reality can get me down. But when I am here in this reality"—my voice starts to get emotional—"I am overwhelmed by the Enormous Beauty of this World."

Suddenly, I feel all of their love reflected back to me and start to get even more emotional. As the wave of emotion builds, something "clicks" and I realize that I'm half out of the lucid dream. I consider struggling to get my complete awareness back in while I still have the visuals but I feel like I should end it and write it down, so I decide to wake.

This book is the result of the "enormous beauty" of the unconscious, the mental space of dreams, and the hidden, yet ever supportive, psyche. This lucid dreaming path, with its fantastic creativity, deep lessons, profound compassion, and awareness, has touched me greatly and encouraged me to give it voice.

I hope to activate your personal curiosity, your own exploration of lucid dreaming, so that you can discover your own answers, beauty, and wonder. By becoming more consciously aware in the dream state, we begin to recognize our wholeness and the broader dimensions of Self. Aware in the dream state, we as a people and a culture have access to a more informed psychological viewpoint reflective of this wholeness. Lucid dreaming allows us another means to achieve the ancient imperative, "Know Thyself."

May this book touch you and inform you as you strive knowingly or unknowingly toward your greater wholeness. I wish you well on your journey.

Appendix A
Frequently Asked
Questions

The following are some of the many questions I have been asked about lucid dreaming. Because lucid dreaming is a vast topic, please feel free to visit my website for more questions and answers at www.lucidadvice.com

What are reality checks?
Reality checks are the practice of assuring yourself that you are dreaming by double-checking the dream reality. Lucid dreamers "check" the reality by floating, flying, placing their hand through a wall, and so on. In such a fashion, they confirm that they are aware in the dream state, since these actions can be performed only in dreaming. Reality checks are an excellent practice to incorporate into your lucid dreaming.

How do I awaken from a lucid dream?
Most people simply decide or intend to wake up, and they do. Others find that they routinely wake if they stare at one object in the lucid dream for a period of time. Still others know that if they engage in certain emotion-producing behaviors while lucid, they will likely wake. In general, lucid dreamers have no problem waking. Most have a greater interest in staying in the lucid dream and avoiding things that make the lucid dream end.

What are false awakenings?
False awakenings describe the experience of believing that you have woken from a lucid dream only to realize that you still dream. Normally, you quickly realize that you are still dreaming and awaken to physical reality. Sometimes, however, it takes a while for the realization to occur, since you may find yourself in a very real seeming environment

or be busily writing down the lucid dream in your dream journal when it occurs to you that you are still dreaming. Some people use the realization of a false awakening to conduct a reality check (as explained previously) and begin a new lucid dream adventure.

What is the void or gray state?
The void or gray state describes the dark, sparkling, normally imageless scene that occasionally lucid dreamers see when the lucid dream collapses and the visual imagery ends. At this point, many lucid dreamers decide the lucid dream is over and wake up. If you wish, however, you can maintain your awareness throughout the gray state and wait for a new lucid dream to emerge. Lucid dreamers do this by touching their sensed body and maintaining a kinesthetic sensation or by singing to keep an auditory sense active, or sometimes they simply maintain their awareness and wait for a new dream scene to appear. (Some lucid dreamers, myself included, wonder if the void or gray state represents unexpressed potential or the dream matrix.)

How long do lucid dreams last?
The length of a lucid dream depends on one's experience and ability at staying focused and aware. For many beginners, I estimate that ninety percent of their lucid dreams last fewer than five minutes. Intermediate lucid dreamers may find that they remain lucid for up to ten to fifteen minutes. Experienced lucid dreamers may go beyond that; some reports suggest as many as fifty minutes of continuous lucid dreaming.

Experienced lucid dreamers sometimes voluntarily cut short their lucid dream because if they stay too long, it often becomes hard to recall exact details that occurred much earlier in the dream. This is why lucid dreamers conducting experiments while lucid will normally tell themselves to awaken after getting the experimental results.

Besides memory limitations, what other cognitive issues do you find in lucid dreams?
When viewed from the waking perspective, it may appear that the lucid dreamer isn't always relating to the dream events in a particularly analytical, rational, or logical way.[1] Similarly, in hypnosis, the subjects often accept considerable logical incongruity as they act in their trance state, something hypnotists call "trance logic." Of course, most of the incongruence relates to suggestions offered by the hypnotist.

As previously noted, your lucid dreaming actions normally follow your existing beliefs and expectation (which seem rational at that moment). For example, if you believe that you can fall, then you will fall, although logically, gravity does not exist in the dream state. Though your concern about falling seems a very rational idea at the time (it *is* rational for you as long as you hold that belief), when awake it appears illogical and irrational.

Since your "belief posture" or set of beliefs and expectations act to largely direct your relation to the dream environment (and possibly the hypnotic one), under the constraints of your beliefs in that state, you do act rationally. Therefore, it seems improper to examine the logic or rationality of a lucid dreamer's behavior without examining his or her "belief posture" at that moment in the lucid dream.

What are dreamsigns?
Dreamsigns refer to any dream object or event that helps you realize you're dreaming. In my early lucid dreaming, seeing my hands acted as my predetermined dreamsign. As soon as I saw my hands, I realized I was dreaming. Sometimes seeing something unusual or a deceased relative in the dream will act as a dreamsign and elicit lucid awareness. If you want to create an effective personal dreamsign, the dreamsign needs to be strongly paired or associated with the realization "This is a dream!"

Most lucid dreams seem fun and exciting. Do you ever have negative or upsetting lucid dreams?
Most lucid dreams are exciting and enjoyable, yet it is possible to have upsetting lucid dreams or lucid nightmares. In these cases, the lucid or semi-lucid dreamer meets a threatening dream figure or situation (a personification of fears, normally) and feels overwhelmed, often failing to consider the various options in dealing with the figure or situation. Since lucid dreams are predisposed to follow beliefs, expectations, and focus, concentrating on the frightful characteristics helps precipitate the frightful situation. If you can suddenly change your beliefs, expectations, or focus, then you will likely resolve the situation. If you remain fearful, you prolong the fearful lucid situation.

What about lucid dreams where distracting dream figures appear?
Some lucid dreamers experience the appearance of "distracters" (a term coined by Ian Koslow in his *Lucid Dream Exchange* interview[2]) or lucid dream figures that seem to work in opposition to your intended goal or your lucid awareness. These dream figures may bother you with questions or doubts; by all appearances, they symbolically represent your own questions or doubts. Normally, distracters become less frequent as you become more comfortable with your lucid dreaming abilities.

Similarly, you might meet the converse in lucid dreams, or "attractors," meaning lucid dream figures who garner your attention by being attractive, seductive, or in some way very noticeable. Depending on the situation, these dream figures often represent (preexisting) feelings of desire. Like most distracters, once you ignore them, they disappear.

How do you respond when you find a frightful figure in your lucid dream?

First, the designation "frightful" is an interpretation of an experience. I have seen monsters in lucid dreams and laughed because I saw them as personified symbolic expressions. Most experienced lucid dreamers encounter unusual experiences and accept them or deal with them as expressions of a fundamentally constructive and unified Self. By changing your mental perspective, interpretation, and emotional response, you can transform situations that some may call frightful into interesting, albeit unusual, lucid dream encounters.

For example, many lucid dreamers successfully deal with the appearance of a hostile figure by projecting love and compassion onto it. In some cases, the hostile figure immediately transforms into something neutral or friendly. I recall a lucid dreaming friend who encountered a very menacing dream figure, whereupon he decided to project a feeling of love onto it. The result? The menacing dream figure began to melt and dissolve, like the Wicked Witch of the West. Mentally projecting the "power of love" or "peace" upon frightful figures can have a dramatic, positive effect.

How can there be something "behind" the lucid dream, if you, the lucid dreamer, are dreaming the dream?

When we realize that we don't control every aspect of the lucid dream (as I discuss at length in chapter 2) and we encounter completely unexpected and unanticipated things, we begin to sense that something else is involved in producing the lucid dream. At first, this something may seem to be an automatic dream-making process that occurs beneath our conscious awareness. However, in those cases when I and others questioned the "dream," it normally responded in a thoughtful, intelligent, purposeful, creative, and often unexpected way, indicative of something much more aware than an automatic dream-imaging process. Moreover, in the cases of lucid dream telepathy, clairvoyance, precognition, and so on, you again find evidence for some awareness behind the dream, which provides an answer that our waking ego self could not know.

You can resolve this for yourself in your next lucid dream by not focusing on the dream figures and objects and instead questioning the dream, "Hey dream! Show me . . ." Choose something open-ended, conceptual, or outside of your awareness (a likely future event) and see what happens. Then, based on your experience, you decide.

I don't remember my dreams. How can I begin to do so?
During a presentation in Colorado a few years ago, a young man asked me that same question. I told him that there were two reasons most people didn't recall their dreams: 1) they felt dreams had no value, and therefore didn't warrant being remembered, or 2) they felt that dreams were naturally scary and they had decided not to recall them. He then realized his lack of dream recall coincided with his parent's divorce fifteen years earlier. So, on the night following our conversation, he mentally told himself that he was now prepared to remember his dreams. In the morning, he was ecstatic. Incredible, wonderful, inspiring dreams had come to him upon falling asleep, he said.

For anyone wishing to become a lucid dreamer, remembering your dreams is the first step. Believing and suggesting that it is easy to remember them will impact your recall positively. Then, when you wake, immediately write your dreams in your journal. If you have too many dreams, you can suggest that you recall the "most important dream of the night" and see what happens.

Appendix B
Tips and Techniques

In the coming pages, you will find a number of successful techniques that lucid dreamers have used to become consciously aware in dreaming. My advice—focus on one technique, practice it consistently but without straining or overexertion, and imagine yourself happily writing down your lucid dream in your dream journal—imagine the joy of your success.

Doing It: Becoming Consciously Aware When Dreaming

Dreaming lucidly seems within almost anyone's ability. Many people who first hear about lucid dreaming have a lucid dream in the next night or two—simply by becoming curious and open to the idea. For others, it takes more time.

While making a presentation in Copenhagen a few years ago, I noticed a prominent psychologist and author on dreaming in the front row. After my talk, we conversed a bit about lucid dreaming. Days later, he announced during a conference presentation that he had experienced his first lucid dream. Similarly, over a dinner conversation with a psychologist trained in psychoanalysis, I discovered he had his first lucid dreaming in the night following our conversation, simply from becoming curious and mentally engaged by the idea.

Following a lucid dream seminar I held at MonkeyBridge Art Studios in Minneapolis, a woman attendee, "ERHS," reported her first lucid dream[1]:

Two weeks ago I celebrated my 60th birthday. A couple of nights after, I had a dream in which I was given a red birthday card. I look inside, but can't read the words. I realize, "I'm dreaming, so I can read anything." I look again and can read what the card says: "Showers of flowers, on your birthday and every day! signed: the Universe." I was still grinning when I woke up. Yes, it was my first, and I hope and expect not my last lucid dream. I am going to try asking out loud for a lucid dream.

Lucid dreaming happens naturally to people of all ages, backgrounds, and interests. If you can remember a dream— if you possess that much awareness in the dream state—then you only need to increase your awareness a few degrees more to become lucidly aware. Consider the "dimmer switch." Once the switch is on, a minor adjustment dramatically increases the amount of light. So, too, with lucid awareness in dreaming. You only need to make a minor increase in your dream awareness to become consciously aware of dreaming.

Let's look at some of the techniques that lucid dreamers find successful.

INFORMAL SUGGESTION

Suggestion comes in two modes, formal and informal. In my example of the psychoanalyst who became lucid the night after our dinner conversation, you find informal suggestion operating. As he listened to the experiences and concentrated upon them—much like you are doing now—he took in this informal suggestion: lucid dreaming happens to curious and interested people of all ages, backgrounds, and viewpoints simply by opening up to and allowing lucid dreaming. By reading this book, you are becoming curious about lucid dreaming and increasing your chances to spontaneously become lucidly aware in your upcoming dreams.

How do lucid dreamers use informal suggestion? Before going to sleep, they read about lucid dreaming or others' lucid dreams. Without thinking about it, they become engaged in the ideas. They might read a lucid dream report and think, "Wow, is it really possible to do that in a lucid dream?" or "No one can do that in a lucid dream—that's baloney!"

This latter point happened to me one evening as I read a copy of *The Lucid Dream Exchange* before going to sleep. A woman wrote that lately her lucid dreams had elements of the next day's newspaper's front page. I thought, "Oh please! There are so many items in the front page. I bet she's just seeing what she wants to see." That night, I had a powerful lucid dream in which I sat in a church pew between a man and a woman. Strangely, I felt the man really wanted to kill the woman, even though they seemed married! Why am I dreaming this and sitting between these two? I lucidly wondered. Upon waking, I went downstairs, opened the Sunday paper, and was greeted by a huge front page article about a battered spouse who first met her husband in church but eventually had to flee him and his controlling personality. Wait a second—that was my lucid dream! The whole article took up almost three pages of newsprint. Once again, I learned an important lesson about the possibilities inherent in dreaming.

How else can you practically use informal suggestion to increase the likelihood of lucid dreams? Besides reading about lucid dreams in books, publications, or online, you can simply play around with the idea of lucid dreaming. What would it feel like to fly through this wall? What would it feel like to shoot out the window and fly around outside? Play with the idea of it. When sitting in a lecture room or office meeting, imagine yourself saying, "This is a dream! I'm having a lucid dream!" Then imaginatively take off and fly around the room. Stand on the podium. Float upside down. (Take a minute to play right now with lucid dreaming—see yourself free and unfettered.) Playing with the idea of lucid dreaming generates valuable emotional energy.

FORMAL SUGGESTION

When we engage conscious techniques to influence our mind, we use formal suggestion. Hypnosis, visualization, dream incubation, dream ritual, all these techniques have an element of formal suggestion. Psychologist and lucid dreamer Patricia Garfield advocated a simple "Tonight I will have a lucid dream" in her groundbreaking book from 1974, *Creative Dreaming*. She found that autosuggestion resulted in an average of four to five lucid dreams a month.[2]

Self-suggestion might include the following: 1) while lying in bed and preparing for sleep, repeatedly say to yourself, "When dreaming tonight, I will realize I'm dreaming," or 2) "Tonight in my dreams, I will be much more critically aware and when I see something odd or unusual, I will realize I'm dreaming," or 3) "Tonight while my body sleeps a portion of me will remain alert and make me realize I'm dreaming."

Choose a suggestion that feels comfortable to you and stick with it every night. Lucid dreamers who consistently use a proper suggestion before sleep invariably report a lucid dream. In fact, every induction technique rests upon the idea of suggestion.

Lucid Dreaming and Hypnosis

In the 1980s at the University of Virginia, Dr. Joseph Dane researched the use of hypnosis to induce lucid dreaming. The participants selected for the study had shown an ability to be responsive to hypnotic induction but had no previous lucid dreaming experience.

After placing each of the women students under hypnosis, Dane suggested, "Tonight, you're going to turn off the automatic pilot in your dreams and fly with awareness. Tonight as you dream, you will somehow manage to recognize that you are dreaming while you're dreaming. Something will happen in your dreams to trigger your awareness, and you will remember that you are dreaming."[3]

Additionally, half of the group was also encouraged while in hypnosis to discover a personal dream symbol in a dream, which would help prompt a lucid dream. One young woman dreamt of a powerful woman in a cape, so that became her dream symbol. The following night, the young woman saw the same caped woman, which triggered her to become lucidly aware and conscious. According to Dane, "The qualitative level of their experience was well beyond what would normally be expected in laboratory experiments."[4] This group experienced longer and richer lucid dreams than those lucid dreamers without a personal dream symbol.

Results seemed extremely promising, since most managed to have a lucid dream within a few nights of the hypnosis. The results also suggest that lucid dreamers may improve their lucid dreaming skills by incubating a personal dream symbol to assist their lucid dreaming. To discover a personal dream symbol, you could suggest something like, "Tonight in my dream, I will clearly see a personal dream symbol that will assist me in becoming lucid."

Castaneda's Finding-Your-Hands Approach

I first learned of the Castaneda technique in this passage from his third book, *Journey to Ixtlan:*

"You must start by doing something very simple," he [don Juan] said. "Tonight in your dreams you must look at your hands."

I laughed out loud. His tone was so factual that it was as if he were telling me to do something commonplace.

"Why do you laugh?" he asked with surprise.

"How can I look at my hands in my dreams?"

"Very simple, focus your eyes on them just like this." He bent his head forward and stared at his hands with his mouth open. His gesture was so comical that I had to laugh.

"Seriously, how can you expect me to do that?" I asked.

"The way I've told you," he snapped. "You can of course, look at whatever. . . . I said your hands because that was the easiest thing for me to look at. Don't think it's a joke. *Dreaming* is as serious as *seeing* or dying or any other thing in this awesome mysterious world. Think of it as something entertaining."[5]

Don Juan certainly seemed serious about such a simple technique. So I tried it every night before going to sleep. Within a few nights, it happened. I became consciously aware in the dream state.

From a psychological perspective, the Castaneda approach establishes a simple stimulus-response associational linkage between seeing your hands and realizing, "I'm dreaming!" Remember the Russian physiologist Ivan Pavlov and his dogs? He was the scientist who trained a group of dogs to associate the presentation of food with the ringing of a bell. Ultimately, every time the dogs heard the ringing of the bell, they began to salivate reflexively, even if no food was present. Pavlov elicited this response by associating food with bell ringing. He created what psychologists call a conditioned reflex or a conditioned response.

When we consistently associate the sight of our hands with the idea, "I'm dreaming!" then, like Pavlov, we set up a mental conditioned response that sparks an aware realization in the dream state. As Pavlov learned, we need to repeat this activity frequently to establish a solid and automatic association. By creating this association in the waking state, we can influence the dreaming state. Here you have my version of a modified Castaneda technique:

1. Sit in your bed and drop the cares and concerns of the day. Take a minute to do this.

2. Casually look at your hands and tell yourself in a caring manner, "Tonight while I dream, I will see my hands and realize I'm dreaming."

3. Continue to casually look at your hands and mentally repeat the affirmation, "Tonight while I dream, I will see my hands and realize I'm dreaming."

4. Don't be bothered if your eyes cross or you begin to get tired. Remain at peace and continue to repeat your intent slowly and gently.

5. After five minutes, or once you feel too tired or sleepy, quietly end the practice.

6. Gently remind yourself of your intention to see your hands in a dream and then realize that you're dreaming, and go to sleep.

7. When you wake up in the middle of the night, gently recall your last dream; did you see your hands? Resume your intention to see your hands and realize that you're dreaming.

8. Repeat this approach faithfully each night, and you should have a lucid dream. When you wake from your lucid dream, write it down in your dream journal. Write the entire dream, how you realized you were dreaming, what you did while aware that you were dreaming, all the details. And congratulate yourself!

Stephen LaBerge's MILD Technique

Although I began with the Castaneda technique in 1975 and used it and suggestion as my initial methods, once I heard about the MILD technique years later, I employed it with considerable success. Within months, I had doubled my average number of lucid dreams.

In the front of my college dream journal, I kept a numeric graph charting my lucid dreaming progress (a remnant of many behavioral psychology courses). I knew my lucid dreaming baseline ranged from four to nine lucid dreams a month. When I switched to the MILD technique, my lucid dreaming numbers began to climb. Eventually, I topped out at thirty lucid dreams in one month—my best numbers ever.

The term MILD stands for Mnemonic Induction of Lucid Dreams and can be more fully explored in Dr. LaBerge's book, *Lucid Dreaming*. (I highly recommend this book for all lucid dreamers.) *Mnemonic* stands for a mental device used to assist the memory; for example, the rhyme "In 1492, Columbus sailed the ocean blue" helps children recall the date of Columbus's voyage. LaBerge felt that the memory of one's desire to become lucid was a key to becoming lucid. My rendition of the MILD technique follows:

1. When you spontaneously wake up during the night, vividly remember your last dream in detail.

2. Intend to become lucid in the next dream by suggesting, "Next time I'm dreaming, I want to remember to recognize I'm dreaming."

3. Now imagine that you are back in the recalled dream and becoming lucidly aware at an appropriate point. Visualize this clearly.

4. Keep doing these steps until your intent feels well established. As you prepare to sleep, expect to become lucid and aware in your next dream.

As a college student, I found it hard to recall this technique, so I wrote it on a note card, placed it on my night stand, and committed it to memory each night. In fact, I found it useful to recall the technique via the MILD acronym in this way: M–Memorize the last dream, I—Intend to become lucid, L—Lucid, I see myself becoming lucid in the dream, D—Do it! By remembering the steps in this way, I could easily perform them when I awoke.

By imagining yourself becoming lucid in your last dream, you help create a very real-seeming mental event. As you mentally play at being aware in a dream, you mimic lucid dreaming. This role-playing seems to prepare a fertile field for lucid awareness, increasing your chances of becoming conscious in the next dream.

THE NAP-TO-LUCIDITY TECHNIQUE

For many lucid dreamers, the "nap to lucidity" technique vastly improves their probability of becoming lucidly aware. The first lucid dreamer to signal from the lucid dream state, Alan Worsley, discovered that if he woke up early in the morning, stayed awake for an hour or two while having a cup of tea or coffee, then went back to sleep, he often became lucid in his morning nap. Many others have independently noticed the same thing.

Research on this technique reported by Lynne Levitan at the Lucidity Institute[6] showed significant increases in the probability of a lucid dream. In the study, lucid dreamers would intentionally wake about ninety minutes before their normal waking. They would spend the next ninety minutes awake and then return to sleep, using a special MILD exercise. Using this technique, the number of lucid dreams skyrocketed in the morning nap when compared to baseline records.

Recently, I woke at 4 A.M. and felt the need to get up and write down some ideas about lucid dreaming for this book. When I finished an hour later, I decided to take a nap on the downstairs couch and proceeded to have a very intriguing lucid dream in which I consciously moved the living room furniture through the air by dream psychokinesis.

Of course, by waking up earlier than normal and then taking a nap an hour and a half later, our chances for lucid dreaming increase most dramatically.

PAUL THOLEY'S CRITICAL-MIND TECHNIQUE

German lucid dreamer and psychotherapist Paul Tholey explored lucid dreaming deeply and originally in some fascinating ways. In 1959, he developed an idea to achieve critical awareness in dreams. He wrote: "If one develops a critical frame of mind towards the state of consciousness during the waking state, by asking oneself whether one is dreaming or awake, this attitude will be transferred to the dreaming state. It is then possible through the occurrence of unusual experiences to recognize that one is dreaming. One month after beginning with this method, I had my first lucid dream."[7]

Tholey translated this idea into various practices such as asking himself numerous times throughout the day or when confronted with an odd event, "Am I dreaming or not?" Then wondering, "How do I know?" Later when dreaming, he found that same attitude beginning to express itself in the dream state and eventually became lucid.

Testing certain dream theories of the time, Tholey calculated, "If one thinks over unsolved problems before falling asleep, a quasi need develops which according to Lewin can be interpreted as a system in a state of tension. In the dreaming state, this system is able to relax more easily which may not only lead to the problem being solved *but also help the dreamer to become aware that he is dreaming*" [emphasis added].[8]

In effect, Tholey wondered if the tension of an "unsolved problem" could act as a vehicle to elicit conscious awareness, assuming that we dream about unresolved issues from the day, as some dream theorists proposed. This psychological vector approach to bringing conscious awareness into dreaming shows his impressive creativity and interest in dreaming processes.

I once experienced this "unsolved problem" influencing lucidity while on a business trip in January 1995. I was watching the evening news before falling asleep when the announcer reported that a major earthquake measuring 7.2 on the Richter scale had hit Kobe, Japan. The details were sketchy. I turned off the television, hoping the earthquake was not too severe. That night, I became lucidly aware and found myself flying to Japan to inspect things; I walked amongst broken concrete and twisted metal. Also, along the way, flying high over the Pacific Ocean by all appearances, I saw a ship far below. The ship appeared to be moving along a southeast to northwesterly line. I flew down to see it and read the ship's name—it was the USS Stark. Although the U.S. Navy had an active frigate by that name at the time, I have not been able to determine whether it was in the Pacific or what its movements were on the day after the Kobe earthquake. (The earthquake occurred on January 17, 1995, at 5:46 A.M., local time.)

MISCELLANEOUS CONDITIONS THAT SEEM TO ASSIST

During my thirty years of lucid dreaming, I noticed certain activities or events seemed to increase the probability of a lucid dream. A few years ago, I wrote an article for *The Lucid Dream Exchange*, mentioning these miscellaneous factors. Oddly enough, within two months of its publication, my dreaming self showed me that I had made an error in the list. In the article, I stated that lucid dreaming seemed *less likely* to occur on the night of the full moon. Guess what? After I wrote that, I had lucid dreams on the night of the next two full moons. Once again, the aware unconscious appears to listen with the intent to educate.

Many lucid dreamers have found the following items boost their lucid dreaming chances:

1. Change in location: It seems that sleeping in a different room, whether in the same house or when traveling, makes one a bit more "vigilant" or aware.

2. Change in life routine: Vacations and holiday periods all seem to increase the likelihood of lucid dreaming.

3. Yoga or energy practices: Many of us have noticed that the night after yoga class or other energizing practice we have a spontaneous lucid dream.

4. Excess physical, mental, or emotional effort during the day: It appears that excess exertion may increase lucid dreams.

5. Normal exuberance: Periods of feeling in good spirits, content, and positive seem to affect the ability to become lucid.

6. Certain foods: Some lucid dreamers have noticed an increase in lucid dreams after eating certain foods. The writer Jane Roberts suggested foods like asparagus might be helpful, and a minor touch of caffeine before sleep may assist some people. Years later, scientists discovered that a plant relative of asparagus contains a chemical useful for increasing awareness in those with Alzheimer's.

7. Vitamins such as B6 before bedtime: Some studies indicate B6 may lead to enhanced memory retention.

8. Weather changes: I have personally noticed a strong connection with approaching storm systems and an increase in lucid dreaming. Perhaps this is due to changes in air ionization or air pressure in the prairie landscape where I reside.

9. Certain locales: Though I would prefer to say that all places seem equal for lucid dreaming, I have had some incredible lucid dreams on various trips that visited ancient Native American sites. It seems impossible to know whether the actual site, or my possible beliefs and expectations about the site, created this increase in lucid dreaming. Others have suggested high altitudes promote lucid dreaming.

These miscellaneous factors create questions about the triggering of lucid dreams. Once a person possesses the basic skill, does mental expectation play the primary role? Or do lucid dreams increase based on one achieving a certain "energy threshold?" Can external forces, such as weather, food, vitamins, and so forth, affect lucid dreaming significantly? Do these factors play only a secondary role to expectation?

DIFFICULTY WITH BECOMING CONSCIOUSLY AWARE

Over time, I have noticed some people seem to take to lucid dreaming with relative ease. These people appear to possess a welcoming mental atmosphere. By that, I mean internally they exhibit a deep sense of allowance, personal acceptance, and active expectation about lucid dreaming. They feel good about trying it. They have goals they want to try. They have a sense of wonder and intrigue. They possess a sense of play about it.

Of course, not everyone initially succeeds at lucid dreaming. The most likely reason is that they fail to recall dreams—any dreams. When someone approaches me with a complaint about being unable to lucid dream, I first ask them about their dream recall. Until they become actively interested in remembering dreams, how can they expect to become lucid dreamers? I encourage them to keep a pen and notebook on their nightstand and to begin to record their dreams upon waking or in the morning—even if only a fragment appears.

When I do meet those who actively recall dreams but seem incapable of having a lucid dream, I ask them, "If you could become lucid tonight, what would you really want to do?" More often than not, they have no specific response, no goal. I ask them to develop a goal that arouses their emotional energy—because if you don't care, then why bother?

Last, I ask about their consistent efforts or persistence. If you try the technique one evening and then forget for the next four evenings before trying again, the lack of consistency or persistence does not bode well. Think of your efforts as an expression of your true intent and gently persist.

If you do *not* succeed in becoming lucid after a month or two of regular practice (or if you have tried to become lucid and never succeeded), you may need to reconsider your mental atmosphere. It may be that your mental atmosphere contains one or more of the following fears or inflexible conceptual blocks:

1. You're interested in lucid dreaming but have fears about it or the subconscious.

2. You're interested in lucid dreaming but philosophically don't agree with it or don't approve of it.

3. You're interested in lucid dreaming but feel it requires too much effort, high spiritual accomplishment, or special permission.

4. You're interested in lucid dreaming but are too tired to do the practices or can't remember any dreams.

5. You're interested in lucid dreaming, but your life feels hectic or in turmoil (due to problems related to work, relationships, family, and so on), and you can't really concentrate.

If any of these conditions apply, it's important to face them fully before proceeding. By facing our fears, expanding our limiting beliefs, and responding to issues in a thoughtful and insightful manner, we grow. Allowing new and interesting experiences requires an inner openness and a sense of wonder. When you feel wonder about lucid dreaming, you draw its realization closer to you.

Seeing Lucidity's Depth: Levels of Lucidity

Experienced lucid dreamers know that there are degrees of lucid awareness in lucid dreaming. Once we recognize the dream environment and become lucid, we may find our awareness fluctuating among varying levels of lucidity. Ed Kellogg explores the varying levels of lucid awareness, which he calls the Lucidity Continuum,[9] which I present here, with Ed's permission, in a condensed format:

> **Pre-Lucid:** Dreamer notices bizarreness as "unusual." Dream Report might read: "I saw a young woman with a hole in her stomach and thought that was weird."
>
> **Sub-Lucid:** Dreamer vaguely realizes he or she dreams. Dream Report might read: "I walked down the street and noticed a flying horse, so I knew this couldn't be real."
>
> **Semi-Lucid:** Dreamer knows he or she dreams but continues to follow the dream plot with very minor adjustments. Dream Report might read: "I walked into the house and saw Uncle Harry, but I realized Uncle Harry was dead, so this must be a dream. Mom asked me if I would set the table, and I did so, even setting a place for Uncle Harry."
>
> **Lucid:** Dreamer knows he or she dreams and realizes choices and ability to make major changes in their dream experience. Dream Report might read: "Sitting in my third grade classroom, I thought, 'I'm not in the third grade anymore! This is a dream!' Then I decide to fly out the window. I meet some people at a crosswalk and tell them, 'This is a dream. To prove it, I will fly to the top of the stoplight.' I do so easily. Standing on the stoplight, I then make all of the traffic stop by mentally expecting it."
>
> **Fully Lucid:** Dreamer can recall his or her physical life and all predetermined tasks to perform and shows high level of dream manipulation. Dream Report might read: "Now lucid, I begin to think, 'What experiment did Jan and I talk about yesterday? Oh yes, she wanted me to ask a dream figure what it represents!' So I approach a dream figure standing at the bus stop and ask, 'Excuse me. What do you represent?'"

Super Lucid: Dreamer shows extremely high level of dream manipulation and personal energy, clarity of thought, creativity, and memory, and so on. Dream Report might say: "Lucid, I have incredible energy, clarity, and flying skill. I recall that I want to experience unconditional love. I ignore the dream figures and objects and shout out to the awareness behind the dream, 'Hey, I want to experience unconditional love.' Suddenly, I felt intense . . ."

At each successive level, you find an improvement in your clarity of thought and overall awareness. Thinking of lucid dreams as a continuum of awareness has other important aspects.

First, beginning lucid dreamers should see that achieving lucid dreaming may come in stages. You may dream of having conversations about lucid dreams—or you may dream of mentioning how "lucid-like" or "dream-like" an event or action appears. So close! These events clearly show that the idea of lucid dreaming has seeped into your awareness. Lucid dreamer John Galleher provides an example of moving through various "levels of lucidity" before finally becoming lucidly aware:

I dreamed I was at a dream retreat center. I was sitting in a lawn chair by a lake which bordered the center. I was writing "lucid dream" in my dream journal, when the director of the center approached me. "Having any dreams?" he asked me. "No, but I'm going to have a lucid dream," I answered. "Why don't you take a walk around the lake and get to know your surroundings," he said.

I got up and began walking and my wife joined me. We walked around the lake until we came to a place where the lake flowed into a river. There was a bridge across the river but it was made of fabric, like a long sheet stretched across the water. I hesitated because this sure looked like an "iffy" proposition, but then I decided that I could swim if I fell in so I crossed over. It was a balancing act, but I made it. My wife saw that I did it, so she joined me.

We continued walking and came to a wooden house along the lakeside. On the porch sat a waking life friend of mine. He was relaxing but in waking life he's a real workaholic and it was this inconsistency that made me lucid. "We're in a dream, look at your hands," I said to him. He looked at me rather doubtfully, so I said "Watch this." I began levitating, but as I pushed off I gave myself a twist in a kind of theatrical way, like "up, up and away." This twist started me spinning as I went up and got faster and faster as I rose. It became more and more ecstatic until finally I lost the dream. I woke up feeling great.[10]

In this example, the dreamer engages in discussing lucid dreams with a dream figure who questions him. But not until he notices his workaholic friend relaxing does it strike him as too unusual. At that point, he shifts levels from the pre-lucid stage to lucidly announce, "We're in a dream . . ."

A second important consideration of the lucidity continuum concerns your ability to move up or down the lucidity continuum. You may lose awareness after becoming lucid or gain greater awareness as the lucid dream progresses. Lucidity does not exist as a steady state—it fluctuates.

A third valuable aspect to the lucidity continuum involves differentiating between standard lucid dreams and fully lucid dreams. In fully lucid dreams, you can recall experimental tasks and use a much broader range of your lucid abilities.

Fourth, the lucidity continuum provides insight into a certain small percentage of people who claim, "All my dreams are lucid!" When questioned, they seemed to understand that they dream while in the dream, but they often act like semi-lucid dreamers: dreamers who know they dream but continue to follow the dream plot with very minor changes.

For beginning lucid dreamers, their strategy should be to remain lucid as long as possible while learning to direct their focus. The initial lesson involves modulating emotions to maintain the lucid dream. The second lesson involves maintaining one's lucid awareness while interacting with the ongoing dream.

Here are some techniques to modulate your emotions and maintain the lucid dream:

Stay focused on lucid awareness. Because excess emotions often lead the lucid dream to collapse, lucid dreamers quickly learn to modulate their emotions by staying focused on their lucid awareness. When lucid dreamers see something exciting, glorious, or disgusting, they can remind themselves, "This is a dream," as a way to stay calm and focused on their awareness. Often that realization seems enough to reduce emotional surges.

Develop a calming practice: In some situations, the lucid dreamer develops a practice that serves to induce calm. Don Juan taught Castaneda to return to looking at his hands whenever the dream seemed ready to collapse. You can do the same thing whenever the lucid dream gets too emotional. Look at your hands or, perhaps, at the floor. In either case, this seems to "ground" the dreamer because it removes one's attention away from a disturbing stimulus and to a peaceful or neutral stimulus.

Place emotional issues to the dream's end: For more experienced lucid dreamers who might wish to do something in their lucid dream that naturally leads to excitement or emotion (e.g., have sex, perform a fantastic feat, confront a serious fear), they can often recall that intent but act on it at the conclusion of their lucid dreaming (since they know that the excitement will be intense). So in the lucid dream, they first perform less emotive tasks before getting to the more emotive tasks.

Handle recurring emotions: For a small portion of lucid dreamers, they may become lucid and soon be confronted by something emotive: an intense sexual desire, a frightful figure, or something exciting. When lucid, you decide how to respond, but when it comes to recurring emotion producing situations or dream figures, it seems most helpful to ask such things as, "What do you represent?" or "Hey Dream! Why am I experiencing this?" and await the response. Dealing with recurring figures or situations seems invaluable for moving forward and creating a proper foundation for growth.

Techniques for maintaining awareness are extremely helpful for beginner and intermediate lucid dreamers as they seek to prolong the lucid state. Most awareness techniques involve manipulating your focus, such as:

Repetition: Many have discovered that one way to maintain awareness involves repeating a comment about your awareness. To avoid losing your lucidity in early lucid dreams, you may wish to repeat every fifteen seconds, "This is a dream. I am dreaming this." Some beginning lucid dreamers make it a practice to look at their hands every now and then during the lucid dream as a reminder.

Having a goal: When we focus on a goal, the goal seems to remain active until the goal is satisfied. For example, if we walk into the Louvre looking for the *Mona Lisa*, we continue with that goal by actively disregarding other artwork until we reach the *Mona Lisa*. In a similar way, when we have an active goal in lucid dreaming, that focus seems to buttress our lucid awareness. We usually ignore or reject competing images and temptations and continue toward our goal, lucidly aware.

Comparison/contrast in the dream: When we become lucid and notice a certain quality about the lucid dream, we can use that to maintain lucidity. For example, flying might be the quality that reminds you that you are lucidly aware. In other lucid dreams, you may touch something and make a natural comparison/contrast between lucid dreaming and waking. If you continue touching things throughout the lucid dream, you continue to reinforce the idea of a comparison/contrast of the two states.

Announcing intent: When lucid, announcing your intent seems to have extra power or extra impact. While some people might yell, "Better lighting" and see light levels increase or "More people" and see more dream figures around them, one could also announce, "Greater awareness!" or "Greater clarity!" and elevate the awareness.

Projecting one's power: In some lucid dreams, I found myself "deciding" that I could more easily maintain lucid awareness if I created a reminder such as carrying a cane or holding a special object. In one lucid dream, I magically created stickers that read, "I am lucid." Then I spent the dream placing the "I am lucid" stickers on items in the dream! You can buttress your awareness by creating a personal symbolic reminder to be aware.

Singing: Some lucid dreamers, like my *Lucid Dream Exchange* coeditor Lucy Gillis, have discovered that singing while lucid dreaming helps them maintain their lucid awareness and make certain activities, such as flying for example, easier. Singing about your lucid activities may help you focus your lucid awareness, provide a sense of directed emotional energy, and allow you to engage specific goals.

Practice makes perfect: With practice, your lucid dreams become easier to maintain and last longer. In a sense, practice makes perfect—or at least, much better—lucid dreamers. Most established lucid dreamers have no trouble maintaining their basic lucid awareness and may hardly give it a second thought.

Dream Reentry

In my early years of lucid dreaming, as a college student, I would sometimes find myself lucidly aware in a dream with a gorgeous young woman. As things progressed and became more amorous, my emotions would rise to a point at which I woke. Oh, if I could only reenter that lucid dream!

Surprisingly, I found that in many instances I could reenter the dream consciously and continue it, often, by all appearances, with the same dream figure and dream setting. Since a beginner's lucid dreams can be relatively short, learning dream reentry is a valuable tool.

Certain behaviors appear to assist the dream-reentry process. First, for some reason, it seemed to help if I matched the exact position of my physical body upon waking from the earlier dream. So to reenter the dream, I would reposition my body to conform to how it had been upon waking. I put my head just so, put my arms here, placed my leg just right, and so on. Now, my body felt ready for reentering the dream.

Then, I found it best to replay the dream in my mind while focusing on an event near the dream's end. At that place in the dream, I would visualize it completely in my mind for a moment while allowing myself to doze off. Often, at this stage, I would slip back into the dream, consciously aware, as if by lucidly intended dream osmosis.

My final trick involved replaying the dream to the end and then "seeing" some portion of the dream as if inside the dream. By that, I mean I would seek to perceive the dream from some symbol or dream figure's viewpoint in the dream. Once I began to see the dream from an inside perspective, I suddenly would find myself back in the dream state. Usually, the dream would reanimate and continue, and my lucid awareness would be in the scene. Sometimes, the dream details would seem slightly altered, but all in all, a fair similitude would exist there.

Later, I discovered other lucid dreamers had created very similar practices for improving their dream-reentry chances. Once again, the dream state and lucid dreaming process showed a common platform of successful principles and activities.

ENDNOTES

Chapter 1: Stepping Through the Gate

1. On June 16, 1973, I dreamed of watching a moon cross the sky three times as a voice said that the event would occur in three years. Then suddenly I found myself in the midst of a ferocious riot with both blacks and whites. As I sought shelter, I noticed a Dutch-type windmill, similar to one in my hometown. Three years later, on June 16, 1976, the Soweto riots erupted in South Africa as students protested the forced teaching of Afrikaans. Because of the numerous deaths and injuries, many historians consider this date *The Day Apartheid Died*, as a BBC broadcast called it. In an odd coincidence, two months later at college, one of my dorm-suite mates was a young black man from Soweto. I never told him about the dream.

2. In fact, sometime later, I overheard one of my older brothers assert, "We're part Indian." I asked him how he knew that, and he replied, "Grandmother told me." I asked my mother about it, and she became very upset. Years later, she admitted that Grandmother was right; we were a small part Native American. She hadn't wanted us talking about it with our schoolmates for fear that some prejudice would occur. As for me, it explained certain experiences.

3. Carlos Castaneda, *Journey to Ixtlan: The Lessons of Don Juan* (New York: Pocket Books, 1974), 266.

4. A fair amount of controversy has ensued as to whether Carlos Castaneda's books constitute fiction, nonfiction, or some blend of both. Critics include author Richard de Mille, *Castaneda's Journey: The Power and the Allegory* (Santa Barbara, CA: Capra Press, 1976), who sought to point out the numerous chronological and logical errors in the writings.

For my part, I can only say that the book's technique of inducing lucid or conscious dreaming worked for me and many others. Also, as I continued to lucid dream on my own, I had experiences that Castaneda's don Juan explains in later books *before* his explanations were published. Because of this, I feel at least some of the books' instructions seem based on valid insights about dreaming consciously.

In many respects, Castaneda's work had a broad and lasting influence, even creating ripples in the approach to the study of anthropology. He inspired others to investigate indigenous knowledge both theoretically and practically. Additionally, he created a greater appreciation of possible psi phenomena and indigenous techniques to explore that mystery.

5. Castaneda, *Journey to Ixtlan*, 100.

6. Quoted in "Conscious Dreaming" by Chandra Shekhar, *Science News 2006* (Santa Barbara: University of California): http://www.nasw. org/users/chandra/Clips/lucid_dreaming.htm.

7. As I was doing some research for this book, I came across various articles by Alan Worsley, the first lucid dreamer to signal lucid dreaming in a sleep lab in the mid-1970s and an extremely talented lucid dreamer.

In his writings, Worsley mentions one of his lucid dream skills, which involved manipulating and elongating his arms to incredible proportions. Reading this prompted me to think I might like to try it myself.

Many lucid dreamers find that if you become really curious about doing a lucid dream task, you're more likely to lucid dream, remember the task, and perform it. Just like that, in my next lucid dream, I recalled the idea:

I find myself walking down a road that seems under construction, like a war has ended and it's being rebuilt. Other people walk along too. I get to a small school house where I see one of my brothers and a little kid wearing an interesting blue and gold shirt. Something about this little kid or his energy makes me realize, "Hey! This is a dream. I'm lucid!" The kid claps when he sees me become lucid.

I feel some excitement at being lucid again and decide to fly through a glass window—I fly right through it but now am in a different room. So I decide to fly through a concrete block wall to see what lies on the other side. I fly through it and experience the interesting sensation of sensing the wall as I do so. But now I seem to be in a storage room. I fly through the wall once more and end up near the entrance of the school.

Standing there, I wonder what to do and recall Worsley's ability to extend his arms while lucid. I decide to try it. Holding out my left arm, I begin to pull on it with my right arm—incredibly, the arm begins to lengthen. I find this interesting and pull some more and then some more. Now my left arm has extended to about seven feet in length. I wiggle my fingers and watch as they move.

I look over at my brother, whom I now notice. While I've been extending my arms, he has been contracting his by pushing his arms into his shoulders! One arm has virtually disappeared down to the wrist and fingers! Suddenly, I can feel the dream ending and I try to hold on but can't manage to reenter it. I shout something like sending love and energy to others. I wake.

8. Castaneda, *Journey to Ixtlan*, 100.

Chapter 2: Does the Sailor Control the Sea?

1. J. Allan Hobson, "Finally Some One: Reflections on Thomas Metzinger's 'Being No One,'" *Psyche* 11, no. 5 (June 2005): 5.

2. Ibid., 7.

3. Various of the Jungian-oriented psychotherapists told me that lucid dreaming reminded them of what Jung called "active imagination," except that I was doing it in the dream state, not, as Jung described it, in the meditative state. The main practice of active imagination involves quieting yourself into a meditative state, then using either a remembered dream image or some imagined starting point (e.g., walking up to a house) and waiting for the imagery to evolve while you consciously maintain awareness and engage the images with questions. With practice, one can become quite adept at active imagination and mentally converse with many interesting symbols and figures that may provide insight into your life situation or emotional state.

4. As quoted by Marc Ian Barasch in his book, *Healing Dreams* (New York: Riverhead Books, 2001), 14.

5. Ryan Hurd, "DreamSpeak Interview," *The Lucid Dream Exchange* 43 (June 2007): 6.

Chapter 3: Moving in Mental Space

1. Lynne Levitan and Stephen LaBerge, "In the Mind and Out-of-Body: OBEs and Lucid Dreams, Part 1," *NightLight* 3, no 2 (Spring 1991): 9.

2. Thomas Metzinger, "Reply to Hobson: Can There Be a First-Person Science of Consciousness?" *Psyche* 12, no. 4 (2006): 3.

3. Susan Blackmore, *Consciousness: An Introduction* (Oxford: Oxford University Press, 2004), 2.

4. Robert Monroe, *Journeys Out of the Body* (New York: Doubleday, 1971; reprint, New York: Broadway Books, 2001).

5. The following are some OBE basics and suggestions for "rolling out."

If you find yourself falling asleep and hearing a constant humming, buzzing vibration about you, just remind yourself that people have reported this for hundreds of years and, thus, there is no reason for alarm. Assuming you don't spontaneously find your awareness outside of your body, you can do this: 1) imagine that you have lifted your arms straight up (you might suddenly see a pair of faded images of arms above you, almost like shadowy outlines); 2) now, imagine yourself quickly moving those arms to the left (or right) so that you can roll out of the bed; and 3) as you throw your arms to one side, the imagined movement of those imagined arms might suddenly "roll" your awareness out of your body! Keep trying until you succeed in moving your awareness.

You may find yourself standing in your bedroom now, feeling light as a feather. Feel free to look back at your bed. You may see yourself there, but in some cases, you won't. Either way, levitate a little bit to be sure that you are in an altered state or stick your hand through the wall to confirm it. Once confirmed by an appropriate "reality check," feel free to explore. You might want to see if you can confirm whether you are in an imagined realm or a physical one.

When it comes to experiences of awareness like lucid dreams or OBEs, if you can simply accept the experience with a feeling of curiosity and be-mused interest, you will likely have an interesting and enjoyable experience. To fight or resist the experience will likely lead to unnecessary concerns and fears. Like many inner experiences, they are rarely discussed openly, even though they are relatively commonplace.

6. Kenneth Ring and Evelyn Elsaesser Valarino, *Lessons from the Light: What We Can Learn from the Near-Death Experience* (New York: Insight Books, 1998; reprint, Needham, Massachusetts: Moment Point Press, 2006), 65–66.

7. Robert A. Monroe, "Wanted: New Mapmakers of the Mind," *Lucidity Letter* 4, no. 2 (December 1985): 49.

8. E. W. Kellogg III, Ph.D., "Mapping Territories: A Phenomenology of Lucid Dream Reality," *Lucidity Letter* 8, no. 2 (December 1989).

9. In recent years, the OBE phenomenon has received new attention from scientists. In one case, they assisted in creating a waking OBE-type experience with virtual-reality goggles. In another, scientists stimulated a region of the brain that resulted in OBE-like sensations in an awake pa-tient. Experiments like these may lead to increased understanding of the possible mechanism. However, on a personal or experiential level, these laboratory-induced copies may not accurately replicate the actual total OBE experience any more than duplicating symptoms of the flu can be equated to having the flu.

10. I discuss the apparent knowledge of some dream figures at length in chapter 11.

Chapter 4: Beyond Freud's Pleasure Principle

1. Actually, when my niece called me the day of the dream, I believe I heard her say to the dream, "Hey dream, show me something good for me to see." But in this written report from weeks later, she gives a more convoluted request to the dream.

2. Robert Van de Castle, *Our Dreaming Mind* (New York: Ballantine Books, 1994), 129.

3. *The Lucid Dream Exchange* (December 1992): 18.

4. Carlos Castaneda, *The Art of Dreaming* (New York: HarperCollins, 1993), 161.

Chapter 5: Independent Agents and the Voice of the Unconscious

1. Years later, Linda Lane Magallón wrote *Mutual Dreaming* (New York: Pocket Books, 1997). Jane Roberts' two-volume *The "Unknown" Reality* was published by Prentice Hall (Englewood Cliffs, NJ) in 1977. It was republished in 1996 by Amber-Allen Publishing (San Rafael, CA).

2. C. G. Jung, "The Relations Between the Ego and the Unconscious," in *The Basic Writings of C. G. Jung*, ed. Violet Staub de Laszlo (New York: Random House, 1993), 196.

3. Ibid., 196–97.

4. Connie Gavalis' lucid dream originally appeared in the May 1993 *Lucid Dream Exchange*.

5. Personal communication (December 12, 2007). Used by permission.

6. Suzanne Wiltink, *The Lucid Dream Exchange* (June 2006).

7. Paul Tholey, "Overview of the Development of Lucid Dream Research in West Germany," *Lucidity Letter* 8, no. 2, (December 1989).

8. Paul Tholey, *Schöpferisch Träumen: Der Klartraum als Lebenshilfe* (*Creative Dreaming: The Lucid Dream as an Aid to Life*) (Niedernhausen, Germany: Falken Verlag, 1987), 237. Thanks to Christoph Gassmann for his assistance in translating.

9. Scott Sparrow, "Letter to the Editor," *Lucidity Letter* 7, no. 1 (June 1988): 8.

10. I'm not sure who coined the term "false awakening," but I feel that it may serve to denigrate a valid experience and keep researchers from considering it and its phenomenological implications. Consider if we replaced the word "imagination" with the term "false thinking." Would you want your child to develop his or her "false thinking" skills? Would you support artists and writers who engaged in works of "false thoughts?" In calling this valid experience a "false awakening," we suggest a prejudgment of an experience about which we know little. I prefer a more neutral term, such as "alternate awakening."

Chapter 6: Feeling-Tones and Review Committees

1. For many years, I had found that the books by Jane Roberts contained particularly helpful advice on lucid dreaming. Not that they focused so much on being consciously aware in the dream state; rather, they offered a different perspective on the nature of reality and reality creation, a topic of special interest, of course, as one goes deeper into lucid dreaming.

2. Jane Roberts, *The Nature of Personal Reality* (Englewood Cliffs, NJ: Prentice Hall, 1974; reprinted, San Rafael, CA: Amber-Allen, 1995). Session 613, September 11, 1972.

3. Carlos Castaneda, *The Art of Dreaming* (New York: HarperCollins, 1993), 64.
4. Ibid., 65.
5. Ibid., 99.
6. Ibid., 107.

Chapter 7: Experiencing the Light of Awareness

1. Deirdre Barrett, *The Committee of Sleep* (New York: Crown Publishers, 2001), 113–14.

2. As I mentioned in chapter 1, lucid dreamers have been able to signal from within a dream that they are dreaming and thus prove the existence of conscious awareness when dreaming. This seems to provide insight into the age-old psychological debate of whether humans have a mind or only a brain. Now consider this: Is the person's conscious awareness inside the dream a physical being? No, he exists mentally in a lucid dream and uses the physical mechanism of eye movement only to "declare" that he exists. However, the lucid dreamer moves his nonphysical, mental eyes in the dream with only the mental intent to make physical eye movement—yet, the physical eyes move. Therefore, by these mental actions, a conscious dreamer seems to prove the separate but concurrent existence of the mind with the brain.

3. Tenzin Wangyal Rinpoche, *The Tibetan Yogas of Dream and Sleep* (Ithaca, New York: Snow Lion Publications, 1998), 149–50.

4. When I read Metzinger's question about the naturally contradictory aspect of someone reporting a "selfless state," it reminded me of my similar concerns from a different perspective. Whereas Metzinger approaches this from logical insight, my wonderings centered on "how." How did the first person to experience this figure it out? How did he or she come to understand this self-less state and give it a name? Without another to discuss the experience or compare notes, how could that person identify it? Did the person question a knowledgeable figure in the dream after the experience and have it explained?

In any case, Metzinger's question is a good one because so many of us would not have the insight to raise this important question. In turn, any response to it raises new questions about the nature of awareness and self consciousness.

5. Thomas Metzinger, *Being No One: The Self-Model Theory of Subjectivity* (Cambridge, Massachusetts: MIT Press, 2004), 566.

Chapter 8: Connecting with the Hidden Observer of Dreaming

1. C. G. Jung, "On the Nature of Psyche," in *The Basic Writings of C. G. Jung*, ed. Violet Staub de Laszlo (New York: Random House, 1993), 53.
2. Ibid., 61.
3. *American Heritage Dictionary* (Boston: Houghton Mifflin, 1976).

4. Wendy Doniger O'Flaherty, *Dreams, Illusion, and Other Realities* (Chicago: University of Chicago Press, 1984), 224–25.

5. Ibid., 15.

6. Ernest Hilgard, *Divided Consciousness: Multiple Controls in Human Thought and Action* (New York: John Wiley & Sons, 1977), 1.

7. Ibid., 4.

8. Ibid., 5.

9. Ibid., 6.

10. Ibid., 10.

11. Ibid., 10.

12. Ibid., 83.

13. Of interest to lucid dreamers who may wonder about the nature of their dream figures as independent of one's self or hallucinated, Hilgard recounts how a hypnotized subject solved this dilemma. When hypnotized and directed to create a duplicate copy of a person in the room, the subject would now report two identical figures. When asked to determine which one was "real," the hypnotized subject hit upon the "ingenious idea" of mentally suggesting that one figure should now raise its hand. The figure that raised its hand would thus identify itself as the hallucination.

14. Ibid., 186.

15. Ibid., 209–10.

16. Ibid., 209.

17. Ibid., 255.

Chapter 9: The Five Stages of Lucid Dreaming

1. IASD, the International Association for the Study of Dreams, was formerly ASD, the Association for the Study of Dreams. (I refer to ASD in chapter 7.) The organization changed its name in 2001 to reflect its international membership.

Chapter 10: Creating the Dream Reality

1. Gordon Globus, *Dream Life, Wake Life: The Human Condition through Dreams* (Albany: State University of New York Press, 1987), 173.

2. Wendy Doniger O'Flaherty, *Dreams, Illusion, and Other Realities* (Chicago: University of Chicago Press, 1984), 118.

3. Ibid., 119.

4. William James, *The Principles of Psychology*, vol. 1 (London: Macmillan, 1890), 402.

5. Stephen LaBerge, *Lucid Dreaming* (Los Angeles: Tarcher, 1985).

6. Marie Louise von Franz, "Science and the Unconscious," in *Man and His Symbols*, ed. C. G. Jung (New York: Dell, 1979), 383.

7. LaBerge, *Lucid Dreaming*, 103.

8. Carlos Castaneda, *The Power of Silence* (New York: Simon and Schuster, 1987), 239.

9. Carlos Castaneda, *A Separate Reality: Further Conversations with Don Juan* (New York: Pocket Books, 1972), 147.

10. Out of curiosity, I asked my fiancée if she had any dreams that night. She said all she could remember was a strange dream with some Chinese people in it.

Chapter 11: Varieties of Dream Figures

1. Connie Gavalis, "Going Over All Parts of You," *The Lucid Dream Exchange* 12 (January 25, 1973): 38.

2. Marc Ian Barasch, *Healing Dreams* (New York: Riverhead Books, 2000), 206.

3. Joscelyne Wilmouth, *The Lucid Dream Exchange* 32 (September 2004), 19.

4. Clare Johnson, Ph.D., "The Ball of Light," *The Lucid Dream Exchange* 34 (March 2005), 34.

5. I say "in general" here because some lucid dreamers make the presumption of calling a dream figure their guide, even though the dream figure has not announced itself as such. Also, some dream guides may challenge the lucid dreamer, which may not necessarily feel caring or teacherly to the lucid dreamer but could be considered such.

6. C. G. Jung, *Memories, Dreams, Reflections*, ed. Aniela Jaffé, trans. Richard and Clara Winston (New York: Pantheon, 1963), 183.

Chapter 12: Fishing for Information

1. From an interview of Epic Dewfall by Richard C. Wilkerson, creator of the online magazine *Electric Dreams* 4 (January 1997), http://www.dreamgate.com/electric-dreams/.

2. pasQuale Ourtane, *The Lucid Dream Exchange* 42 (March 2007): 4

3. Ibid, 5.

4. Ibid, 5.

5. From my personal email correspondence with pasQuale Ourtane (December 16, 2007).

6. Ibid.

7. E. W. Kellogg III, Ph.D., "Exploring the Bizarre Physics of Dreamspace, Part 3: 'Dreamspace,'" *The Lucid Dream Exchange* 39 (June 2006): 17.

8. David L. Kahn, *The Lucid Dream Exchange* 41 (December 2006): 4.

9. Stephen LaBerge and Howard Rheingold, *Exploring the World of Lucid Dreaming* (New York: Ballantine Books, 1990), 178.

10. Justin M. Tombe, *The Lucid Dream Exchange* 31 (June 2004): 15.

11. Ibid., 15.

12. "Phenomenology as a discipline aims at clearly seeing, and rigorously describing, the essential structures of one's life-world," Kellogg explains.

"To accomplish this, phenomenologists perform the *epoché* (or transcendental phenomenological reduction) which involves a fundamental shift in perspective by *suspending judgment* in the 'thesis of the natural attitude.' Basically, this meta-schema describes our ordinary everyday attitude toward the world. For example, the judgments that we live physically as human beings in 'objective reality,' that physical objects exist independent of our awareness of them, that events juxtaposed in space-time exist in some sort of a cause and effect relationship, and that we experience a 'physical universe' directly and without significant distortion. Thus, the *epoché* brings about a radical suspension of belief in this ordinary, deeply ingrained, and usually unconscious attitude toward the life-world."

In his lucid dream, Kellogg performs the *epoché* "while also attempting to suspend the autonomous operation of 'Functioning Intentionality.'" (Ed Kellogg, "Lucid Dreaming and the Phenomenological Epoché." Lecture, Society for Phenomenology and the Human Sciences conference, Eugene, OR, October 7– 9, 1999).

13. E. W. Kellogg III, Ph.D., "Lucid Dreaming and the Phenomenological Epoché" (Lecture, Society for Phenomenology and the Human Sciences conference, Eugene, OR, October 7– 9, 1999).

14. Ibid.

15. Jane Roberts, *The "Unknown" Reality*, Session 700.

Chapter 13: Healing Yourself and Others

1. Jeremy Taylor, *Dream Work: Techniques for Discovering the Creative Power in Dreams* (New York: Paulist Press, 1983), 215.

2. Stephen LaBerge, *Lucid Dreaming* (Los Angeles: Tarcher, 1985), 90.

3. I use the term *dream body* only as a means to identify the body form as a representation in the dream state. Though some may suggest that the dream body exists as a type of "energy body" or "etheric body," and Western psychology might make room for a "symbolic body" or "body model," the question at this point seems moot.

4. Patricia Garfield, *The Healing Power of Dreams* (New York: Fireside, Simon and Schuster, 1992), 256.

5. Keelin, *The Lucid Dream Exchange* 32 (September 2004): 5.

6. E. W. Kellogg III, Ph.D., "Lucid Dream Healing Experiences: Firsthand Accounts." Abstract. 1999 ASD Conference, Santa Cruz, CA. http://www.asdreams.org/documents/1999-_kellogg_lucid-healing.htm. Used by permission.

7. Ibid.

8. Ibid.

9. Ibid.

10. Ibid.

11. Ibid.

12. Ibid.

13. E. W. Kellogg III, Ph.D., "A Personal Experience in Lucid Dream Healing," *Lucidity Letter* 8, no. 1 (June 1989). Access this article online at http://www.spiritwatch.ca/Lucidity%20Letter%20Vol.%208(1)/A%20 Personal%20Experience%20in%20Lucid%20Dream%20Healing-Kellogg. htm or by going to http://www.spiritwatch.ca and clicking the appropriate edition of the *Lucidity Letter*. Used by permission.

14. Ibid.

15. Jayne Gackenbach and Jane Bosveld, *Control Your Dreams* (New York: Harper & Row, 1989), 13.

16. Beverly Kedzierski Heart D'Urso, Ph.D., "My Lucid Dream Geometric Healing Experience," *The Lucid Dream Exchange* 35 (June 2005): 17.

17. Ibid, 17.

18. Ibid, 17.

19. Ibid, 19.

20. Personal communication (November 8, 2007). Used by permission.

21. Ibid.

22. *The Lucid Dream Exchange* 24 (September 2002): 20–21.

23. *The Lucid Dream Exchange* 35 (June 2005): 31.

24. Personal communication (February 11, 2008). Used by permission.

25. Ibid.

26. E. W. Kellogg III, Ph.D., "Lucid Dream Healing Experiences: Firsthand Accounts."

27. Ibid

28. Ibid.

29. My thanks to Ed Kellogg for the use of his lucid dream accounts. For more on Dr. Kellogg's experiences with healing lucid dreams, go to www.asdreams.org (click Member Pages and E. W. Kellogg).

30. Patricia Garfield, *The Healing Power of Dreams* (New York: Fireside, Simon and Schuster, 1992), 256.

Chapter 14: Consciously Connecting via Telepathy

1. Montague Ullman, M.D., and Stanley Krippner, Ph.D., with Alan Vaughan, *Dream Telepathy: Experiments in Nocturnal ESP* (New York: Macmillan, 1973; reprint, Charlottesville, VA: Hampton Roads Publishing, 2002), 51. Citations are to the Macmillan edition.

2. Ibid, 53.

3. Ken Kelzer, "East Meets West, Buddhism Meets Christianity: The Lucid Dream as a Path for Union," *Lucidity Letter* 7, no. 2, (December 1988), http://www.spiritwatch.ca/Issue7_2/LL7_2_Kelzer_1.htm.

4. Ibid.

5. Ibid.

6. Peter Gay, *Freud: A Life for Our Time* (New York: Norton, 1988), 445.

7. Ullman and Krippner, *Dream Telepathy: Experiments in Nocturnal ESP*, 28.

8. Retired professor Robert Van de Castle, Ph.D., notes in his book, *Our Dreaming Mind* (New York: Ballantine, 1994, page 405) that "several prominent dream theorists, such as Freud, Jung, Stekel, and Boss, have strongly asserted the existence of paranormal dreams." Van de Castle himself played a prominent role as a talented dream telepathy receiver in Ullman and Krippner's scientific studies at the Maimonides dream laboratory.

9. Ian Koslow, *The Lucid Dream Exchange* 41 (December 2006), 23.

10. I want to also point out that Ian and the young woman had agreed, in the waking state, to do this experiment. (In other words, Ian did not just approach her in the dream without her knowing beforehand.) As I have mentioned in previous chapters, whenever performing experiments in the lucid dream state, it's important to get the complete approval of the other party involved, if for no other reason than to have a clear mind, knowing the other party agrees with and approves of the action.

11. Ian Koslow, *The Lucid Dream Exchange* 44 (September 2007): 4.

12. Clare Johnson, Ph.D., "Dream Telepathy and Tree Shouting," *The Lucid Dream Exchange* 34 (April 2005), http://www.improverse.com/ed-articles/clare_johnson_2005_apr_lde_novel_writing.htm.

13. Robert Van de Castle, *Our Dreaming Mind* (New York: Ballantine, 1994), 413.

14. Ullman and Krippner, *Dream Telepathy: Experiments in Nocturnal ESP*, 223.

Chapter 15: Forward-Looking, Precognitive Lucid Dreams

1. *Proceedings of the Society for Psychical Research*, Vol. 26, 1913, http://www.lucidity.com/vanEeden.html.

2. "It's What You Think About What You Eat," *The Lucid Dream Exchange* 41 (December 2006), 23.

3. C. G. Jung, "Approaching the Unconscious," *Man and His Symbols* (New York: Dell, 1979), 37.

4. I use the term *precognitive* only for convenience's sake in this book. Unfortunately, the word precognitive (or foreknowing) suggests that one knows that an event is predestined to occur. Since I believe in free will, I feel events are not predestined; rather, events are probable (though some may be so probable as to be nearly certain). Therefore, I use *precognitive* in a probabilistic sense of likely future actions.

5. Daniel Oldis, *The Lucid Dream Manifesto* (iUniverse: New York, 2006), 66, http://books.google.com/books?q=%22lucid+dream+manifesto%22.

6. For more information, I suggest visiting http://www.sheldrake.org/ homepage.html: "Rupert Sheldrake, one of the world's most innovative biologists, is best known for his theory of morphic fields and morphic resonance, which leads to a vision of a living, developing universe with its own inherent memory." As I discuss, in ambient precognitive lucid dreams, we may wander into dream settings that we later physically see.

7. Stanley Krippner, Fariba Bogzaran, and André Percia de Carvalho, *Extraordinary Dreams and How to Work with Them* (Albany: State University of New York Press, 2002).

8. Ibid, 35.

9. Ibid, 36.

10. E. W. Kellogg III, Ph.D., "A Lucid Dream Incubation Technique," *Dream Network Bulletin 5*, no. 4, 16.

11. E. W. Kellogg III, Ph.D., "LDE Quarterly Lucid Dreaming Challenge: The Lucid Dream Information Technique," *The Lucid Dream Exchange* 33 (December 2004), 8.

12. E. W. Kellogg III, Ph.D., "A Lucid Dream Incubation Technique," *Dream Network Bulletin 5*, no. 4, 16.

13. Patricia Garfield, *The Universal Dream Key: The 12 Most Common Dream Themes Around the World* (New York: HarperCollins, 2001), 206.

14. In particular, Patricia Garfield addresses the issues of eyes in lucid dreaming. See her book *Pathway to Ecstasy: The Way of the Dream Mandala* (New York: Fireside, Simon and Schuster, 1990).

15. Tenzin Wangyal Rinpoche, *The Tibetan Yogas of Dream and Sleep* (Snow Lion Publications, Ithaca, NY, 1998), 62.

16. This is a concept put forth by E. W. Kellogg III, Ph.D., in "Mutual Lucid Dream Event," *Dream Time* 14 (1997), 32–34.

Chapter 16: Mutual Lucid Dreaming

1. Linda Lane Magallón, *Mutual Dreaming* (New York: Pocket Books, 1997), 39. Used by permission.

2. Ibid, 24.

3. Ibid, 25.

4. Stanley Krippner, Fariba Bogzaran, and André Percia de Carvalho, *Extraordinary Dreams and How to Work with Them* (Albany: State University of New York Press, 2002), 91–92.

5. Dale Graff, *River Dreams: The Case of the Missing General and Other Adventures in Psychic Research* (New York: Houghton Mifflin, 2000), 25.

6. Ibid, 27.

7. Personal email communication with Ed Kellogg (July 1998). Used by permission.

8. This entire account by Ed Kellogg, in which he recounts his own and Harvey Grady's dreams and analyses, comes from his paper "Mutual Lucid Dream Event," in *Dream Time* 14, no. 2 (1997), 32–34.

9. Robert Waggoner, "Meeting Dreamers in the Dream State: A Lucid Quest," *The Lucid Dream Exchange* 35 (June 2005), 23–26.

10. Stephen LaBerge, *Lucid Dreaming* (Los Angeles: Tarcher, 1985), 227.

11. Ed Kellogg, Linda Lane Magallón, and I developed a structure for mutual lucid dream experimentation, or the "Lucid Mutual Dream Protocol," which I invite you to view at http://www.asdreams.org/documents/1999_kellogg_lmdp_protocol.htm.

Chapter 17: Interacting with the Deceased

1. Lucid dream submission, *The Lucid Dream Exchange* 33 (December 2004), 15.

2. Lucid dream submission, *The Lucid Dream Exchange* 20 (September 2001), 23.

3. "An Interview with Beverly D'Urso: Part One," *The Lucid Dream Exchange* 29 (December 2003), 4.

4. Lucid dream submission, *The Lucid Dream Exchange* 33 (December 2004), 14.

5. From the appendix of Ed Kellogg's 2004 presentation to IASD's online PsiBer Dreaming Conference, "Psychopompic Dreaming: Visits with Those Who Have Passed On?" http://www.asdreams.org/telepathy/2004kellogg_psychopomp.htm.

6. Ibid.

7. Ibid.

8. Ibid.

9. "Psychopomp" refers to a guide for the soul of the deceased, a mediator between conscious and unconscious realms.

10. Ed Kellogg, "Psychopompic Dreaming."

Chapter 18: The Unified Self in a Connected Universe

1. C. G. Jung, ed. *Man and His Symbols*, 53.

2. In *The Essential Mystics* by Andrew Harvey (New York: HarperCollins, 1996), 14.

3. John Sanford, *Dreams: God's Forgotten Language* (New York: HarperCollins, 1989), 182–83.

4. Ibid, 52 and 53.

5. Sigmund Freud, *The Interpretation of Dreams*, trans. Joyce Crick (Oxford: Oxford University Press, 1999), 405.

Appendix A: Frequently Asked Questions

1. Deirdre Barrett, "Just How Lucid Are Lucid Dreams: An Empirical Study of Their Cognitive Characteristics," *Dreaming* 2 (1992): 221–28.

2. Ian Koslow, *The Lucid Dream Exchange* 44 (September 2007), 3.

Appendix B: Tips and Techniques

1. Personal communication with ERHS (September 9, 2007). Used by permission.

2. Patricia Garfield, *Creative Dreaming* (New York: Simon and Schuster, 1974).

3. Jayne Gackenbach and Jane Bosveld, *Control Your Dreams* (New York: Harper & Row, 1989), 33.

4. Ibid., 34.

5. Castaneda, *Journey to Ixtlan*, 98.

6. Lynne Levitan, "Get Up Early, Take a Nap, Be Lucid," *Nightlight* 3, no. 1 (1991).

7. Paul Tholey, "Overview of the German Research in the Field of Lucid Dreaming," *Lucidity Letter* 7, no. 1 (June 1988). http://www.spiritwatch.ca/Issue7_1/LL7_1_Tholey.htm. Many papers written by Paul Tholey (1937–1998) can be found on the Internet, some in English, many in German.

8. Ibid.

9. E. W. Kellogg III, Ph.D., "Mapping Territories: A Phenomenology of Lucid Dream Reality," *Lucidity Letter* 8, no. 2 (December 1989).

10. John Galleher, *The Lucid Dream Exchange* 45 (December 2007), 18.

SELECTED BIBLIOGRAPHY

Barasch, Marc Ian. *Healing Dreams*. New York: Riverhead Books, 2001.

Barrett, Deirdre. *The Committee of Sleep*. New York: Crown, 2001.

Blackmore, Susan. *Consciousness: An Introduction*. Oxford: Oxford University Press, 2004.

Castaneda, Carlos. *The Art of Dreaming*. New York: HarperCollins, 1993.

Journey to Ixtlan: The Lessons of Don Juan. New York: Pocket Books, 1974 and 1991.

The Power of Silence. New York: Simon & Schuster, 1987.

A Separate Reality: Further Conversations with Don Juan. New York: Pocket Books, 1972.

Delaney, Gayle. *All About Dreams*. New York: HarperCollins, 1998.

Erickson, Milton, Ernest Rossi, and Sheila Rossi. *Hypnotic Realities: The Introduction of Clinical Hypnosis and Forms of Indirect Suggestion*. New York: Irvington Publishers, 1976.

Faraday, Ann. *The Dream Game*. New York: Harper & Row, 1974.

Freud, Sigmund. *The Interpretation of Dreams*. Edited by Ritchie Robertson. Translated by Joyce Crick. Oxford: Oxford University Press, 1999.

Gackenbach, Jayne, and Jane Bosveld. *Control Your Dreams*. New York: Harper & Row, 1989.

Gackenbach, Jayne, and Stephen LaBerge, editors. *Conscious Mind, Sleeping Brain*. New York: Springer, 1988.

Garfield, Patricia. *Creative Dreaming*. New York: Simon & Schuster, 1974.

The Dream Messenger: How Dreams of the Departed Bring Healing Gifts. New York: Simon & Schuster, 1997.

The Healing Power of Dreams. New York: Simon & Schuster, 1991.

Pathway to Ecstasy: The Way of the Dream Mandala. New York: Prentice Hall, 1989.

Gay, Peter. *Freud: A Life for Our Time*. New York: Norton & Co., 1988.

Globus, Gordon. *Dream Life, Wake Life: The Human Condition Through Dreams*. Albany: State University of New York Press, 1987.

Gordon, David. *Mindful Dreaming: A Practical Guide for Emotional Healing Through Transformative Mythic Journeys*. Franklin Lakes, New Jersey: Career Press, 2007.

Graff, Dale. *River Dreams: The Case of the Missing General and Other Adventures in Psychic Research*. Boston: Element Books, Inc., 2000.

Hilgard, Ernest. *Divided Consciousness: Multiple Controls in Human Thought and Action*. New York: John Wiley & Sons, 1977.

Hoss, Robert J. *Dream Language: Self-Understanding Through Imagery and Color*. Ashland, OR: Innersource, 2005.

Jung, Carl G. *The Basic Writings of C. G. Jung*. Edited by Violet Staub de Laszlo. New York: Random House, 1993.

Man and His Symbols. New York: Dell, 1979.

Memories, Dreams, Reflections. Edited by Aniela Jaffé. Translated by Richard Winston and Clara Winston. New York: Vintage, 1989.

Kelzer, Kenneth. *The Sun and the Shadow: My Experiment with Lucid Dreaming*. Virginia Beach: ARE Press, 1987.

Krippner, Stanley, Fariba Bogzaran, and André Percia de Carvalho. *Extraordinary Dreams and How to Work with Them*. Albany: State University of New York Press, 2002.

LaBerge, Stephen. *Lucid Dreaming*. Los Angeles: Tarcher, 1985.

LaBerge, Stephen, and Howard Rheingold. *Exploring the World of Lucid Dreaming*. New York: Ballantine Books, 1990.

Magallón, Linda Lane. *Mutual Dreaming*. New York: Pocket Books, 1997.

Metzinger, Thomas. *Being No One: The Self-Model Theory of Subjectivity*. Cambridge: The MIT Press, 2004.

Monroe, Robert. *Journeys Out of the Body*. New York: Doubleday, 1971.

Moss, Robert. *Conscious Dreaming: A Spiritual Path for Everyday Life.* New York: Three Rivers Press, 1996.

Norbu, Namkhai. *Dream Yoga and the Practice of Natural Light.* Edited by Michael Katz. Ithaca, New York: Snow Lion Publications, 1992.

O'Flaherty, Wendy Doniger. *Dreams, Illusion, and Other Realities.* Chicago: University of Chicago Press, 1984.

Oldis, Daniel. *The Lucid Dream Manifesto.* New York: iUniverse, Inc., 2006.

Ring, Kenneth, and Evelyn Elsaesser Valarino. *Lessons from the Light: What We Can Learn from the Near-Death Experience.* Needham, MA: Moment Point Press, 2006. First published 1998 by Perseus Books.

Rinpoche, Tenzin Wangyal. *The Tibetan Yogas of Dream and Sleep.* Ithaca, NY: Snow Lion Publications, 1998.

Roberts, Jane. *The Nature of Personal Reality.* San Rafael, CA: Amber-Allen Publishers, 1994. First published 1974 by Prentice-Hall.

Seth Speaks: The Eternal Validity of the Soul. San Rafael, CA: Amber-Allen Publishers, 1994. First published 1972 by Prentice-Hall.

Ryback, David, and Letitia Sweitzer. *Dreams That Come True.* New York: Dolphin-Doubleday, 1988.

Sanford, John A. *Dreams: God's Forgotten Language.* New York: Harper & Row, 1989.

Sparrow, G. Scott. *Lucid Dreaming: Dawning of the Clear Light.* Virginia Beach: ARE Press, 1982.

Taylor, Jeremy. *Dream Work.* Mahwah, NJ: Paulist Press, 1983.

Tigunait, Pandit Rajmani. *The Power of Mantra & The Mystery of Initiation.* Honesdale, Pennsylvania: Yoga International Books, 1996.

Ullman, Montague, and Stanley Krippner, with Alan Vaughan. *Dream Telepathy: Experiments in Nocturnal ESP.* New York: Macmillan, 1973.

Van de Castle, Robert. *Our Dreaming Mind.* New York: Ballantine Books, 1994.

von Franz, Marie Louise. "Science and the Unconscious." In *Man and His Symbols.* Edited by Carl G. Jung. New York: Dell, 1979.

INDEX

About the Author

Robert Waggoner is President-elect of the International Association for the Study of Dreams (IASD) and a graduate of Drake University with a degree in psychology. Over the past thirty years, he has logged more than a thousand lucid dreams. He is a frequent speaker at national and international dream conferences and the coeditor of *The Lucid Dream Exchange*.

To learn more about the IASD and its conferences and publications, including the journal *Dreaming*, visit www.asdreams.org.

To view the current issue of *The Lucid Dream Exchange* and submit lucid dream accounts, articles, questions, or comments, visit www. dreaminglucid.com.

To contact Robert Waggoner, visit his website, www.lucidadvice.com.

A portion of the author's royalties from this book are being donated to www.replanttrees.org.

Moment Point Press
publisher of books that help us all
consciously create limitless lives
in a limitless world

momentpoint.com